P9-DNY-941

YOUR
AGING
CAT

*How to Keep Your Cat Physically
and Mentally Healthy Into Old Age*

Kim Campbell Thornton

and

John Hamil, DVM

HOWELL
BOOK HOUSE
NEW YORK

Howell Book House
A Simon and Schuster Macmillan Company
1633 Broadway
New York, NY 10019

Copyright© 1996 by Kim Campbell Thornton and John Hamil, DVM

All rights reserved. No part of this book shall be reproduced, stored in a retrieval system, or transmitted by any means, electronic, mechanical, photocopying, recording, or otherwise without written permission from the publisher. No patent liability is assumed with respect to the use of the information contained herein. Although every precaution has been taken in preparation of this book, the publisher and authors assume no responsibility for errors or omissions. Neither is any liability assumed for damages resulting from the use of the information contained herein. For information, address Howell Book House, 1633 Broadway, 7th Floor, New York, NY 10019-6785.

MACMILLAN is a registered trademark of Macmillan, Inc.

Library of Congress Cataloging-in-Publication Data
Thornton, Kim Campbell.
    Your aging cat: how to keep your cat physically and mentally healthy
into old age/Kim Campbell Thornton & John Hamil.
       p.   cm.
    Includes index.
    ISBN 0-87605-085-2
    1. Cats.   2. Cats—Aging.   3. Cats—Health.   4. Veterinary geriatrics.
I. Hamil, John.   II. Title.
SF447.T49   1997
636.8'089897—dc20   96-34091
                                                CIP

Manufactured in the United States of America

98 97   9 8 7 6 5 4 3 2

Book Design: Heather Kern
Cover Design: Michael Freeland
Cover photo: Renee Stockdale

To Mr. Boo,
the best introduction to
the world of cats
a little girl could have.

Table of Contents

Foreword

Age is a state of mind, as the saying goes, so for a cat that is a healthy, contented, beloved pet, life must seem endless. Free from worries about basic survival and from such human frailties as vanity, dreams and unfulfilled expectations, most cats age gracefully, adapting to life's inevitable changes with barely a flick of the whiskers or a purr.

If you share your home with a cat who is eight to ten years or older, consider yourself lucky, and give yourself a pat on the back. You've already taken steps to ensure that your feline friend will be with you for years to come. But as adaptable as it is, a cat may need help handling the physiological and mental changes it will undergo as it ages, and you need to be aware of these transformations so you can understand and adjust to your cat's evolving appearance, behavior and needs.

This book will help you do just that. Both ardent cat lovers, Kim Campbell Thornton and John Hamil, DVM, have a long association with and thorough knowledge of older cats. Their expertise will guide you through the medical, behavioral and care challenges of living with a senior cat, as well as help you discover and enjoy the special benefits that only companionship with a mature feline friend can bring. Even if your cat is still young, reading this book can help you provide proper care now to ensure a long, happy relationship with your furry companion.

As the owner of three cats—two seniors and one "middle-aged"—I know I will keep this book handy as an invaluable reference and cat care guide. If you do the same, you can rest easy in the knowledge that you have thoroughly prepared yourself for your cat's golden age.

Debbie Phillips-Donaldson

Group Editor, *Cat Fancy* Magazine

Acknowledgments

The written word has ever been my guide in the care of my cats and throughout my years as a cat owner. And, during the year spent writing this book, I have consulted many books, journals, magazine articles and newsletters about cats. My deep appreciation goes to those writers who came before me and who inspired me to write my own book about cats.

This book couldn't have been written without the help and input of many people. Dr. Hamil and I are grateful to the veterinarians who shared their knowledge and experience: Sarah Abood, DVM; Bonnie Beaver, DVM; Jimmy Conrad, DVM; Deborah Edwards, DVM; Thomas H. Elston, DVM; Larry Glickman, DVM; Johnny Hoskins, DVM; John Limehouse, DVM; Susan McDonough, VMD; Amy Marder, VMD; Margaret Muns, DVM; Gary Patronek, DVM; Andrew Rowan; Lenny Southam, DVM; Priscilla Taylor, DVM; Vickie Valdez, DVM; Diana Webster, DVM; Elaine Wexler-Mitchell, DVM; and Christine Wilford, DVM.

Also generous with their time and knowledge were Susan Phillips Cohen, director of counseling at New York City's Animal Medical Center; Jamie Pinn, Humane Animal Rescue Team; Balinese breeder Mary Desmond, as well as many other cat breeders who shared information about their breeds' lifespans; Martha Jordan, licensed massage therapist; Joan Miller, president of the Winn Feline Foundation; Don Noah, Centers for Disease Control; Peter Drown, International Association of Pet Cemeteries; cat judge Caroline Osier; Paul Glassner, San Francisco SPCA; the Morris Animal Foundation; the online cat owners who shared information about their cats' lifespans, medical problems and behavior; the helpful staff and veterinarians at the veterinary schools at the University of California, Davis; the University of Florida, Gainesville; the University of Illinois, Urbana; Cornell University; Purdue University; and Tufts University. Many thanks are also due to our hardworking photographers, Wayne Guidry and Jerry Thornton, and the cats and their owners who modeled for us. Our apologies to anyone we have omitted.

Special thanks are due to friends who offered support, encouragement, and advice during the writing of this book: Betsy Sikora Siino, Jane Calloway, Audrey Pavia, Lisa Hanks and Mordecai Siegal. And last but not least, we are most grateful to our ever-patient spouses: Jerry Thornton, who gave up computer time and took on more than his share of pet care during the past year, and Susan LaCroix Hamil, who offered much constructive criticism and editing of the manuscript.

Introduction

Thirty years ago at the age of five, I acquired my first cat, Mr. Boo. Back then, not much was known about the feline lifespan or the care of geriatric cats. That's primarily because cats were not as valued as pets as they are today. Back then, cats spent most of their time outside, sunning themselves on sidewalks, hunting birds and, because few were neutered, getting into fights with each other. Naturally, this outdoor lifestyle left cats open to a number of dangers: speeding cars, disease, and infected wounds. Most cats used up their nine lives in nine years or less.

Today, it's a different story. The popularity of cats as pets has risen over the decades. Numbering 60 million in the United States, they are the fastest growing group of pets, with predictions of further growth through the end of this decade. Cats are found in more than one-third of American homes, outnumbering dogs by about three million. Cats have a well-deserved reputation as low-maintenance pets—a high priority in today's busy society—and they are healthy and long-lived when cared for properly. In a country where pets are often given equal status with children, such longevity is a plus.

Results from a recent survey by the American Animal Hospital Association showed that 69 percent of cat owners spend 45 minutes or more each day interacting with their pets. Sixty percent responded that they give their cats as much attention as they do their children. A survey conducted by the Center for Animals in Society at the University of California, Davis, School of Veterinary Medicine discovered that people like cats because they are easy to care for, provide their owners with affection and companionship, and have interesting personalities. Survey respondents said their cats gave them unconditional love, undivided loyalty and devotion, and total acceptance. The conclusion? A relationship with a cat brings important emotional and even physical benefits to people. Heart patients with pets live longer and have lower blood pressure. It's no wonder that more and more owners are taking steps to ensure that their beloved pets live long lives.

Health awareness is very popular in this country, and pet owners are no exception. Twenty-five percent of the typical small-animal practice is made up of geriatric patients: At least 11 percent are cats. Cats live longer now because they receive better nutrition, better medical care and, perhaps most important, lead more protected indoor lives. Today, indoor cats have every chance of living to be greater than fifteen years old. The average age of outdoor cats is significantly less, especially when they are unneutered males. And stray cats that must fend for themselves usually survive for only two years.

Ensuring that a cat lives to a ripe old age requires care that begins in kittenhood, but even if your cat didn't get the best start in life, you can take steps to help it have a healthy, happy old age.

What are the secrets to a cat's long life? Factors that affect longevity include an indoor lifestyle, regular veterinary checkups and vaccinations, a high-quality diet, and sharp owner observations, which can lead to discovery and treatment of problems before they become life-threatening. It is our hope that this book will help you recognize problems or avoid them in the first place.

While writing this book, we asked veterinarians around the country to give us the one piece of advice they believed was most important to owners of geriatric cats. Look for their advice at the end of each chapter. Each veterinarian had a different angle, but all said much the same thing: Love your cat. By being aware of your cat's condition, by providing preventive care, by making life a little bit easier when the going gets tough, you are taking positive steps to ensure that your cat lives a long and full nine lives.

Your cat's golden years can be some of the finest for the two of you because you have built a loving relationship over the years. With preventive care, you can enjoy each other's company for years to come.

Secrets 1
to *Longevity*

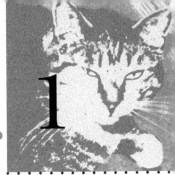

Age will not be defied.
—*Francis Bacon*

Once upon a time, so the story goes, before vaccinations and commercial pet foods, cats used to live for a long time. They lived outside, caught their own food, and lived the vagabond life that is the due of every cat. At a ripe old age, they would go off alone to a secret place to die. It was a wonderful, if fictional, life.

Reality was not so wonderful. Thirty years ago, back when cats were not as highly valued as pets as they are today, they were lucky to live for more than five or six years. They got hit by cars, died of distemper, or just wandered off and were never seen again, presumably the victims of predators, diseases, or accidents. The cats that lived long lives were the exceptions. Perhaps that is why we remember them.

Today, thanks to their higher value in society, cats are living longer and better—long enough to have a true old age. When they are healthy and well cared for, cats can live up to twice as long as dogs and other types of pets (with the exception of parrots and tortoises). That's a boon to the loving pet owner, who can enjoy a cat's company for many years before its inevitable loss.

FACTORS DETERMINING LIFE SPAN

Cats are most likely to suffer their major health problems in kittenhood, from birth until the age of two years. It is during this time that most congenital or hereditary problems will make an appearance, and it is when cats are most susceptible to respiratory diseases. If you can get them safely past the age of two, they are likely to live a long time, given proper care and diet.

How can you start your cat on the road to a long life? Cats live longer today than ever before, but a long life span is no accident.

Much of a cat's longevity is determined by whether the cat spends its time indoors or outdoors and whether it is intact or altered (spayed or neutered). Why? Because longevity is dependent not only on heredity, but also on how well a cat is protected from disease and injury.

THE LINK BETWEEN LONGEVITY AND AN INDOOR LIFESTYLE

After being missing for three days, Boise dragged herself over the stone wall into her backyard. She wasn't walking properly, so her owner, Kathy, took her to the veterinarian. He speculated that Boise had been hit by a car, breaking her pelvis. Boise would have to heal on her own unless Kathy opted for expensive surgical repair.

■

One-year-old Alice always came running when her owner whistled. One day he came home for lunch and whistled for the small black-and-white cat. She answered his call, but on her way across the street she was hit by a car and killed. He was heartbroken and guiltridden. From then on, his cats were kept indoors.

■

Cricket enjoyed visiting the neighbors and roaming the neighborhood. On their evening walks, her owners often saw her "in conference" with other cats. Recently, however, they noticed that their once-healthy cat wasn't eating much. She had lost weight and didn't have much energy. A trip to the veterinarian pinpointed the problem: Cricket had feline leukemia virus.

■

Cleo, now 14, has survived a mammary tumor and overcome obesity. Her owners say she has no problem jumping to her favorite spots and so far they have seen no obvious signs of aging. She has been an indoor cat her entire life.

More and more cat owners are keeping their beloved pets indoors, safe from disease, cars, and predators. A 1994 survey conducted by researchers at the School of Veterinary Medicine at Purdue University showed that 62 percent of the Indiana cat owners surveyed kept their pets strictly indoors. A similar survey taken in Massachusetts in February 1994 indicated that 51 percent of the owners interviewed had cats that spent all their time indoors. In a 1995 survey of *Cat Fancy* magazine readers, 50 percent of the respondents reported keeping their cats indoors at all times and 25 percent let their cats outdoors only under supervision, on a leash, or in an enclosure.

Much of a cat's longevity is determined by whether the cat spends its time indoors or outdoors and whether it is intact or altered (spayed or neutered).

According to Andrew Rowan, DVM, director of the Center for Animals and Public Policy at Tufts University School of Veterinary Medicine, the above-mentioned Massachusetts survey indicated that the median age of death for cats from illness or euthanasia was 13 years, while the median age of death for cats struck by cars was only three years.

THE BENEFITS OF NEUTERING

Altered cats—those who have had their reproductive organs surgically removed—that live indoors are most likely to live to a ripe old age. It is rare to see unneutered cats reach a greatly advanced age because they usually live primarily outdoors, which exposes them to danger and injury. This is

Surveys have shown that most cat owners keep their pets indoors all the time.

especially true of unneutered male cats, whose territorial natures make them likely to be crossing the street or fighting with other cats. A cat that stays indoors avoids many risks, including speeding cars, most diseases, and fights with other animals.

Unaltered cats are also more likely to suffer from disease, especially various forms of cancer. Spaying, especially before a cat's first heat, can prevent such health problems as mammary tumors, uterine cancer, and pyometra, a potentially fatal uterine infection. One Siamese cat breeder reported that her cats lived to be 16 or older if they were neutered or spayed by five years of age. Like neutered toms, spayed queens allowed outside are less likely to fight and wander the neighborhood.

Harry came limping home after a night out carousing with the boys. The next day he wasn't his usual chipper self, but his owner didn't notice a problem until she was petting him the next day and hit the sore spot on Harry's leg. The veterinarian diagnosed the painful lump as an abscess, no doubt incurred from a fight with another male cat. He drained the wound, which was filled with smelly pus; showed Harry's owner how to clean the area until it healed; gave the cat a shot of antibiotics; and recommended that Harry be neutered when he was feeling better.

Battle scars are another result of outdoor living. Neutering reduces roaming and fighting behaviors, both of which can lead to serious injury: torn ears, scratched eyes, bite wounds that abscess. Not only are these painful conditions a threat to the cat's health and longevity, but they are also expensive and time-consuming to treat, requiring a course of antibiotics, regular cleansing of the wound, and sometimes surgery. The veterinary bill for an abscess that requires anesthesia, surgery, and antibiotics can be $100 or more. By comparison, altering the cat at an early age is an inexpensive method of prevention.

PARASITE PREVENTION

Parasites are another problem for outdoor cats. A cat that roams brings home unwanted guests, such as fleas, ticks, and ear mites. The resulting itching, biting, and scratching isn't pretty, and it's most annoying when it occurs in the middle of the night. Treating the cat and the home for flea infestations is time-consuming and expensive, not to mention difficult. Few cats willingly submit to being sprayed and powdered, let alone medicated for ear mites. And exposure to insecticides on a frequent, long-term basis doesn't do anything for improving the cat's longevity.

A number of cat owners have found that their flea problems decreased dramatically—and sometimes disappeared—when they began keeping their pets indoors. The fact that fleas spread disease and internal parasites, such as tapeworms, is another reason to keep them away from older cats.

DANGER FROM PREDATORS AND PLAGUES

Trouble lived in a nice neighborhood in one of the many canyons of Southern California. The neighbors were always commenting on the friendly, talkative nature of the Siamese mix, and they enjoyed watching her make her rounds each day. When she didn't appear for a few days, they asked her owner if she was all right. "I think a coyote got her," he said sadly. "I heard a scream the other night, and I haven't seen her since."

Widespread development in once-wild areas has exposed outdoor cats to dangers many people don't think about until it's

Outdoor cats are exposed to seemingly harmless wildlife, which can carry fatal diseases such as rabies.

too late. They are at risk of falling prey to coyotes, mountain lions, and roaming dogs. Cats are predators and their claws can certainly inflict pain, but they are no match for the larger predators. It's important to remember that wild animals that prey on pets are not deliberately being cruel or vicious. Just as humans go to fast food restaurants, coyotes and mountain lions roam their habitat in search of an easy meal, which in many cases, is a free-roaming cat.

To discourage coyotes and other wildlife from scavenging the neighborhood and preying on pets, keep trash containers tightly closed, don't leave pet food and water outside, and don't let pets roam without supervision. Another consideration, albeit from the reverse point of view, is that cats are among the greatest killers of urban wildlife, especially songbirds. By keeping your cat indoors, you not only protect it from predators, you also protect other animals from feline predation.

Seemingly harmless wildlife can present problems, too. Rodents and skunks have widespread habitats and are found in most areas of the United States. Rodents can carry the plague, and skunks are well-known for spreading rabies. The wandering cat is likely to be exposed to both these fatal diseases, even in seemingly urban areas.

Most communities do not require cats to be vaccinated for rabies and licensed. This is surprising, because according to 1994 figures from the national Centers for Disease Control and Prevention in Atlanta, there were 267 reported cases of rabies in cats, compared to only 153 in dogs. A rabies vaccination can protect cats from that disease, but there is no preventive medicine for the plague.

DISEASE PREVENTION

Of course, a rabies vaccination isn't the only one important for cats. The number one hazard faced by outdoor cats—ahead of dogs, cars, or coyotes—is other cats, because they carry infectious feline viruses. For this reason, vaccinations are an important element in the long life of the modern cat. Feline distemper (cat fever) and upper respiratory viruses once killed cats in large numbers. But with the rise in the cat's popularity as a pet, more frequent veterinary care, including regular vaccinations, has almost eliminated these diseases. Research in feline medicine and development of new vaccines, such as the one for feline leukemia in 1985, are protecting cats even further.

Unfortunately, not every disease spread by cats has a preventive vaccine. Feline immunodeficiency virus, or FIV, is one such fatal disease that can't be prevented—except by limiting exposure to it, and that's difficult to do when a cat goes outdoors. Because cats are territorial—even those that are spayed or neutered—they run

How Old is Your Cat?

How old is your cat in human years? Cats age differently than humans. A one-year-old cat is comparable to a 15-year-old human; at two years of age, a cat is roughly equivalent to a 24-year-old person. After that, relative aging slows to a ratio of four human years to each cat year. So a nine-year-old cat is approximately the same physical age as a 52-year-old human.

With this in mind, it is important to remember that because pets age more rapidly than humans, an older cat that goes a year between physical exams is like a human going from age 60 to 65 without ever seeing a doctor. More frequent veterinary exams can catch problems before they become serious.

The average cat life span is 10 to 14 years, but protected cats frequently live into their 20s. One cat is reported to have lived to age 36. With preventive care, cats can live 15 to 20 years.

the risk of a close encounter with a stray cat that wanders onto their property.

This country's large feral cat population, including unowned neighborhood cats, is a reservoir for all kinds of fatal diseases, from FIV to feline infectious peritonitis (FIP). There is a vaccine for FIP, but it is not 100 percent effective. Until the feral cat population is brought under control, or vaccinations or treatments are available for all feline diseases, it will remain unhealthy for a cat to have free access to the outdoors.

A Balanced Diet

Yesterday's working cat lived a primarily rural outdoor existence. Its purpose in life was to keep down the vermin on the farm, and the cat lived on scraps and what it could catch. Back then, that diet was natural for the cat's lifestyle and status, but few pet cats in the 1990s live in similar circumstances. Most live sedentary lives in urban homes and neighborhoods. The availability and quality of wild "game" is not comparable to that on a farm.

Today's cat food manufacturers offer a variety of complete, balanced diets designed to take the pet cat from kittenhood to old age, through sickness and in health. It's unlikely that cat experts and owners will stop arguing any time soon over which type of food is best, but the fact remains that today's name-brand cat foods, whether they are found in grocery stores, pet stores, or veterinary offices, offer excellent nutrition and help provide the foundation for good health and a long life.

Heredity definitely plays a role in determining a cat's life span.

Breed, Heredity, and Longevity

Does breed affect life span? In some cases it can. Veterinarians who run cats-only clinics report that the cats in their practices that live the longest are Siamese, domestic shorthairs, and Siamese/shorthair mixes. These cats often live into their late teens and early twenties. Not many other breeds live that long, with most having life spans ranging from 12 to 16 years. Some breeds, such as the American Curl and the Sphynx, have not been in existence for very long, so it is unknown yet whether they will have similar life spans.

Sex plays a role, too. As with humans, females tend to live longer than males. A final factor is heredity. Breeding and genes play an important role in determining a cat's life span. There is no doubt a link between genetics and certain life-shortening diseases.

VETERINARY TIP

"I really believe in preventive care. Finding out that a cat has a disease before it becomes debilitating can slow progression dramatically. Preventive care can make all the difference. Cats are more wonderful the older they get. Give them lots of love; that's real important."

—*Deborah A. Edwards, DVM, All Cats Hospital Professional Association, Largo, Florida.*

Keeping 2
a *Cat Young*

"Live long and prosper."—Vulcan salutation,
Star Trek television series

The Vulcans on the *Star Trek* television series often reminded me of cats. They had the same pointy ears, logical minds (to them), and freedom from emotion. They too were known for their long life spans. Perhaps they knew the same secrets that lead to feline longevity: regular observation and maintenance.

In Chapter 1, we talked about how environment, nutrition, and vaccinations can affect a cat's life span. But keeping a cat indoors or in a protected outdoor environment is only one of the steps involved in keeping it healthy into old age. Grooming, regular veterinary care, and simple observations made on a regular basis are also integral to a cat's longevity. Although they can't stop

Playing with your cat is a simple way to keep him healthy.

aging completely, they can delay its onset.

Like a car, a cat that receives routine inspection and maintenance will run better and longer. Regular care is important throughout a cat's life, but as it grows older its health depends more and more on what may seem like simple, routine activities: brushing and combing, dental care, weight control, and play.

PAYING ATTENTION

All these activities involve paying attention to your cat. The more observant you are, the more likely you are to notice problems before they become unmanageable. No one knows your cat better than you do. By establishing routines for grooming, exercise, feeding, and veterinary care, you can develop habits of observation that will allow you to notice variations from what you know to be normal for your cat.

GROOMING

As Alicia combed Cleveland's fur, she noticed that he flinched when the comb touched a spot near the back of his neck. Upon closer examination, Alicia found a small lump that she hadn't noticed the previous week. She called her veterinarian, who advised that she bring Cleveland in immediately for an exam. Lumps in cats, the veterinarian explained, were more likely to be malignant than in dogs, and an early diagnosis was Cleveland's best defense against future complications.

Grooming is one of the first lines of defense when it comes to keeping a cat healthy. Regular grooming familiarizes you with the cat's body so that you come to know what's normal and what's not. As your hands move the brush or comb through your cat's fur, you will learn how your cat's body feels normally, and the texture and condition of its fur.

Depending on your cat's condition, you will notice reactions of pleasure or discomfort. The grooming session is a good time to examine your cat for lumps, parasites, and sores. Combing and brushing also strengthen the bond between you and your cat.

In addition to the emotional benefits of the human-animal bond, grooming is psychologically important to cats. They like to be clean and will spend hours licking their coats into shape. An unkempt cat is usually an unhealthy, unhappy cat. If your cat has no desire to groom itself, it may actually be sick.

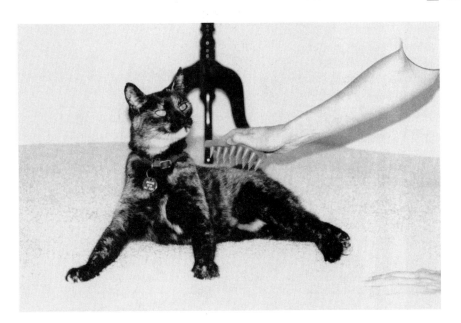

Even though cats are clean by nature, they enjoy being groomed, and it's a good way for you to detect problems of the fur or skin.

Of course, grooming has physical benefits, too. Regular brushing also helps prevent hairballs, which can be more serious in older cats than young ones. An older cat's digestive system may be less able to remove the hairball, either by regurgitation or defecation. A buildup of hairballs can eventually cause an intestinal blockage, a dangerous situation for any cat but more so for an older cat, which may be less able to withstand the surgery required to resolve the problem. A regular dose of a petroleum-based hairball remedy can also help keep hairballs to a minimum. (If your cat is prone to hairballs, ask your veterinarian how frequently you should administer hairball medications. Overuse of hairball remedies containing petroleum jelly can prevent absorption of fat-soluble vitamins.) Grooming also stimulates blood circulation and distributes natural oils for a healthier skin and coat.

Some cats produce less saliva as they age and can't groom themselves as thoroughly as they did when they were younger. Brushing and combing on a regular basis helps keep them in good condition. Depending on your cat's coat type, grooming should take place daily or weekly. Cats with coats that mat easily, such as Persians, may need daily care, while shorthairs and some longhairs can get by with combing or brushing just once a week.

Some cats produce less saliva as they age, making them less able to thoroughly groom themselves.

THE BRUSHING ROUTINE

When brushing your cat, use a wire slicker brush, grooming mitt, rubber curry brush, or a fine-toothed comb. Start at the cat's head and work your way over the body to the tail. Most cats enjoy a good grooming session, although kittens may find it difficult to sit still for any length of time. If that's the case, just do one small area and continue the grooming session later.

When cleaning the eyes, check for discharge or filminess. Gently wipe away dried mucus using your finger or a tissue. Persistent tear stains beneath the eyes may indicate irritation, and the condition should be brought to your veterinarian's attention. Other symptoms to look for include redness, cloudiness, squinting, and pain.

NAIL CARE

Nail care is an important part of grooming. Even though cats shed their nails and usually use a scratching post to loosen them, older cats may not scratch as frequently as they once did. Encourage your cat to scratch by providing a rope or bare wood scratching post.

Run your fingers up and down the post to entice your cat to scratch. The noise and action will attract its attention. Waving a feather or fishpole toy up and down the post serves the same purpose. If your cat loses interest in the scratching post, try moving it to a new area. Sometimes a new location piques a cat's interest.

Encourage your cat to scratch by providing a rope or bare wood scratching post.

Examine the nails weekly and trim them if necessary, using either a nail clipper for humans or one made for cats. If the nails get too long, the cat may end up walking on the sides of its toes and feet. This uncomfortable situation can contribute to joint problems. And in rare instances, the nails can actually grow into the pads.

TRIMMING NAILS

When trimming nails, choose a time when your cat is relaxed or sleepy. As it lies on the bed or in a sunny spot, gently grasp its paw with your left hand, holding the nail clippers in your right hand. (Reverse this if you are left-handed.) Gently press upward on the pad and down behind the nail bed to extend the nail, and clip just where the nail curves. Don't clip too far past the curve or you will hit the quick, causing the cat to bleed and yowl. If this happens, don't panic. Have a styptic stick or styptic powder close at hand so you can stop the bleeding. If you don't have styptic powder, cornstarch or flour will do in a pinch.

If they are accustomed to regular nail trimming and have never been quicked, most cats will put up with nail trimming without much fuss. If your cat is the exception, try holding it between your knees to keep it still, or ask a friend or family member to help hold the cat or trim the nails. Also, wrapping the cat in a towel is a good way to confine it and prevent scratches.

GROOMING TIPS

To get the most out of grooming your older cat, keep in mind the following tips.

- Keep grooming sessions short, especially if your cat has a long coat. Your cat's body is more sensitive to aches and pains now, so go gently and slowly.

- Don't hold the cat too tightly or brush too forcefully. Trim matted hair carefully; it's easy to cut the skin.

- Be patient if your cat seems less than willing to be brushed or combed. Resume the session later when your cat is in a better mood.

- If you take your cat to a groomer, be sure he or she is sensitive to your cat's needs.

BRUSH THOSE FANGS!

Don't forget to clean the teeth! Food leaves a soft, sticky, bacteria-filled residue called plaque on cats' teeth. When plaque hardens, it forms a substance called calculus (or tartar). If tartar is not removed from teeth, the result is gingivitis, an inflammation of the gums. Left untreated, this condition erodes the tooth sockets, eventually leading to periodontal disease and tooth loss. The major cause of tooth loss in cats is plaque, and about 75 percent of cats develop periodontal disease by age four.

Of even more concern is the fact that dirty teeth can affect every other organ system in a cat's body. Severe gum disease can lead to the spread of bacteria to internal organs via the bloodstream, causing serious infections. Oral bacteria are associated with certain diseases of the kidneys, liver, and heart.

Although you can't teach your cat to floss, daily or weekly brushing can significantly reduce plaque buildup. Studies show that daily cleaning reduces the formation of plaque by 95 percent, while weekly cleaning reduces it by 76 percent. Interestingly, the formation of tartar on a cat's teeth is often related to the way it eats. A cat that swallows its food whole is less likely to develop plaque than one that chews slowly. And dry kibble is less likely than canned food to contribute to plaque formation.

To clean your cat's teeth, wrap a small piece of gauze around your finger and use diluted hydrogen peroxide, salt water or a special cat toothpaste to rub gently against the teeth. Go slowly and be patient and gentle.

Beginning home cleaning in kittenhood is the best way to promote dental health, but it's never too late to start if you have a compliant cat with mild plaque. Otherwise, professional veterinary cleanings will be needed more frequently to keep the cat's mouth healthy. A good professional cleaning can improve the cat's immune response by reducing the amount of bacteria the body must contend with, giving the cat a better chance of staying healthier longer.

To clean a cat's teeth at home, use a soft cloth or a piece of gauze wrapped around your finger. Gently wipe the teeth with a solution of diluted hydrogen peroxide, salt water, or a toothpaste made especially for cats that is available from your veterinarian. Never use toothpaste made for humans. The foaming action can scare your cat, making it unwilling to undergo further tooth cleaning, and the toothpaste can cause gastrointestinal upset if swallowed. Avoid using baking soda, too. Its high sodium content may cause problems in cats with heart conditions.

Be patient and go slowly and gently as you introduce your cat to its oral hygiene program. As your cat becomes used to the cleaning procedure, you can scrub more firmly to be sure you remove as much plaque and tartar as possible. Don't forget the molars back under the cheeks. When you're through brushing, reward your cat with praise or a treat.

KEEPING THE WEIGHT OFF

You can keep your cat in good physical condition by monitoring its food intake and providing opportunities for activity. It's an old wives' tale that spaying or neutering causes a cat to gain weight. Fat cats get that way because they eat too much and don't get enough exercise. Remember, not even the brightest cat can operate a can opener.

If your old cat is gaining weight, you need to examine your feeding habits and the cat's lifestyle. A cat that has moved from the wildness of kittenhood to the sedate behavior of old age may need a change in the amount and type of food it receives.

Ask your veterinarian what your cat's optimum weight is, and check your cat's weight quarterly or any time it appears to have changed. A change of 10 percent—which may be less than a pound for a cat—up or down may be significant. To determine a cat's weight, weigh yourself on your bathroom scale. Then pick up your cat and weigh yourself again. Subtract the difference to get an accurate weight for your cat. Write the cat's weight on your calendar or in the cat's record book for future reference.

Kittens and young cats usually don't have weight problems because they are full of energy. At age four or five, however, your cat may start becoming less energetic. This is the time to begin encouraging it to play and run on a regular basis. Consider reducing the amount of food it receives if it is less active, particularly if there is any tendency toward weight gain.

If your cat is overweight or has health problems, ask your veterinarian for advice. Begin an exercise plan gradually and watch closely for signs of overexertion such as rapid, open-mouth breathing, which can indicate respiratory distress.

PLAY IS IMPORTANT

Robin's indoor cats demand occasional walks outdoors on a leash. Kathy built an enclosed "cat run" to give her indoor cats a taste of the great wide open.

▪

*Frances and Bob made use of the abundant air space in
their home by placing "cat walks" along the walls, which
allowed their pets to scale the heights while safely indoors.*

To ensure that your cat stays active, schedule daily play
time. Provide a climbing area and rotate toys so the cat doesn't
get bored.

Test your cat's agility with a fishpole-type toy. Few cats can
resist chasing and leaping after the bouncing line, and some
even become addicted to these toys, meowing pitifully until
the beloved toy is brought out. Some cats like to retrieve, and
they are easily entertained—and exercised—with a thrown
piece of wadded up paper or a small ball. Ping-pong balls
make "lively" playmates, too. Also, a cat trained to wear a
leash and harness can accompany you on a daily walk. A cat
does not need as much exercise as a dog, but it shouldn't be a
total couch potato, either.

Playing with your cat increases his longevity.

Use playtime as an opportunity to evaluate your cat's physical condition. Can its eyes still follow the course of the Kitty
Tease? Does it tire quickly or begin to breathe heavily after
only a few minutes of play? Tailor playtime to your cat's physical abilities, and seek your veterinarian's advice if you notice
a marked decrease in your cat's desire or ability to play.

Flexibility in the body leads to flexibility in the mind as
well. Cats are never too old to learn. Keeping their brains

stimulated through games and toys can increase their life expectancy by re-awakening their kittenish interest and delight in life. Sometimes we think that because cats are old, they're not capable of doing things. Certainly they can't run as fast or jump as high as they used to, but gentle play will help keep them motivated.

The benefits of exercise and play are many. Increased blood flow nourishes the organs, keeping them healthier longer. Obesity, the cause of many health problems, is prevented or reduced. Activity helps keep the cat limber and young at heart. It takes only five minutes a day to exercise your cat—five minutes that can add years to your cat's life.

REGULAR VACCINATIONS

Many people believe that only kittens need vaccinations, but a cat's immune system weakens with age, making the cat more susceptible to disease. Regular vaccinations can prevent conditions that the aging cat might have difficulty fighting, especially if it is an outdoor cat that is exposed to many viruses and bacteria. Regular vaccinations also provide an opportunity for veterinary examination of your cat and discussion of its health.

A common misconception is that indoor cats don't need vaccinations. But without exposure to viruses, immunization can be lost over time. Airborne viruses can infiltrate homes and viruses can even be brought in on shoes.

Although modified live virus vaccines offer longer, better protection, inactivated vaccines are safest for old cats. With these there is no chance the vaccine will revert to being virulent or that it will shed the vaccine virus. The most important vaccines for old cats are those for upper respiratory viruses (feline rhinotracheitis virus, or FRTV; feline calicivirus, or FCV; and chlamydiosis); panleukopenia; rabies; and feline leukemia virus, or FeLV, especially for outdoor cats.

Rabies in cats is a serious problem, with the number of annually reported cases of rabies in cats regularly exceeding that of dogs. Few states require rabies vaccinations for cats, and it is estimated that only 4 percent of all cats nationwide are immunized against rabies. Even if your cat stays indoors, there's always the chance that it could slip out one day and come in contact with a rabid animal, especially in a rural area. A cat that regularly goes outdoors is in even greater danger. The roaming and nocturnal nature of a cat makes it likely to come into contact with wild animals, and its celebrated curiosity means it is likely to investigate a dead or dying rabid animal. The cost of a vaccine is a small price to pay for peace of mind, especially if your cat goes outdoors.

HOW TO CONDUCT A HOME EXAM

Routine is the key to keeping your cat healthy. By performing a regular home examination, you can develop a sense of your cat's well-being. Your knowledge of its body will enable you to catch problems when they are minor and prevent them from developing into something serious.

To examine your cat, begin at the head and use both hands to feel your cat. Be gentle but firm. Feel for lumps, bumps, scabs, and mats. Note whether your cat startles or exhibits pain in any area. If you find something unusual, examine it for size, shape, color, and texture. Is it hard or soft? Oozing or scaly? Look for flea dirt (pepper-like specks that turn red when you squish them), dandruff, and hair loss.

When you are finished with the body, look more closely at the head. Are the ears clean, and the eyes and nose free of discharge? Does the cat shake its head or scratch its ears frequently? Lift the lips and examine the teeth and gums. Are the gums a healthy pink, or do they look white, yellow, or bluish? The gums should not be red or swollen. The teeth should be reasonably white, with few or no brown

Maintenance Notes

Groom your cat regularly. If it has short hair, brush or comb it weekly. If it has long hair, brush daily or at least twice a week. Don't forget to trim the nails and brush the teeth.

Keep your cat in good condition by playing with it regularly. A brief, daily session playing with a ping-pong ball or chasing a fishpole-type toy will help keep your cat limber.

Keep diseases at bay by having your cat vaccinated yearly. Ideally, the vaccinations will be combined with a physical exam. A vaccination clinic, where the cat receives shots only, is better than no shots at all, but it offers no guarantee of catching any other health problems.

Conduct a regular home exam. By knowing what's normal for your cat and paying attention to the body's physical changes, you can detect many illnesses before they become serious.

tartar stains. Don't forget to check the molars beneath the cheeks.

It is important to familiarize yourself with what is normal. You may wish to keep a diary of your cat's condition, recording such things as eating habits, weight, litterbox habits, hairball frequency, and activity levels. Such a record will be invaluable in case of illness, giving the veterinarian a solid foundation on which to build a diagnosis.

Finish the home exam with a massage. Your cat will love it, and the stroking will be good for you, too. It's a wonderful way to relieve tension after a difficult day at the office. Soon both of you will look forward to this ritual.

VETERINARY TIP

"The one piece of advice I often give to owners of geriatric cats is to have regular health exams that pay particular attention to the dental health of the cat. Many of the preventable problems I see in old-timers are directly related to untreated dental problems."

—*Jimmy Conrad, DVM, Florence, Oregon.*

A Time 3
of Change

Old age comes on little cat feet.
—with apologies to Carl Sandburg

The changes appeared gradually. Bob didn't even realize that Boise was nearing her 14th birthday until he noticed that after taking a nap, she seemed to struggle to stand up and would limp for a few seconds before walking normally. When he consulted his veterinarian, she reminded him of the pelvic injury Boise had suffered a few years back after being hit by a car. "Boise is just starting to show the signs of old age," she said. "She doesn't weigh as much as she used to, and her coat isn't as thick and shiny as it once was. Have you noticed any changes in her eating and drinking habits?"

Cats age gracefully, but no matter how well we care for them, the signs of age will begin to appear. Perhaps the fur is less lustrous and the eyes not quite as bright. The skin may hang a little more loosely. The cat that once took the stairs two at a time now ascends in a slow, stately manner. These changes are not necessarily cause for alarm. However, they may be early warning signs of degeneration and disease, alerting you to be on the lookout for more serious problems. Typically, age first begins to show when the cat is between 12 and 15 years old.

WHEN IS A CAT OLD?

As with people, the definition of "old" varies from cat to cat. Some people seem to be old when they're 45, while others don't seem to be old even when they're 85. The same is true with individual pets. Many cat owners don't think of their pets as being "old." But, in general, a cat's geriatric years begin when it is 8 to 10 years old. That's when the aging process begins to occur. Aging can be defined as a faster rate of cell deterioration than repair; in effect, it is a decrease in the rate of bodily functions. Because cats spend up to 18 hours a day sleeping, it's sometimes difficult to notice that their activity level has decreased or that their movements are a little slower than they once were. In fact, the aging process can be so gradual that owners don't even notice it until an illness or injury shocks them into awareness.

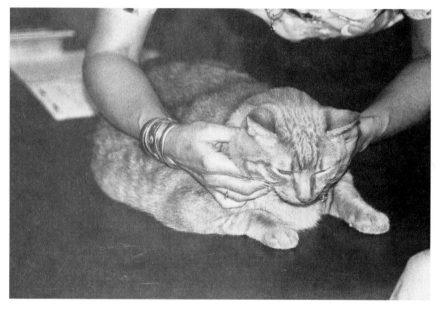

Use your hands to help you gauge your cat's well-being. Notice if he's feeling bonier or sore, or is developing any unusual bumps.

Rather than letting your cat's old age creep up on you, make it a habit to use not only your eyes, but also your hands and nose to gauge your cat's well-being. You may notice that Smoky is feeling a little bonier than usual when you pet him, or that his breath is not too appealing when he snuggles up on your pillow in the morning. If you observe such seemingly minor signs of a change in health, it's time to start looking more closely at Smoky's overall condition. His lifestyle, the care he has received over the years, and your observation skills will all determine whether Smoky goes through his golden years with flying colors.

How can you tell if your cat is beginning to show its age? Changes you may notice include worn, yellowing teeth, weight loss and a change in attitude. The pupils of the eyes may change from black to blue or gray. In advanced age, the cat may increase its water consumption and urination. A cat that was once agile and sinewy may lose muscle tone or become unsteady on its feet. Reaction time is often decreased.

Inactivity is also more common, but an old cat that just lies around all the time should not necessarily be viewed as normal. Lethargy is the hallmark of some diseases. Therefore, it's important to be aware of a cat's normal behavior, so it can be differentiated from that caused by illness. Otherwise, the cat may not receive needed veterinary care until a disease has progressed to the point where it is untreatable.

Age brings a decline in the metabolic rate. Tissues lose water and become more fibrous, causing stiffness in the joints, and the skin is less elastic. The reduction in moisture manifests itself in flaky skin and lackluster fur. Also, nails become more brittle, the haircoat begins to thin, and the muzzle may turn gray. And, muscle is edged out by fat as a percentage of body weight.

Organs—especially those that secrete hormones, such as the pancreas and thyroid—become less efficient, leading to conditions like hyperthyroidism and diabetes. A decrease in kidney size leads to reduced renal function. And there is often a decrease in liver function, as well. Also, digestive motion in the esophagus, stomach, and colon slows. Vision, hearing, and smell diminish. And the lens of the eye as viewed through the pupil may seem bluish-gray instead of jet-black. Finally, bones become more brittle.

This slowing down and wearing out of the cat's system means reduced caloric needs, less tolerance of temperature variations, and decreased protection from disease. In most cases, it is not indicative of serious problems, but it does mean

Signs of Increasing Age

- *Dry fur*
- *Flaky skin*
- *Slower movement*
- *Worn or yellowing teeth*
- *Increased thirst*
- *Loss of muscle tone*
- *Stiff joints*
- *Thinning coat*
- *Weight loss*
- *Inactivity*
- *Diminished hearing and vision*
- *Blue or gray pupils*

that you must pay closer attention to your cat's physical needs so you can limit the effects of some of these aging processes. As discussed in the last chapter, regular brushing helps distribute body oils, and exercise, even small amounts, can reduce loss of muscle tone.

It is also a good idea to consider taking your cat in for a geriatric exam. Aging disorders can begin appearing as early as 8 to 10 years of age, although most cats don't show definite signs of aging until they are about 15 years old.

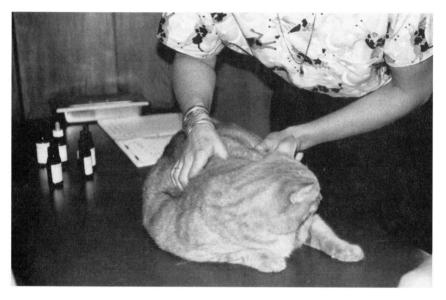

Your veterinarian will recommend that you bring your cat in for a geriatric physical exam when he's reaching his golden years.

THE GERIATRIC EXAM

Janice has two indoor/outdoor cats, Spot and Blue, who are both 10 years old. Because they are allowed outdoors, her veterinarian likes to see the two littermates at least twice a year. This year, Janice plans to ask her veterinarian to give the cats a geriatric profile so he will have a basis for comparison if they become ill.

The best way to begin your cat's old-age health care plan is to plan ahead. When you begin to notice signs of aging in your cat—or better yet, before you notice such signs—it's a good idea to take stock of the situation by asking yourself some questions about your cat's condition. Depending on the answers, you may want to schedule your cat for a geriatric exam. Most veterinarians recommend bringing a cat in for a physical exam and lab work when it is 7 to 10 years old.

The earlier its state of health is established, the more can be done to prevent problems. Even if your cat seems healthy, things are noticed during physicals that, in some instances, can make a difference in whether a cat lives or dies.

Another reason for performing lab work on an aging cat is to identify any problems that might be exacerbated by anesthesia. If your cat is seven years or older, your veterinarian may recommend bloodwork before scheduling a dental cleaning or other surgery.

Ask Yourself These Questions

To decide whether your cat is ready for a geriatric exam, evaluate its condition. Examine your cat and its habits, using the following list as a guideline:

- *Has your cat gained or lost more than a pound in the past year?* A cat that is overweight is more prone to disease, especially diabetes and congestive heart failure. On the other hand, a cat that is eating well but losing weight may be suffering from diabetes or hyperthyroidism. Rapid weight loss in an obese cat can lead to a condition called hepatic lipidosis, which occurs when fats accumulate within liver cells. (See Chapter 7 for a more complete explanation of this disease.) Weight loss can also be an early warning sign of cancer.

- *Does your cat vomit frequently, despite use of a hairball remedy?* Frequent vomiting can be a sign of megaesophagus, hyperthyroidism, inflammatory bowel disease or kidney disease.

- *Is your cat drinking more water than usual?* Among other conditions, excessive thirst can indicate diabetes or kidney disease.

- *Has your cat's appetite changed? Is it picky or hungry all the time?* A cat that isn't eating well could have dental problems. If its teeth hurt, the cat won't want to eat, especially if it eats a diet of dry food. Also, lack of appetite and excessive appetite are signs of a number of diseases.

- *Does your cat have a hard, dry stool; a soft stool; diarrhea; or a bloody stool? Are there changes in stool color or frequency? Does your cat strain to defecate?* Constipated cats strain to defecate, or they produce a hard, dry stool. Diarrhea can be a sign of intestinal disease or hyperthyroidism.

- *Does your cat make frequent trips to the litter box to urinate, or does it urinate outside the litter box? Is there less or more urine than usual? Does the urine have an abnormal color?* Excessive urination often occurs in conjunction with excessive thirst. It can indicate a bladder or kidney infection, or diabetes. Very dark urine can be a problem sign, as can colorless urine.

- *Does your cat have bleeding gums, loose or broken teeth, or bad breath? Does it drop food while eating?* Gum and teeth problems may be signs of periodontal disease, a common ailment in cats. If it gets bad enough, it can affect their ability to eat.

- *Is your cat's coat dry, dull, or flaky? Does it have bald patches?* Skin problems can indicate vitamin, mineral, or fatty acid deficiencies. Or, it might be a sign of hormonal diseases, allergies, or parasites.

- *Is there a change in your cat's energy level? Is it lethargic? Does your cat rarely jump to high places? Does it sleep more and hide from attention? Is your cat nervous, agitated or hyperactive?* Lack of energy can signify a number of problems, including anemia or cancer. Excessive activity or agitation can be a sign of hyperthyroidism.

If you answer yes to any of the above questions, a visit to the veterinarian should be your next step. The veterinarian can help you anticipate changes and evaluate water consumption, food consumption, stool volume, hair coat, and teeth. Such an exam, before your cat begins to show signs of aging, can serve as an early warning system for disease. Conditions that commonly affect older cats include kidney disease, hyperthyroidism, cancer, and dental problems.

THE EXAM PROCESS

If your cat is an older animal, you are probably familiar with veterinary exams. If your cat is young and you want to ensure its good health for years to come, regular veterinary exams are a good idea. Whatever the case, you may have questions about the exam process. The following section is a step-by-step explanation of each stage of the examination and why it is necessary. By knowing the types of questions your veterinarian is likely to ask and being prepared with complete information, you can be certain your cat gets the most out of the exam.

A geriatric exam usually begins with an assessment of your cat's level of health. Your veterinarian will either ask a series of questions or ask you to fill out a form describing your cat's condition, activity level, eating and elimination habits, and so on. This medical history becomes part of your cat's permanent record. The information you provide gives the veterinarian a starting point for the examination and will be used as a baseline for future evaluations.

Have you noticed a change in your cat's energy level? Does he seem more lethargic than usual?

The Medical History

"Begin at the beginning," said the King in Lewis Carroll's *Alice in Wonderland*. Indeed, that is the very same place your cat's medical history should begin. Certain disorders are more likely to affect cats of a certain age, breed, or sex, so the medical history will begin with this information.

The same is true of geographic location. Where your cat lives can affect its health. For instance, a cat with respiratory problems that lives in the Mississippi basin is more likely to be tested for histoplasmosis than one living on the coast of Maine. A jaundiced cat in south Florida is more likely to be infected with a liver fluke than a jaundiced cat in New York City. If you and your cat have recently moved or traveled to another part of the country, it's important for the veterinarian to know.

Where you acquired the cat is also important. Did it come from a pound or a pet store? Did you find it as a stray or buy it from a breeder? What was the quality of its previous care? Knowing the cat's original environment can help pinpoint certain problems. You may not have acquired your cat as a kitten, but as much information as you can provide will be helpful.

Next on the list is the cat's home environment. Is it allowed outdoors? Does it live with other cats? How many? The free-roaming cat is more likely to bring home parasites such as fleas, worms, and flukes, or to have a traumatic encounter with a car. On the other hand, the incidence of infectious respiratory diseases, feline leukemia virus, and feline infectious peritonitis is higher in multi-cat households and catteries, especially if new cats are not isolated before being introduced to the home.

The veterinarian will also want to know your cat's dietary habits. What does it eat and how frequently? A cat that eats a generic food or table scraps may not be getting the proper amount of vitamins and minerals. Cats that dine on raw meat or the occasional rodent, rabbit, or bird are most likely to develop salmonella poisoning or toxoplasmosis. A fat cat may not receive enough physical activity, or it may be eating too much food or a food that is too high in calories for its needs.

There is a reason this inquisition is called a history. Not only does your veterinarian need to know what's going on with your cat now, he or she also needs to know the cat's past medical problems and their outcome. This information helps the veterinarian know what has and hasn't worked in the past, which is important for recurring problems. It also gives the veterinarian an idea of the types of health problems the cat has had, which can indicate the direction the veterinarian should take in making a diagnosis. For instance, a past history of recurrent infections, unresponsive anemia, or unexplained weight loss might suggest testing the blood for feline leukemia virus infection.

The cat's vaccination and parasite status provide important information, too. Has it been vaccinated in the past year? When was the last time it had a fecal exam or worming treatment?

Taking a history is like detective work. The information that is provided lays the groundwork for further investigation.

The Physical Examination

The physical exam involves looking at the ears and teeth, listening to the heart, and taking the temperature. The veterinarian will also palpate the cat, manually examining the entire body to check the condition of the organs and to search for lumps.

Although your cat may appear to have a problem in a specific area, it's important for the veterinarian to examine the entire body, from head to tail. To get the big picture, the veterinarian may observe the cat from a distance, noting its attitude, posture, and body condition. Then the cat's temperature, weight, pulse rate, and respiration are recorded.

Starting at the head, the veterinarian examines the cat's eyes, ears, nose, and mouth, checking for such signs as discharges, inflammation, nasal obstructions, foreign bodies, dental disease, bad breath, or abnormal growths. A stethoscope is used to evaluate the heart and lungs. Moving down the rest of the body, the veterinarian will palpate each area, feeling for organ position and size, abnormal lumps, and painful areas. Then the genital area is checked for discharges and growths.

While examining your cat, the veterinarian may ask you questions about its condition. Your ability to provide concrete answers is an important part of the process. It's not enough to merely say that the cat is lethargic, that it isn't eating, or that it is hiding. These signs could indicate a variety of illnesses, so the veterinarian will ask specific questions about the cat's behavior or symptoms.

For instance, abnormal urination may elicit questions about the amount and frequency of urination; whether the urine contains blood or is an abnormal color; whether the cat is urinating away from its box; whether the cat is straining during urination; and whether the cat's diet has changed. The answers, combined with the physical examination, are the key to the diagnosis. If you think of something later, even if it seems minor, don't hesitate to call with the information.

Keeping a daily diary of pet behavior is a good habit. Be sure to record even minor changes in activity, such as choosing an unusual spot to sleep. Noting even normal behavior is important, because it indicates development of patterns. If a cat later becomes ill, this record can help pinpoint when its activity started to change. Take the diary to the veterinarian's office for quick, easy reference about the cat's behavior and the length of time since the symptoms started. Such a diary need not be elaborate. It can be a simple spiral-bound notebook with a paragraph written each night.

During the exam, your veterinarian will feel your cat's body for anything unusual — inside or out.

Diagnostic Tests

Depending on the information provided in the history and the findings of the exam, the veterinarian may order diagnostic tests. Such tests may include a complete blood count, a chemistry profile, a urinalysis, a chest X ray, ultrasonography, endoscopy, or an electrocardiogram. These diagnostic aids can help the veterinarian identify such conditions as kidney disease, diabetes, hyperthyroidism, and heart disease. Unless the problem is external—an abscess, for example—some form of diagnostic test will probably be required.

Making a Diagnosis

When the laboratory results are in, the veterinarian can pull together the information from the tests, the exam, and the history to diagnose a cat that is ill or make care recommendations for geriatric cats. Your veterinarian should discuss the results with you and offer advice on the steps you need to take to keep your cat in good health. A written evaluation of the health assessment, along with written short-term and long-term plans, will keep you and your cat on track. The veterinarian may suggest a follow-up exam in six months to a year to evaluate your cat's condition and ensure that the plan is still appropriate.

Annual examinations, plus a well-kept medical history, can put your old cat on the fast track to a long life. If your cat goes outdoors all or part of the time, your veterinarian may recommend more frequent examinations. Careful observation, good care, and regular checkups can help you nip problems in the bud or avoid them altogether.

CHOOSING A VETERINARIAN

If you have just acquired your cat, whether it is a kitten or an adult, or if you have moved recently, finding a good veterinarian should be at the top of your list of priorities. The relationship you build with the veterinarian, as well as his or her relationship with your cat, can make a big difference in your cat's health over the years. It's important not only to be confident in a veterinarian's abilities, but also for your cat to be comfortable in his or her care.

As your cat ages, keep a diary of his behavior so you can log anything unusual, such as whether he's eating more or less. This is vital information for the vet should your cat become ill.

To begin your search, ask friends or neighbors for recommendations. If you are moving to a new area, ask your former veterinarian if he or she can recommend a colleague in that area. The American Animal Hospital Association can refer you to affiliated veterinarians or clinics. Membership in AAHA is not automatically a sign that a clinic is well-run, but it does indicate that the hospital has met certain standards established by AAHA.

Another good place to search is in the Yellow Pages of your phone directory. An advertisement can tell you how long a veterinarian has been in practice, whether the clinic offers boarding or grooming, and if any specialists are on staff. It's also a good way to locate clinics near your home.

When you have chosen a few prospects, call the clinic and make an appointment to interview the veterinarian and tour the clinic. During the interview, ask about the veterinarian's interest in cats and whether he or she has an interest in geriatrics. This is not a field in which a veterinarian might be a board-certified specialist, but he or she should be familiar with the problems of age and keep up with the advances made in the care of older cats. In addition, the veterinarian should be comfortable handling an old cat.

Note whether the veterinarian answers your questions readily and clearly. A good veterinarian is a good communicator. Brief, mumbled answers without any details do not inspire confidence. The staff, too, should communicate clearly and courteously. Do they answer the telephone promptly and greet clients in a friendly manner when they enter the clinic? Do the veterinarian and the staff have a good rapport with the animals they treat?

Cleanliness, of course, is vital. All veterinary clinics have an odor, but there's a difference between the normal scents of disinfectant and animal aromas, and the smell of urine, feces or vomit that hasn't been cleaned up.

Summary of Care Concerns

- *Evaluate your cat's condition when it is 7 to 10 years old. Schedule a geriatric exam if you notice any physical changes, such as weight loss, increased thirst, or urination.*
- *Be prepared to give the cat's complete medical history at the exam.*
- *Keep a log of your cat's behavior and physical condition.*
- *Choose a veterinarian with an interest in geriatrics.*

If you are satisfied with your tour of the clinic and the responses to your questions, make an appointment to bring your cat in for an examination. Even if the cat is up-to-date on its vaccinations, it's a good idea for the veterinarian to see your cat when it's healthy, so he or she can have a baseline against which to judge its health.

Also, if you are new to an area, the veterinarian may be able to advise you about concerns facing cat owners there. For instance, outdoor cats in Florida may encounter the Bufo toad, which secretes a poisonous substance on its skin. The unlucky cat that tries to bite this toad will suffer such symptoms as drooling, vomiting, diarrhea, and convulsions. Cats that go outdoors in the western United States, especially in New Mexico, Arizona, Colorado and Utah, run the risk of contracting the plague, transmitted when the cat eats an infected rodent or is bitten by a flea from an infected rodent.

This type of information and interaction is invaluable. Ideally, your cat will see the same veterinarian for its entire life. The relationship the three of you build should have a foundation of trust and communication.

VETERINARY TIP

"As cats get older, that yearly exam gets more and more important. It can pick up a lot of things, as can the questions the veterinarian asks about the cat's lifestyle."

—*Vickie Valdez, DVM, All Cat Veterinary Clinic, Orange, California.*

Personality

4

and *Behavior*

Old friends are best . . .
—John Selden

In her younger years, Shelby was fearful of all strangers and new situations. She still doesn't like trips away from home, but now in her eleventh year, she has mellowed considerably.

■

Misty never liked the vacuum cleaner. She ran and hid every time it was pulled out of the closet. At age 13, however, she has made her peace with it. Instead of running down the stairs when it appears, she makes a stately exit after it is turned on.

■

Maxwell is 17. The once fastidious cat is now starting to miss the litterbox more often than not. His owner is baffled by this uncharacteristic behavior. Is Maxwell senile, is he getting lazy in his old age, or does he have a urinary tract infection?

■

Peter once flipped through the air with the greatest of ease, chasing and tumbling after the elusive Kitty Tease. These days, the 10-year-old diabetic cat still anticipates the appearance of this much-loved toy, but his double-flips are no more.

One of the pleasures of living with a cat for many years is watching its personality grow and its habits change. In kittenhood, which can sometimes last through age four, a cat is bold and brave, always exploring, never taking no for an answer. A kitten is usually too busy to sit in a lap—at least, not for very long.

In middle age, the cat becomes more dignified and sedate. It may become a lap cat at this time, or it may remain the cat that walks alone: aloof, reclusive, and independent.

Old age, however, can bring surprises. The standoffish cat may become friendly, often settling into a lap for hours on end. The fearful cat may finally develop confidence, no longer running at the sound of the doorbell or the sight of the vacuum cleaner.

As cats age, their personalities change. For example, a standoffish cat may welcome more attention.

It's unlikely that age will bring a major personality change in your cat, but you will probably notice it slowing down some. Cats are known for sleeping a lot, but an aging cat may sleep even longer and sounder than it did in its younger days.

Old cats may become less social or even downright cranky, especially around children or younger animals. Provide these cats with quiet, comfortable sleeping areas away from high-traffic areas, and confine them when visiting children or pets are around. Reducing its stress level will help keep your cat happy.

Some cats may become clingy, following you through the house and demanding to sit in your lap at every opportunity. Playfulness may decrease, too. Your cat may still show interest in its favorite ping-pong ball, but fantastic flips and pounces are probably a thing of the past. Continue to offer your cat opportunities to exercise and play, but don't push it past its limits.

Some older cats become cranky—especially around children. It's up to you to safeguard the child and the cat.

HEALTH AND BEHAVIOR

Behavior changes, especially in older cats, are an indication that something is wrong. Behavioral signs of disease include aggression, irritability, fear, disorientation, lethargy, personality changes, changes in urinary or bowel habits, repetitive behaviors, and pacing or circling.

The most common behavior problems in old cats are inappropriate elimination and excessive vocalization. Hyperthyroidism may make cats agitated and grouchy. Excessive vocalization is sometimes related to hyperthyroidism or liver disease. Increased water consumption and subsequent increased urination resulting from kidney or bladder disease can lead to litter box problems. Brain tumors, although uncommon, can affect a cat's actions, causing such personality or behavior changes as dullness, pacing, circling, and inability to recognize familiar people and objects. If your cat's behavior changes suddenly or becomes extreme, schedule a thorough veterinary exam to rule out any physical causes.

As any animal ages, its sensory functions decrease. Often, behavior problems are related to these changes. Some older cats seem to become bewildered, especially at night. They are wakeful, wandering and yowling, as if lost or confused. These may be senile changes, or they may have a physical cause. Changes in sight or hearing can make a cat feel isolated, nervous or disoriented, causing it to vocalize more or to hide. Signs of senility usually appear in cats of advanced age, from 17 to 22 years.

Loss of housetraining is sometimes a problem with old cats. This may be the result of physical problems or an inability to reach the litter box in time. A senile cat may forget where the litter box is located. Incontinence is another possibility. Generally, incontinence is indicated when the cat dribbles urine or drops stool in its sleep or while at rest. A cat that is incontinent or suffering from a medical problem cannot control its actions and should not be punished. Fortunately, medication can help. Commonly used drugs to treat incontinence are phenylpropanolamine, an appetite suppressant and decongestant, and diethylstilbestrol, a synthetic form of estrogen. Your veterinarian can help you identify the problem and recommend a treatment. Be sure to ask about the possible side effects of any drugs that you give.

If your cat's change in behavior is not health-related, do some detective work. In the case of a cat that yowls at night, examine the circumstances. Are there any stimuli associated with the vocalization? This can be a tough process, given the inscrutable nature of the cat, but look for such seemingly simple things as changes in furniture placement or alteration of a routine. A cat that is losing its sight may well be confused by a new piece of furniture or a change in family routine.

When you are having a problem with your cat, talk about it with your veterinarian or write down what is happening. A new perspective can give you insight into the situation. You may need the fresh eyes of a third party, but the answer is there. Observe your cat's behavior without judgment. For the time being, there is no right or wrong; the situation just *is*. For whatever reason, the problem behavior at that moment is normal for the cat. That doesn't mean things are the way you want them to be, but it does allow you to step back and look at the problem. Frequently, misbehavior occurs because the cat is frightened. This is especially true of old cats, whose diminished senses no longer serve them as well. Deafness, for instance, can cause excessive vocalization.

Grief can be another cause of misbehavior or excessive vocalization. Without anthropomorphizing, it is fair to say that cats develop attachments to people and to each other. When a familiar face, whether it is human or feline, goes away or dies, a cat is likely to express its loss in long and loud meows. One cat, a Siamese whose housemate had died, expressed its grief in just such a way. Cats grieving for their owners may wander aimlessly or seem lost and lonely. In these cases, only time can heal the loss.

Cats develop deep attachments to people. (Photo by Faith A. Uridel.)

If the death of another pet means that the cat is now alone, consider whether it might enjoy having a new feline or even a canine companion. Animals do get lonely, and the addition of a new cat or dog may help ease the sense of loss. If the new pet is a kitten or young cat, it may even serve to increase your older cat's activity level and interest in life. Tips on introducing a new pet are covered in Chapter 5.

CHANGING THE ENVIRONMENT

When excessive vocalization cannot be linked to health, environmental stimuli or loss of a companion, try changing its environment to transform the cat's behavior. Often, cats yowl at night, keeping everyone awake, so take steps to encourage sleeping at night. Be sure the cat has a comfortable sleeping area. Give it a heating pad, turned to low so it doesn't burn itself. Hunger may also trigger yowling at night. Try offering a light meal of milk and turkey before bedtime. Both foods are high in tryptophan, an amino acid that is an integral component of serotonin. Serotonin is a chemical in the brain that regulates appetite and sleep cycles. Tryptophan promotes sleepiness by raising serotonin levels. Veterinary behaviorist Amy Marder says this technique isn't guaranteed to work, but it's worth a try. If yowling occurs primarily at night, try leaving on a light. This may not help, however, if the cat's vision is greatly decreased.

THE PROS AND CONS OF DRUGS

In severe cases, a veterinary behaviorist may prescribe an antidepressant such as Elavil, which is known to be relatively safe for use with cats. In general, though, veterinary behaviorists are cautious about prescribing drugs for behavior problems. Although they have their place in treatment, there are drawbacks to pharmacological fixes. Often, side effects aren't discovered until a drug has been in use for many years, as was the case with megestrol acetate, a progesterone that was frequently prescribed in the past for cats that sprayed. Today, it is less commonly used since many cats have side effects, ranging from increased thirst and weight gain to development of diabetes.

Another consideration is a cat's physiological reaction to a drug. The way a cat metabolizes a specific drug can be compromised because of its age. With careful observation, you can help your veterinarian determine whether the dosage should be increased or decreased. Drugs should never be used as a quick fix, but only as an adjunct to proper behavior modification techniques.

LITTER BOX PROBLEMS

To solve litter box problems, use the same techniques. After ruling out medical problems, investigate the circumstances surrounding the behavior. If the litter box is located in the basement or garage, an arthritic cat may have difficulty gaining access to it, causing inappropriate elimination elsewhere in the house. You wouldn't ask your 80-year-old mother to go hurdling to get into the bathroom, so minimize the amount of effort your cat must make to get to the litter box.

A change in the location of the litter box can also trigger spraying or other inappropriate elimination. The solution can be as simple as putting the litter box in a more accessible spot or moving it back to the original location. Another technique is to confine the cat with the litter box in a very small area, such as a bathroom, until the cat is retrained.

EXAMINING AGGRESSION

Aggression caused by illness or irritation is another behavior problem that can affect older cats. A cat that is sick or in pain may react aggressively to what would otherwise be a normal situation. Irritable aggression can be triggered by hospitalization; pain from arthritis, periodontal disease, or the strain of constipation; and even by minor changes in routine, such as a late meal. A major change, such as the introduction of a new pet, disrupts not only an older cat's routine, but also its territorial boundaries. In such a situation, a cat is even more likely to develop irritable aggression.

When a sick cat shows irritation, the best thing to do is to recognize the cause and grant the cat the seclusion it needs until it feels better. If the cat is hospitalized, it may help to cover the front of the cage or give it a place inside the cage where it can retreat, such as a large paper bag or box. In cases where aggression is triggered by a change in the cat's environment or routine, the most important thing the cat needs is time to adjust to the new situation. Over time, the cat will adapt to the new routine or become accustomed to the change in surroundings.

FINDING A BEHAVIORIST

If your cat's actions are not caused by disease and you have been unable to correct the behavior, consider seeking the help of an animal behaviorist. The trained, unbiased observations of an professional can be invaluable. But before you write a check to the first person whose ad you see in the Yellow Pages, ask about his or her qualifications. Credentials are important, especially because no state or federal government agency requires animal behaviorists to be licensed or certified. Anyone can hang out a shingle declaring himself to be an animal behaviorist, even without any training in the field.

Ideally, an animal behaviorist will have both academic training and real-world experience. For instance, a degree in psychology indicates that the behaviorist probably has an understanding of behavior modification. Someone with experience as a veterinary technician probably has worked with many

Looking at Behavior

- *Note any personality changes and make any necessary adjustments in your cat's lifestyle, such as keeping children away from it or ensuring ease of litter box access.*

- *If you notice a sudden or unusual behavior change, schedule a veterinary visit to rule out any health problems.*

- *Consult a qualified behaviorist if you and your veterinarian are unable to determine the cause of a behavior change.*

different animals and gained an understanding of their behavior. Length of time in practice is important, as is affiliation with professional organizations. Ask about continuing education. Someone who earned a degree 20 years ago and hasn't kept up with changes in the field is missing out on a number of advances in behavior modification techniques. With cats, it's especially important to find qualified people, because the techniques used with dogs generally do not work or are the wrong techniques to use with cats.

Ask your veterinarian for a recommendation. Some veterinarians work closely with behaviorists or are certified behaviorists themselves. Because of the potentially complicated medical problems in old cats, a veterinarian whose main area of interest is in behavior may be ideal. Look for a veterinarian who is board-certified by the American College of Veterinary Behaviorists. In addition to their veterinary training, board-certified veterinary behaviorists complete a residency program that includes working with animals that have behavior problems, educational learning theory, and neuropharmacology, the use of drugs to treat behavior problems. Veterinary behaviorists must be knowledgeable about anatomy, physiology, pathology, pharmacology, medicine, neurology and behavior, and it's critical that they have good interviewing skills to diagnose behavioral problems.

If a board-certified veterinary behaviorist is not available, look for a psychologist who works closely with veterinarians. Applied animal behavior consultants certified through the Animal Behavior Society have a Ph.D. in a biological or behavioral science with an emphasis in animal behavior and five years professional experience, or a doctorate in veterinary medicine with a two-year residency in animal behavior. They are active researchers or practitioners in the diagnosis and treatment of behavior problems in pets.

BEHAVIOR RESOURCES

A nearby college of veterinary medicine may have behaviorists on its staff. Veterinary colleges and animal behavior consultants are listed in the Appendix. For more information on finding a veterinary behaviorist, contact one of the following organizations:

American College of Veterinary Behaviorists, Bonnie V. Beaver, DVM, College of Veterinary Medicine, Texas A&M University, College Station, TX 77843-4474.

American Veterinary Society for Animal Behavior, Wayne Hunthausen, DVM, Westwood Animal Hospital, 4820 Rainbow Blvd., Westwood, KS 66205; or Gary Landsberg, DVM, Doncaster Animal Clinic, 99 Henderson Ave., Thornhill, ON L3T 2K9 CANADA.

Animal Behavior Society, John C. Wright, P.O. Box 180 MU, Macon, GA 31207; (912) 752-2973.

VETERINARY TIP

"Continue loving them like you have in the past. They may have some special needs."

—*Bonnie Beaver, DVM, American College of Veterinary Behaviorists, Texas A&M University.*

Physical, 5
Mental, and
Emotional Well-Being

"There are so few who can grow old with a good grace."—Sir Richard Steele

Your cat's emotional well-being and dignity is just as important as its physical well-being. Its mental, physical and emotional health can make a big difference in how your cat adapts to old age. By enabling the cat to continue doing the things it enjoys, while also keeping it safe, you can offer it a number of happy, contented years.

> *Wendy's 19-year-old cat, Zoot, is nearly deaf and has chronic cystitis. Because of a heart murmur, Zoot's circulation is reduced, making her seek more warmth than the average cat. The small black mixed-breed has arthritis and can't jump as well as she once did. And although she still goes up and down stairs and on beds and couches, she can't make it up to the kitchen counter anymore.*

If your cat is no longer able to jump to her favorite high spot, such as the bed or sofa, help her out by providing steps or some other way of climbing up. Be sure the favored spot isn't at a height that would be dangerous if she fell. If it is, you may need to determine some way of making it safer or consider barricading it to prevent access.

Older cats often like to be in warm places, so make sure your cat has easy access to a sunny window or, in wintertime, a comfortable place near the heater.

Heated, washable cushion beds are available from pet stores or pet supply catalogs. If Smoky likes to curl up in front of the fireplace, keep an eye on him so his whiskers don't get singed.

Older cats like comfy spots, whether it's a warm patch of carpet, a sunny window, or a favorite chair.

Make the litter box more accessible, too. If you have a multi-story home, place a litter box on each floor so your cat doesn't have to make trips up and down the stairs. Increased water intake means increased urination, so you may also need to change the litter in the box more frequently. Similarly, make food and water available both upstairs and downstairs.

DEALING WITH STRESS

Stress is defined as a physical, chemical, or emotional factor that causes bodily or mental tension. It is believed that stress can play a role in the development of disease or decreased resistance to disease. For instance, stress can be related to development of colitis, and excessive thirst and urination. Helping your cat maintain a normal lifestyle will contribute a great deal to its physical and mental health by reducing stress—an important part of ensuring longevity.

The Causes of Stress

The ability to tolerate stress varies from cat to cat. For some cats, any change in routine, however minor, is stressful. Common stress-inducing situations include conflicts with other cats and separation from the familiar, whether that is a person, another pet, or the home. Behavioral changes can result from changes in feeding or care schedules; the move to a new home; and confinement in a carrier for transport, noise, and lack of attention.

Not all stress is harmful—in fact, some stress is believed to be beneficial—but the trick is recognizing when and why stress is causing a problem.

Old cats especially like a strict routine and an unchanging environment. As they age, they can become less willing or

Cats can become stressed by being confined in a carrier for too long.

able to adapt to situations they once took in stride, such as visitors, boarding, remodeling, or a new baby. Some simple adjustments can help both of you adapt.

For instance, a week's stay in a boarding kennel might be replaced by visits from a pet sitter, allowing the cat to stay in familiar surroundings. This can be especially important for cats with health problems such as diabetes, because their well-being is dependent on a set diet at specified times. A cat that is unwilling to eat because of changed circumstances can quickly become ill.

Advise visitors and children beforehand that the cat prefers to be left alone. If necessary, confine the cat to another room about half

As they age, cats can become less willing or able to adapt to situations they once took in stride.

an hour before visitors arrive. That way, your cat won't associate company with being banished.

Other examples of stressful situations include the addition of a new pet to the household or a move to a new home. With planning and patience, however, you can help your cat adapt to these situations.

INTRODUCING A NEW PET

The addition of a new pet can be especially stressful for an aging cat. Used to ruling the roost, Clementine may view the intruder—especially if it is another cat—as competition. Even if she doesn't, some friction is unavoidable, simply because most animals are creatures of habit and dislike the disruption of their routine. Knowing what to expect can help you minimize or prevent problems.

First, be sure your home is large enough for another cat. Cats are territorial by nature and they each need a certain amount of space to call their own. As demonstrated in human and animal population studies, when a situation gets crowded, tempers flare and fights break out. A good rule of thumb is to allow 400 to 600 square feet per cat.

Isolate the new cat—whether it is a kitten or an adult—until your veterinarian can examine and vaccinate it. You don't want to expose your older cat to any diseases, even if she is vaccinated. This means keeping the new cat in an inaccessible area and providing a separate litter box.

Once the new cat has a clean bill of health, you can begin your introduction campaign. Rather than just throwing the cats together and hoping they get along, gradually accustom them to each other, starting with scent.

For the first few days, keep them in separate rooms so they can smell but not see each other. Next, put the new cat in a carrier for the first face-to-face meeting. Cats generally are not very social creatures, so there may be quite a bit of hissing and growling, even though they are separated. This is normal, so don't scold the cats for it.

Continue to separate the cats for two or three days, but allow frequent meetings via the carrier. With any luck, the hissing and growling should decrease. When they seem to ignore each other or at least don't appear to be aggressive, you can allow the cats to meet nose to nose. Once this meeting takes place, there may be some disagreements, but for the

The addition of a new pet can be especially stressful for an aging cat.

most part, the cats will be accustomed to each other's scents and will mind their manners.

Feed them together so they can be in the same room together doing something enjoyable. Fortunately, unlike dogs, most cats are not threatened by the presence of another cat while they are eating. Some behaviorists recommend bathing both cats before introducing them, the theory being that they will then smell alike. If you are willing to make the effort, it can't hurt.

Another technique is to make both cats smell as much like you as possible. Wipe them down with a sweaty T-shirt. That way they smell alike and they smell like you.

If you are unable to follow this program, you can let the cats get to know each other on their own terms, but this method is not recommended as it is likely to take longer and may involve many spats before territorial disputes are settled. If your cat is more than eight years old, or is gentle or unhealthy in some way, you may need to protect it from an overly-aggressive or playful younger cat. But too much interference may delay the settling of their differences. Keep each cat's claws trimmed short.

Introducing a new cat of any age to your household is a matter of patience. Sometimes cats bond quickly; other times they reach a truce only after months of discord. Unless you are very lucky, you can count on two solid weeks of hissing, growling, and spitting. If you can get over that quickly, you have a match made in heaven.

There are other steps you can take to promote a harmonious relationship. Spay or neuter the new cat. This will help reduce the friction that can occur between cats of the same sex, especially if your old cat is also neutered.

Provide separate beds, toys, food dishes and, if possible, litter boxes. Quite often, fights take place over who is going to use the scratching post or litter box first. These territorial creatures don't always like to share. Be sure to give your older cat extra love and attention so it doesn't feel neglected.

Don't forget to discipline the new cat. Your older cat may be so well-behaved that you have forgotten how much training it took to get her that way. Slacking off on the new arrival can lead to both cats developing bad habits. Pull the water squirter out of retirement and use it as needed.

Much of the above advice applies to introducing a puppy or dog to your older cat. Keep the dog crated for the first couple of meetings, and keep it on a leash when dog and cat meet face-to-face so you can control its actions. Never hold your cat out to the dog. The dog may view the cat as a toy— or as prey—and snap at it.

Patience is the key to peace in a multi-pet home. Good relationships are not built in a day. But with careful refereeing, your pets are likely to learn to tolerate each other, and they may even become friends.

Potential Problems

Although most cats will learn to get along without undue behavior problems, some can become so stressed by a new addition to the household that they begin spraying or eliminating away from the litter box. If this happens, don't panic and don't punish the cat. Remember that the cat is stressed, and take steps to relieve that stress.

Take the cat to the veterinarian to make sure no physical problems are causing the behavior. If the cat is healthy, think back to when the problem began. Was it when the new cat was brought into the house or when the two cats were first introduced? Has your older cat ever had to share its litter box? If not, the trauma (from the cat's point of view) could lead to such behavior. Provide a new litter box at a time when the new cat isn't around, and reward your cat for using it. The addition of a new box may nip the problem in the bud.

Another potential problem caused by the introduction of a new pet may be a change in the way your cat eats. At one extreme it may begin eating too much, running the risk of obesity; at the other, it may stop eating altogether, exposing it to other health risks. Keep an eye open for such changes in behavior and be prepared to deal with them. Strictly control the portions received by the cat that is overeating, and be willing to offer a few tasty tidbits to entice the cat that is not eating. It's also a good idea to take the cat in for a veterinary exam to ensure that the loss of appetite isn't health-related.

Irreconcilable Differences

In some cases, your cat may be downright unwilling to tolerate another cat in the home. If you can't keep them separated, you may have to consider finding another home for the new cat.

EASING THE STRESS OF MOVING

Americans are a mobile people, moving on average once every seven years. Some move even more frequently; one 11-year-old cat has lived in five homes during her life. Although a move can be stressful for an older cat, there are ways you can ease the transition to a new home.

You may wish to board the cat while you are packing and moving furniture. If you are moving only a short distance, you can set up some familiar furniture—as well as the cat's litter box and scratching post—before bringing the cat into the new home. The familiar items and scents will help the cat adjust to its new surroundings.

If boarding is not possible, or if you are moving a long distance, you can still take steps to make the move less traumatic. Confine the cat to one room while the movers are working. The cat will be less disturbed by the commotion and less likely to slip out through an open door. When you arrive at your new home, again confine the cat to a single room—preferably with a familiar piece of furniture—until the movers are finished unloading your possessions.

Moves are particularly stressful for cats. This one is hiding between pieces of furniture.

Car and Air Travel

A long-distance move may require a road trip of several days or a flight of several hours. In either case, preparation and common sense will ensure that your cat arrives safely.

Car Travel

When traveling by car, prepare a comfortable carrier for the cat to ride in during the trip. Never allow your cat to ride loose in the car. It takes only a second for the cat to escape out an open door or window, or to be ejected from the car during an accident. The carrier should be sturdy, well-ventilated, and escape-proof.

During a long car trip, pay attention to the carrier's location in relation to the path of the sun. Keep it on the shady side of the car, or shield the carrier from the sun's rays. If you want to give the cat an outing at rest stops, attach a strong, well-made harness (not a collar) and leash before getting out of the car. Never leave the cat alone in the car on a hot day, even with the windows cracked. The temperature inside a car can rise quickly to dangerous levels, leading to heat stress, suffocation, and death.

While you are on the road, try to stick to the cat's regular routine. As much as possible, feed and groom it at the same times each day. Bring along plenty of the cat's regular diet, as well as bottled water to prevent any digestive upsets.

If your cat is prone to carsickness, ask your veterinarian to prescribe a tranquilizer or motion sickness medication. Reactions to these drugs vary from cat to cat, so you may wish to give the medication a trial run before the trip. Ideally, of course, your cat will have been accustomed to car rides since kittenhood and will not find them stressful. One couple frequently took their two kittens for car rides to a nearby drive-in restaurant. When it came time to move cross-country, the cats adapted quickly to life on the road.

Air Travel

Air travel doesn't take as long, but it requires similar plans and precautions. A cat traveling by air will need a health certificate, available from your veterinarian. The certificate verifies that the cat is healthy and properly vaccinated. Make your reservations as far in advance as possible, so you can reserve a spot in the cabin for your cat. Most airlines permit a limited number of pets per cabin on each flight. The cat must ride in a carrier that fits beneath the seat in front of you.

If you cannot reserve space in the cabin for your cat, especially if it is old, consider taking a different flight or airline. The stress of flying in the baggage compartment may be too much for an old cat. If a flight in the baggage compartment is unavoidable, be sure the crate is clearly labeled as containing a live animal. Inform airline employees at both the departure city and the destination of your cat's presence, and ask them to take good care of it. By personalizing your cat to the employees, you increase the chances that they will recognize it and give her extra attention.

Fill the cup inside the crate with ice. This will prevent spillage and provide your cat with water throughout the flight.

Avoid flights during extremely hot or cold weather, and try to get a direct flight so you don't risk the airline losing the cat during delays, stopovers, or plane changes.

Identifying Your Cat

Before any trip, provide your cat with an ID tag that lists not only your new address and phone number, but also a contact name and number from your previous neighborhood. If your cat gets lost along the way, rescuers may not be able to reach you immediately at your new address. Look for temporary or permanent write-on tags at your pet store or advertised in cat magazines. These should be used any time you are traveling with your cat or when you are away from home and want to leave identification directing finders to your petsitter or veterinarian. Microchipping is a relatively new form of permanent identification that you may also wish to consider.

This cat wears a collar and tags even when indoors.

Microchip I.D.

One of the newest and best technologies available for identifying cats is the microchip. Cats are especially good at removing collars and tags, and their fur covers any tattoo. A microchip provides permanent identification that cannot be removed. With the growth of microchip technology since 1990, this new method of identification could save the lives of thousands of cats that would otherwise die in shelters, unrecognized or unclaimed.

A microchip is tiny, about the size of a grain of rice. It is programmed with a unique, unalterable code number, as well as the electronic circuitry required to send out the code number. A small copper coil serves as an antenna, and a capacitor is used for tuning. There are no batteries to be replaced. A microchip can be expected to last for 25 years.

Available only through veterinarians, microchips can be implanted within seconds in cats six months or older. They are injected beneath the skin in the scruff of the neck, between the shoulder blades. The injection is no more painful than a vaccination, and no sedation or anesthesia is required.

Before the microchip is injected, the veterinarian scans it to confirm the code. Once the microchip is implanted, it is scanned again to verify the code and ensure that the microchip is working properly. It's a good idea to have cats microchipped at the time they are adopted or when they receive their annual vaccinations.

A microchip serves as a tracking device, or transponder, sending a signal only when activated by a compatible scanning device. Unfortunately, no universal scanner is yet in place, but some scanners identify the presence of other chips in addition to reading their own chips. When a microchip is activated, the scanner decodes the signal and displays the identification code on a liquid-crystal display window.

In many cases, pet product manufacturers are working with microchip/scanner companies and animal welfare organizations to ensure that shelters nationwide are equipped with scanning devices. Veterinary and animal humane organizations recommend microchipping as a safe and effective way of identifying lost pets and ensuring their return.

Microchip Registries

There are advantages to listing a microchipped cat with a national registry. These services usually provide 24-hour notification, a tag notifying finders that the cat is microchipped and instructions on how to contact the registry, and are usually affiliated with a number of shelters across the country. However, even if you choose not to register your cat with one of these organizations, a shelter or laboratory can still locate and notify the veterinarian who implanted the chip. The following manufacturers and organizations offer microchip registration.

The HomeAgain Companion Animal Retrieval System is managed by the American Kennel Club, but its services are open to all pets, including cats. The microchip is programmed with a unique identification code that is displayed when read by a compatible scanner. The HomeAgain scanner can detect the presence of other microchips in addition to its own,

Stress Beaters

- *Take steps to make life easy for your cat by making sure its food, water, and litter box are easily accessible.*

- *Provide comfortable bedding in a warm spot that is easy to get to.*

- *Keep stressful situations to a minimum while recognizing that stress can never be totally avoided and that some stress is beneficial.*

- *If lost, ensure your cat's safe return by providing it with a collar and identification tags or microchip identification.*

- *Even if your cat is a strictly indoor pet, it should still wear a collar and identification tags in case a door is accidentally left open or a delivery person lets the cat out. Some owners put tags on their cats that read, "If I'm outdoors, I'm lost," along with a phone number or address.*

although it cannot read them. All identification codes are kept on file in a database with nationwide, 24-hour access by phone or fax. Schering-Plough Animal Health is distributing the HomeAgain scanner free of charge to a broad network of animal shelters, humane societies, and animal control agencies across the country, as well as providing veterinarians with directories listing nationwide locations of scanners.

When the microchip is implanted, the owner completes an enrollment form stating the cat's breed, sex, color and markings, as well as the owner's name, address and telephone numbers. The form also requests the telephone numbers of an alternate contact and the cat's veterinarian, in case the owner cannot be reached.

Cats enrolled in the HomeAgain program are given a free collar tag imprinted with their identification code and the toll-free number for the database. If a cat is found with a HomeAgain collar, the tag provides all the information the finder needs to have the animal identified by the database. If the tag is missing, the cat can be scanned at the nearest shelter, veterinary office, or animal control agency. Once the cat is identified, network operators can notify the owner so he or she can set up a meeting with the finder to reclaim the cat.

The implantation and enrollment cost is about $50 per pet. For more information, write to Schering-Plough Animal Health, Attn: HomeAgain, 1095 Morris Ave., P.O. Box 3182, Union, NJ 07083-1982; or call (800) 566-3596. The AKC also provides information, available by writing to AKC Companion Animal Recovery, 5580 Centerview Dr., Ste. 250, Raleigh, NC 27606-3394; faxing a request to (919) 233-1290; or calling (800) 252-7894.

InfoPET literature notes that as many as 70 percent of the animals arriving at shelters have no identification, making it difficult or impossible to return them to their owners. Membership in InfoPET's registry requires a one-time fee for the procedure, charged by the veterinarian who implants the microchip, and a membership fee, which can be paid all at once or renewed annually. Benefits include a 24-hour nationwide database and recovery hotline, a collar tag with your cat's registry number, and access to a veterinary referral network. For more information, write to InfoPET at 415 W. Travelers Trail, Burnsville, MN 55337; (800) INFO-PET.

PETtrac is a national computerized registry for pets identified with the AVID microchip. It has a one-time $35 lifetime membership cost per cat. Your veterinarian may charge a separate fee to implant the chip. Once your cat is chipped and registered with PETtrac, its unique identification number is entered in AVID's database. When a lost cat is scanned, its ID number is displayed on a screen so that the owner, veterinarian, or other contact person can be notified. Owner address and phone number can be updated as needed for a small fee. The AVID scanner can also read chips manufactured by Destron. For more information, call (800) 336-AVID.

VETERINARY TIP

"Some owners don't like to see their cats get old, and they expect them to be exactly as they were when they were young. Recognize that they are older and may not be able to do many of the same things, such as hopping up on the bed or navigating the stairs to use the litter box. You can then take steps to make things easier for them."

—Amy Marder, VMD, veterinary behaviorist, Cambridge, Massachusetts.

Nutrition

"Cats, no less liquid than their shadows,
Offer no angle to the wind.
They slip, diminished, neat, through loopholes
Less than themselves..."—A.S.J. Tessimond

Amanda fed her cat the cheapest food she could find.
After all, it was all the same inside those bags and cans,
wasn't it? The only difference was that some companies
had bigger advertising budgets than others. One day,
Amanda was visiting her friend Susan when Susan's
two cats strolled into the room. "Wow! They're beautiful,"
Amanda said. "Are they purebred?" "Oh, no," Susan
said with a laugh. They just showed up at my door one
day when they were kittens." "But their coats are so
shiny," Amanda said. "Misty doesn't look anything like
that." "What do you feed her?" Susan asked. "Just
whatever's on sale," Amanda replied. "Why, what does
food have to do with it?"

RELATIONSHIP TO HEALTH

We all learn in grade school that "you are what you eat."
That saying holds true for cats as well. Good nutrition plays a
major role in your cat's good health. The right diet can make
a dramatic difference in a cat's appearance, activity level, and
resistance to disease. Many cat owners have seen a tangible
change in their cat's health after switching to higher quality
foods. Indeed, researchers are finding that nutrition is often
an important factor in the prevention and treatment of diseases such as kidney disease and diabetes.

A cat's overall health is affected by his diet, which contributes to his appearance, energy level, and soundness.

NUTRITIONAL NEEDS

No one knows the exact nutritional needs of geriatric cats. The American Association of Feed Control Officials, which regulates the contents and labeling of pet foods, has no specific recommendations or requirements for geriatric cats. In most cases, the older cat that is healthy and maintaining its weight may continue eating food formulated for adult cats.

However, as with people, age can bring changes to a cat's digestive capabilities. Just as pizza and beer may no longer sit well on an aging athlete's stomach, excess vitamins, minerals, and other nutrients may not be tolerated as well by older cats.

To reduce stress on body organs and metabolic processes, it's important to maintain proper nutrient levels, which is not always as easy as it sounds. Because older cats tend to have a decreased metabolic rate and lower activity levels, they require less food to maintain proper body weight. This does not, however, mean that they require less protein or other nutrients. Because a cat is eating less, it may not be getting the amount of nutrients it needs. High quality, nutrient-dense food is a must.

Another casualty of age is the cat's senses of taste and smell. You may notice that your cat is not as drawn to its food bowl as it once was. Or it may leave food in its dish instead of licking the bowl clean. Because the ability to taste is closely linked to the sense of smell, as these senses diminish, the appetite is affected. Food must be highly palatable to tempt an old cat.

The abrasive action of dry food can help prevent the build-up of tartar on the teeth.

The act of eating may also be affected by the aging process. A decrease in saliva production can make it difficult for the cat to swallow. Poor teeth can limit the ability to chew. Enjoyment of food is just as important for cats as it is for people, and a dry mouth and aching teeth aren't conducive to a pleasant mealtime.

And everyone knows that cats are individual in their tastes. Their eating habits may change over the years. In effect, old cats don't always eat as well as young cats. For all these reasons, selecting an appropriate food is one of the easiest steps you and your veterinarian can take to help slow or prevent the onset of disease, improve existing problems, and maintain optimal body weight as a cat enters its geriatric years.

DRY FOOD VS. CANNED FOOD

The scientist prepared his equipment. If his experiment worked, the findings would be revolutionary. He braced

himself for the onslaught. As he twisted the can opener,
Pavlov's cats came running, licking their chops as they
circled him hungrily.

The feline partiality for anything in a can is well-known to anyone who has seen cats come running to the sound of a can opener. If cats had their druthers, they would probably choose to eat the junk food of the cat world: canned tuna in oil.

But is canned food better for cats than dry food? Not necessarily. Each has advantages and disadvantages. Dry diets generally contain less fat and more carbohydrates, while canned diets contain more fat and fewer carbohydrates. There is no evidence showing that cats do better on one type of food than another. The choice depends on a cat's dietary needs and preferences, as well as owner preference and budget. What is most important is whether the food meets all the cat's nutritional needs.

The benefit of dry food is that it helps prevent plaque and tartar buildup on the teeth. Plaque-induced gingivitis and periodontitis are the most common oral diseases of the cat, and studies show that animals fed a hard, abrasive diet form plaque at a slower rate than animals fed a soft diet. For the cat that likes to snack all day long, dry food can be left out without spoiling, or it can be left in a timed feeder by owners who work erratic schedules.

Because dry food contains less fat, it may also be the best choice for a cat that tends to be pudgy. If you have fed your cat a dry diet all its life to help keep its teeth in good condition, you can continue this diet for as long as the cat's mouth is healthy. There are a number of nutritious, digestible, palatable dry cat foods on the market. On the flip side, dry foods can seem boring to the owner who wants to give a cat something special at mealtime.

If your cat's teeth are deteriorating or if your cat is losing weight, a canned food can make chewing easier. Finicky cats may be tempted by the aroma and palatability of canned food. But not all canned foods are nutritionally complete. Some contain only fish, muscle meat or animal by-products, ingredients that often have addictive effects on cats. This type of canned food contains none of the vitamins and minerals that make up a balanced diet. It should be offered only in small amounts, as a supplement to a cat's regular diet.

A food product that is not complete and balanced must state on the label "not to be fed as a sole diet," "for intermittent feeding only," or a similar phrase. If a canned food is your cat's primary diet, be sure it provides complete and balanced nutrition.

One disadvantage to canned food is the smell. The aroma may be tempting to tabbies, but it doesn't do much for humans. Wet food also has a tendency to dry out in the can, but manufacturers are working to improve this by making foods with "gravies" that help keep the food moist even after refrigeration. Keeping a tight plastic lid on an open can may also help prevent drying. The need for refrigeration is another disadvantage. Canned food can't be left out for long periods without risk of spoilage. However, some timed feeders have refrigerated containers so wet food can be left out for the cat that prefers it to dry food. Price must also be considered. Canned food is more expensive than dry food.

If you like the cost and benefits of dry food but feel the need to give your cat something special, there's nothing wrong with mixing the two types of food. Just be sure you don't end up feeding the cat more calories than it needs. Most food labels offer guidelines on how to mix quantities of dry and wet food, but sometimes the amounts are on the high side. Although cats are similar in size and shape, they are individuals. Experiment until you discover the right combination and amount for your cat.

NUTRIENTS

The components of food are proteins, fats, carbohydrates, vitamins, and minerals. Although some nutrients are found in greater quantities than others, each plays a pivotal role in the body's functioning. Together, these nutrients help the body grow and maintain its systems. Providing high-quality nutrients in the correct amounts is one of the best ways to promote longevity when a cat is young, and it becomes increasingly important as a cat ages. Each food element and its functions are discussed below.

PROTEIN

Cats are descended from meat-eating desert animals. They have relatively shorter intestines than humans, allowing them to easily digest animal-based foods. They are *obligate carnivores*, unable to obtain all the nutrients they need from a vegetarian diet. If they are to get enough taurine, arachidonic acid, and vitamin A to meet their bodies' needs, cats must have some high-quality, meat-based protein in their diets.

Proteins are the building blocks of enzymes, hormones, and antibodies. They form protective and structural tissues such as skin, hair and nails, as well as connective tissues such as tendons. In addition, proteins carry oxygen and iron to the tissues and form the antibodies the body uses to fight disease. The flavor, or palatability, of a food is also dependent in large part on protein. Generally, the more protein in a food, the better it tastes.

Proteins can be broken down into amino acids, which play an important role in tissue growth and repair. Without amino acids, the body could not function. These multifunctional units can be used directly for energy, or stored as fat or glycogen for later use as energy. Of the 22 amino acids found in proteins, 12 can be synthesized in the cat's body. The other 10—called the "essential" amino acids—must be provided by the diet. Taurine and arginine are two essential amino acids that are especially important to cats. Arginine controls the urine cycle and lack of taurine can lead to a condition called dilated cardiomyopathy, a form of heart disease.

Cats require high amounts of protein, exceeding the needs of dogs and humans. This is especially true for older cats, whose food intake may be less than that of younger cats. Thus, the percentage of protein in their diet must be even higher to maintain adequate protein levels. For best results, a cat's diet must contain high-quality protein—such as eggs, dairy products or poultry—that is easily digestible. The better the protein quality, the less protein is required to meet the cat's dietary needs. High-quality protein also means there is less residue to be eliminated by the kidneys, an important factor for cats with kidney disease.

Sources of Protein

Protein can come from animals, grains, or a combination of the two. The quality of animal protein varies, ranging from excellent to poor. For example, the protein quality of chicken depends on whether the food contains chicken flesh and skin, or chicken feathers, bones, heads, and feet. Because bone and feathers are made up of collagen, a protein that is not digested well by cats, they are not a good source of protein. Common animal-protein ingredients include beef, chicken meal, meat by-products, fish, and meat and bone meal.

The protein quality provided by grain does not vary as much as that provided by animal sources. It is not comparable to high-quality sources of animal protein, but it is better than low-quality sources of animal protein. Plant-protein ingredients include corn gluten meal, ground whole brown rice, and soybean meal.

How Much Protein?

Because of its association with kidney disease, some people believe that geriatric cats need reduced levels of protein, but not all researchers agree that this is correct. Restricting the amount of protein in an old cat's diet is controversial. Studies do not show that reduction of protein in the diet of a normal, healthy cat will *prevent* the development of kidney disease. An old cat that shows no evidence of renal disease can and should eat a diet containing a normal level of protein.

However, if kidney and liver functions are already compromised, too much protein can adversely affect them. Because old cats are especially prone to kidney disease, some researchers believe their diet should contain high-quality protein at somewhat reduced levels. Again, this is not a theory that is agreed upon by all veterinary nutritionists. Unless you and your veterinarian agree that your cat's physical condition and laboratory test results warrant a change, you should continue feeding your cat its regular food. Whatever diet you feed should contain protein of high biological quality.

It's a good idea to make routine screening tests for kidney function part of your older cat's annual exam, particularly if the cat's water consumption appears to have increased. Slight changes in BUN-creatinine levels may not indicate an immediate need to change the cat's diet; rather, the level should be monitored before a decision is made. If the BUN-creatinine levels have increased slightly and have not changed at the next checkup, it could be that the levels have changed to a new normal level. On the other hand, a drastic increase in BUN-creatinine levels, as well as an increase in water consumption and urination, are signs of kidney failure. Once a definite diagnosis is made, your veterinarian can initiate the appropriate treatment, which may include a low-protein medical diet. (The term BUN stands for blood urea nitrogen, an end product resulting from protein catabolism that is normally excreted by the kidney. An increased BUN level indicates decreased renal function. Veterinarians measure creatinine for much the same reason. Creatinine, which results from the catabolism of creatine, a muscle extractive, is also excreted by the kidney. Again, an increased creatinine level suggests that renal function is decreased.)

Fat

High amounts of fat, although we may shun it in our own diets, are essential for cats. About 40 percent of a cat's calories should come from fat. Fats provide energy and make food taste good. Fat serves as padding, protecting the vital organs from injury, and as insulation, conserving body heat. The body also uses fat to help transmit nerve impulses and transport nutrients.

Fats also contain the essential fatty acids: linoleic acid, found in vegetable oils such as safflower oil; and arachidonic acid, found in animal tissue membranes. (Unlike dogs, cats cannot manufacture arachidonic acid from linoleic acid, so they must have meat protein in their diets.) The fatty acids contain the fat-soluble vitamins A, D, E, and K, which are essential for a number of bodily functions. Fatty acid compounds play a role in muscle contraction, gastric acid secretion, and control of inflammation.

Because cats require more and different fatty acids than dogs, dog food is never an adequate diet for a cat. If your cat has a greasy or flaky coat, is underweight, or its wounds become infected easily or heal slowly, the reason may be a lack of essential fatty acids. A fatty acid deficiency can be caused by pancreatic, intestinal or liver disease, or by a diet high in "people" food. If this is the case, your veterinarian may recommend a change in diet or a fatty acid supplement.

Although fat is important to a cat's health, not all fats are equally beneficial. Fish oils, for instance, in conjunction with a vitamin E deficiency, are related to the development of pansteatitis. This condition causes yellow fatty deposits in the soft tissues, resulting in inflammation and death of the fat cells. A cat with pansteatitis develops a fever and loses its appetite. It becomes sensitive to touch and reluctant to move. Fish and fish-based foods must be removed from the cat's diet, and a course of oral vitamin E supplements and prednisone will improve the condition. Pansteatitis can be fatal if left untreated. Avoid feeding your cat a diet consisting solely of fish, especially red tuna, or one high in polyunsaturated fats.

Sources of Fat

The fat in pet foods is provided by animal fats or vegetable oils. Sources of fat include animal fat, chicken fat, corn oil and soybean oil. The animal protein sources in foods also contain fat. If a single type of fat is used—chicken fat, for instance—it must be described that way on the label. Otherwise, the general term "animal fat" is used.

PRESERVATIVES

Because fats become rancid quickly, pet foods must contain preservatives to maintain their shelf life and prevent contamination by bacteria and toxins. By preventing spoilage, preservatives improve the quality of foods.

Antioxidants are one such group of preservatives. These substances retard the deterioration, rancidity, or discoloration that occurs when oxygen comes into contact with fatty acids, which causes food to develop unpleasant odors, flavors and changes in texture.

There are two types of antioxidants: natural (vitamin E and ascorbic acid) and synthetic (BHA, BHT, and ethoxyquin). Synthetic antioxidants are much more potent than natural antioxidants, so lesser amounts are needed to preserve food. If a fat source has been preserved with an antioxidant, it will be indicated on the label.

CARBOHYDRATES

Carbohydrates provide an easy and efficient source of energy. Most dry foods contain 30 to 60 percent carbohydrates, while canned foods contain up to 30 percent. Carbohydrates can take three forms: simple sugars, such as glucose; complex sugars, such as lactose and sucrose; and polysaccharides, such as starch, glycogen, dextrins and dietary fiber.

Glucose provides energy for tissues and is essential to the functioning of the central nervous system. Glycogen, which is stored in the liver and in muscle, provides emergency energy for the heart and cells. Plant fiber consists of such carbohydrate components as cellulose (an insoluble fiber) and pectin and plant gums (soluble fibers). This fiber is broken down in the large intestine, where the resulting product helps stimulate bowel movements and speeds waste through the system.

In addition to serving as an energy source, carbohydrates help form the nonessential amino acids produced by the cat's body. When joined with proteins or lipids, they play a role in the construction of body tissues. Without carbohydrates, the body couldn't synthesize DNA, RNA, and other essential body compounds.

Sources of Carbohydrates and Fiber

Grains such as corn, rice, wheat and oats are the primary sources of carbohydrates in cat foods. They provide the body with complex carbohydrates in the form of starch. These starches are cooked during the food's processing to enhance their digestibility and palatability. Other plant sources provide fiber, which helps the gastrointestinal tract function more efficiently.

Fiber sources include beet pulp; rice, oat or wheat bran; peanut hulls; and cellulose. As with most things, moderation is the key when it comes to fiber in the diet. Too much fiber can cause diarrhea and flatulence.

VITAMINS AND MINERALS

Vitamins and minerals are sometimes present only in tiny amounts, but they pack a powerful punch. They facilitate such metabolic processes as tissue formation, synthesis of hemoglobin, and cell maintenance and growth. They help convert proteins, fats and carbohydrates to energy, and muscle and nerve functions are dependent on the proper level of minerals. The levels of vitamins and minerals needed by older cats may change, as can their absorption of these nutrients, especially the water-soluble vitamins. Consider the following:

- A zinc deficiency may lead to loss of taste acuity, which may be one reason older cats eat less. The body also uses zinc to help maintain the immune system, and it plays a role in healing wounds.

- Excessive phosphorus can cause kidney damage.

- Too much calcium can decrease thyroid function.

- An iodine deficiency can lead to hypothyroidism.

- Without potassium, muscle function and electrolyte balance deteriorate. Heart failure can result from a severe potassium deficiency, which can be caused by kidney disease, diarrhea or use of diuretics.

Obviously, proper mineral balance is vital, but this does not mean that you should begin adding or subtracting vitamins and minerals in your cat's diet. The use of vitamin and mineral supplementation is quite controversial. In general, feeding a diet that is nutritionally complete is all that is necessary to avoid imbalances. Such a diet should meet or exceed American Association of Feed Control Officials (AAFCO) standards for cats and testing requirements. Healthy older cats that eat complete, balanced diets do not need vitamin or mineral supplements.

Should You Supplement?

Adding vitamin supplements to an already nutritionally complete diet can throw off the balance of nutrients. Because no controlled blind studies have been performed to evaluate the effects of vitamin supplements, it is difficult to know whether vitamin supplements really help old or sick cats.

To be on the safe side, do not give vitamin or mineral supplements unless your veterinarian recommends them for a specific condition or confirms that there is no danger of giving too much. For instance, because they tend to drink large amounts of water, older animals often need supplementation of the water-soluble B-vitamins. Vitamin B is inexpensive and won't harm the cat if it is given daily. Excess water-soluble vitamins are excreted daily in the urine, so there is no danger of a toxic buildup. On the other hand, fat-soluble vitamins are stored in the body, primarily in the liver. Thus, supplementation can quickly cause toxic excesses, especially of vitamins A and D. If a multi-vitamin supplement containing vitamins A and D is given every day, the risk of toxicity is increased.

Vitamin Research

One area of interest in veterinary nutrition, especially among holistic veterinarians, is the use of antioxidant vitamins to fight oxygen free radicals. Free radicals are described as reactive and potentially injurious molecules that cause oxidation, or the corrosion or destruction of cells, in much the same way as metal rusts or fruit browns. Oxidation has been described as "biological rust."

It is believed that the action of free radicals plays a role in the development of age-related diseases such as cancer, cardiovascular disease, reduced immune response, cataracts, and arthritis. Among the body's defenses against free radicals are vitamins E and C, and beta-carotene, which are natural antioxidants. These vitamins operate by reacting with free radicals and neutralizing them, thus preventing oxidation.

Scientists theorize that increasing the intake of antioxidants enhances the body's defense against the ravages caused by free radicals. For instance, researchers studying the prevention of certain types of tumors in animals have found that beta-carotene can affect the frequency as well as the regression of those tumors.

For some conditions, veterinary nutritionists may recommend high levels of vitamins E and C and beta-carotene. These include exocrine pancreatic insufficiency, liver disease, and discoid lupus erythematosus. Some veterinary nutritionists believe that high levels of antioxidant vitamins can boost immune response, but research is needed to confirm this theory.

Veterinary nutritionists argue that providing pets with high amounts of antioxidants can't hurt and can play a role in preventive health care. The catch is that use of antioxidant vitamins must begin early in the cat's life for them to do any good, because most conditions are irreversible once they occur. Unfortunately, no studies have been done to determine the level of antioxidant vitamins necessary to affect health. If you are interested in pursuing this subject further, your veterinarian may be able to advise you or to refer you to a veterinary nutritionist.

Sources of Vitamins and Minerals

Vitamins and minerals are found naturally in most of the major cat food ingredients. To ensure a balanced diet, vitamins and minerals in purified or semipurified forms are added to the formulation. Processing and storage can destroy or decrease the efficacy of nutrients, so manufacturers add vitamins at higher levels to ensure an adequate amount at the time the food is eaten.

The amount of vitamins and minerals contained in pet foods is almost always 125 percent to 200 percent higher than AAFCO requirements. Common sources of vitamins that you may see on a cat food label include choline chloride, alpha tocopherol, niacin, folic acid, and biotin. Mineral sources include potassium chloride, calcium carbonate, manganese sulfate, and potassium iodide.

WATER

Although we may not think of it as such, water is the most important nutrient in the cat's diet. Making up almost 70 percent of a cat's body, water plays a vital role in cell and organ function. It helps maintain body temperature, aids in digestion and circulation, transports nutrients, lubricates body tissues, and facilitates elimination of waste products. It is an essential element in the feline diet. Cats can go for weeks without food, but without water they can die within days.

A number of factors control water intake: thirst, hunger, metabolic activity such as pregnancy or growth, and environmental conditions such as temperature and humidity. Water intake and loss vary depending on the amount of food the cat eats each day. That's why it's important to make sure your cat has an ample supply of fresh water daily. If your cat doesn't seem to be drinking very much water, sneak it in by moistening the cat's dry food or offering some wet food. Cats that eat primarily canned food, which is about 75 percent water, drink less water than those fed dry foods.

Observing water intake and paying attention to other fluid losses are good ways to spot problems early. Cats that have diarrhea or that are vomiting or urinating excessively can easily become dehydrated. A cat that drinks excessive amounts of water—look for a dramatic increase in water consumption and urinary output—may be showing early signs of diabetes, kidney disease, or hyperthyroidism. If your cat is making an unusual number of trips to the litter box, monitor his water intake and schedule a veterinary exam if it seems unusually high.

Cats can go for weeks without food, but without water they can die within days.

Another consideration is the source of your cat's water. According to the Environmental Protection Agency and the Centers for Disease Control, the cleanliness and safety of tap water cannot always be guaranteed. Drinking water in some areas of the country has been found to contain high levels of lead, nitrates, and herbicides. Parasites and other contaminants have also been found in tap water. More and more people are offering their pets the same bottled or filtered water they drink themselves. A holistic veterinarian advises that one of the most important things cat owners can do to safeguard their pets' health is to provide them with filtered or bottled water.

SIGNS OF DEFICIENCIES

Deficiencies of protein or essential fatty acids can affect the quality of the skin and coat. Too little protein results in hair loss, while a lack of essential fatty acids causes the hair coat to become dry, dull and brittle, and the skin to become dry, scaly and inflamed. Fatty acid deficiencies are not common and usually take a long time to develop. When they occur it is often because the food is low in quality or has been stored improperly. Disease can also be a factor. Pancreatitis and liver disease are among the conditions that can cause fatty acid deficiencies. Protein deficiencies are also rare and stem from the same source as fatty acid deficiencies: poor-quality foods. Cats fed low levels of protein—for instance, a diet of dog food—will also develop deficiencies.

Scaly skin, ulcerated lips, and thin, slow-growing fur can indicate a zinc deficiency. Cats whose diets lack biotin may develop dry, scaly skin, thinning hair or small skin lesions. If your cat develops any of these skin conditions, discuss its diet with your veterinarian. A change of foods may solve the problem, but if you are feeding a complete, balanced diet, the problem may not be dietary in origin.

SPECIAL MEDICAL DIETS

Fiona's cat, Bob, is 17 years old and his kidneys are beginning to fail. Based on the veterinarian's advice, Fiona began feeding the cat a medical diet formulated to help control the condition. Bob's mouth ulcers, caused by the kidney problems, cleared up only four days after he began eating the new diet.

The dietary management of disease and the use of nutritional therapy to cope with disease are receiving more attention than ever before. Diet can increase the chance that a cat will respond well to treatment, extend the amount of time available for other therapies, and shorten convalescence. However, diet is not a magic bullet. It is a component of medical or surgical management, and therapeutic diets should not be used indiscriminately without appropriate diagnostics.

An aging cat may need a special diet for such conditions as obesity, megacolon, heart disease, kidney disease, cystitis or feline urinary syndrome, or diabetes. Such diets are specially formulated to help cats with these conditions digest, absorb, or process nutrients. Some medical diets are merely short-term stopgap measures to provide cats with a tasty, high-fat or high-energy food that it can tolerate. Others must be used for the rest of the cat's life. A food that carries any type of health claim must undergo specialized testing and regulatory review by the Food and Drug Administration's Center for Veterinary Medicine.

To ensure that the cat eats them, medical diets tend to be highly palatable. This can result in a fat cat if intake isn't monitored. On the other hand, not every cat likes the taste of its special diet. Bob's owner adds a tiny amount of a gourmet canned food to the medical diet to give it added interest. Other ways to tempt a cat's taste buds include chopping, warming, or pan-frying the meal. Try adding such flavor enhancers as garlic or powder (not salt), or sweeteners such as honey or syrup. The parsley you find on your plate in a restaurant is not just a decoration but is often a complement to the food. Try adding it to your cat's meal as well. Oregano is another herb that can be appealing to cats.

If a cat requires dietary therapy for a number of illnesses, the most life-threatening disease should take priority. For instance, dietary therapy for chronic renal failure, heart failure or chronic pancreatitis is more important than for diabetes, because the diabetes, although benefited by a high-fiber diet, can be controlled with insulin. Cats with multiple problems are difficult to manage, but by working closely with your veterinarian and following his or her recommendations, you can help keep your cat on an even keel.

There is a difference between feeding old cats that are healthy and feeding old cats that have a condition such as kidney disease or diabetes. Medical diets are available only from veterinarians. They are not designed as maintenance diets and should never be fed to healthy cats of any age. Many cats go through life without ever developing serious organ malfunctions, and there is no reason to assume that feeding a medical diet will prevent disease in a healthy cat.

FAT CATS

When the body weight of humans rises by 15 percent or higher above normal weight, medical problems begin to increase. The same pattern applies to cats as well, leading to increased risk of health problems such as diabetes.

The average healthy adult cat weighs 8 to 10 pounds. But a 1993 study by researchers at Cornell University's Veterinary School showed that 25 percent of the cats seen by veterinarians are overweight and 5 percent are obese, meaning their weight is more than 20 percent higher than normal. According to the study, the cats most likely to be overweight are neutered, male, mixed-breed house cats, usually between 4 and 10 years of age.

Why are today's cats getting fat? Factors include the increased palatability of cat foods and the practice of offering dry foods free-choice (available at all times). Also, an adult house cat's lifestyle is usually sedentary, although it may eat the same amount of food it received when it was an energetic kitten.

A cat at ideal weight. Ribs have a slight fat covering, and the waist is discernible behind the ribs.

A heavy cat. The ribs are well-padded and the waist almost gone. Also, the abdomen is rounded and, from the side, you can see a layer of fat hanging down.

An obese cat looks swollen from all sides, with thickly padded ribs, no waist, and a bulging abdomen and fat deposits.

Other factors affecting a cat's tendency toward obesity include owner attitudes and misconceptions. Among them are the beliefs that it is "normal" for a cat to gain weight as it ages and that a cat will eat only as much as it needs.

Many people equate eating not only with good health, but also with love; it gives them pleasure to see their cats chowing down. In some cases, cats become spoiled when their owners respond to finickiness by feeding delicacies, such as chicken livers and scrambled eggs, instead of cat food. Whatever the cause, the combination of too much food and too little exercise is a recipe for obesity and may have medical consequences as the cat gets older.

A fat cat has layers of padding covering its spine and ribs. It waddles when it walks, or it doesn't walk much at all because of a lack of energy. Fat cats are often unkempt because they have difficulty grooming themselves. It's hard to lick your tail when your stomach keeps getting in the way! Another sign of a cat that is overweight or prone to obesity is an excessive desire to eat, even when meals are given regularly. Food is often very important to this cat.

The Fat-Cat Test

To tell if your cat is overweight, give it the hands-on test. If you can feel the ribs through a slight covering of fat when you run your hands along the cat's sides, your cat's weight is probably normal. (However, the ribs should not be visible; if they are, your cat is underweight.) Ideally, a cat is well-proportioned, with its waist observable behind the ribs. Abdominal fat should be minimal, as well.

If you must push through a layer of fat to feel the ribs, or if all you can feel is a soft, squishy cat, a weight problem is likely. An overweight cat has a moderate covering of fat over the ribs and a rounded stomach. The cat that is obese has a heavy layer of fat covering the ribs. Fat deposits fill out its face and limbs, and no waist is visible. The abdomen has extensive fat deposits. Other signs of obesity include difficulty breathing after only mild exertion and deposits of fat on either side of the tail where it joins the body. An obese cat has difficulty grooming itself and may develop dry, scaly skin at the areas it can't reach.

Excess body weight strains joints, ligaments, and tendons. It contributes to heart problems, increases twofold the risk of development of diabetes, and can worsen arthritis. Anesthetic and surgical complications are more likely, as is heat or exercise intolerance. Keeping a close eye on your cat's food intake and exercise level can help you stop problems before they become unmanageable. If your cat must go on a diet, however, the following tips will help both of you survive the ordeal:

- Reduce the amount of food given or offer a diet food. The AAFCO recommends feeding cats 32 calories per pound of body weight daily. Thus, a cat whose ideal weight is 10 pounds should receive no more than 320 calories per day. Remember that the objective is to safely return the cat to its optimal weight. Rapid weight loss can be dangerous to its health.

- Change the diet gradually over a 10-day period. Begin by mixing 75 percent of the old diet with 25 percent of the new diet for the first three days; half-and-half for the next three days; and 25 percent of the old diet with 75 percent of the new diet for the last three days. Begin feeding only the diet food on the tenth day.

- Feed the same type of food your cat is used to getting. If Samantha is used to getting canned food, don't switch her to a dry diet food.

- To help a new food seem more palatable, wet it with water, chicken broth, or the juice from waterpacked salmon or tuna (don't use milk), or warm it in the microwave.

- Feed small amounts several times a day. The act of eating increases the body's metabolic rate, so a cat that eats the same number of calories in four meals instead of one or two will burn more calories. The extra meals may also prevent begging. If your cat does beg, don't reward the behavior. Wait to give food until the cat isn't pestering you.

- Weigh your cat regularly. A weekly weigh-in will give you an incentive to continue the cat's diet. A monthly weigh-in at the veterinary clinic allows your veterinarian to adjust the diet if necessary.

- If you must give treats, try offering raw vegetables such as broccoli, carrots or green beans, or fruit, such as cantaloupe. Some cats love them. Be sure to include any treats in your cat's daily calorie count. Treats should not make up more than 10 percent of any cat's diet.

- Pay attention to your cat's activity level or lifestyle. Its caloric needs will vary throughout its life. Feeding the same amount and type of food without regard to the cat's age or physical status can contribute to obesity.

Another important aspect of reducing a cat's weight is refraining from investing the cat with your own thoughts and feelings. Remember to separate your emotions from those of your cat. Rainbow isn't going to wonder what she did wrong to be receiving canned diet food instead of meatballs in marinara sauce, and Misty isn't going to hate you because her diet has been changed to something more healthy. Yes, your cat may react negatively to the change in food, but it is because the food is different, not because of any emotions associated with the change.

Light or Geriatric Diets

Should you switch your cat to a weight loss or geriatric diet when it hits old age, even if the cat shows no signs of obesity or reduction of kidney function? Not necessarily. If a cat can maintain a normal weight and has no health problems, there is no reason to change its diet. There is no evidence showing that high-protein diets cause or contribute to renal failure. The body's cells, especially those of the immune system, are dependent upon a steady source of nutrients. By feeding a diet that is very low in protein (20 percent or less), you run the risk that the cat will lack the resources it needs to fight off disease or make replacement cells.

However, if your cat is overweight, your veterinarian may recommend a weight reduction food. Before putting your cat on a diet, ask your veterinarian to recommend a weight loss plan over a period of weeks or months. Sudden weight reduction, especially in obese cats, can lead to a serious and sometimes fatal condition called hepatic lipidosis, which is discussed more fully in Chapter 7. According to feline nutrition expert Michael S. Hand, DVM, Ph.D., weight loss should not exceed two-tenths of a pound per week, with an obese cat receiving a diet containing at least 70 percent of the recommended dietary requirements.

A number of diets on the market are specifically designed for older or less active cats (see the listing at the end of this chapter), and they generally fall into two categories: low fat/high carbohydrate and low fat/high fiber. The advantage of both types of diets is the lower amount of dietary fat, usually less than 10 percent on a dry-matter basis. This is desirable because fat contains more than twice as many calories as carbohydrates or protein. Less fat means fewer calories, even if you are feeding the same amount of food.

Looks can be deceiving, however. Labels for reducing diets are not standardized, so make careful comparisons when choosing a food. At Cornell University's Feline Health Center, a recent study of 15 commercially available brands showed that some "light" foods contain more calories and fat than regular diets.

The AAFCO, in partnership with the FDA, is working to redefine or clarify the words used to describe weight-loss diets. In the meantime, the FDA advises cat owners to carefully scrutinize claims such as "lite" on cat food products. Compare fat and calorie levels between products to determine the level most suitable for your cat's needs. When choosing a low-fat diet, look for a food that contains 8 percent to 11 percent fat on a dry-matter basis. If a food described as "lite" or "low calorie" does not include a calorie content statement (which is permitted but not required by the AAFCO), look for one that does.

Diet foods containing high levels of complex carbohydrates, such as corn or rice, are easy to digest. Foods that are low in fat and high in indigestible fiber are formulated based on the theory that the bulk provided by the fiber will help the cat feel full, even though it has taken in fewer calories. Although cats do not appear to require dietary fiber, a high-quality, high-fiber diet can aid the cat's digestive system by preventing or relieving constipation, a common problem in aging cats. The fiber absorbs water, and its bulk helps move hairballs and accumulated stools through the cat's system. However, pet food manufacturers and veterinary nutritionists are split on the effectiveness of high amounts of fiber in weight loss diets. Some argue that too much fiber can cause excessive stool production and diarrhea.

In most cases, however, either type of diet will work well to reduce a cat's weight. Much depends on the pet owner's situation and attitude toward the cat's meals. For instance, in families where mealtime is associated with love and companionship, the idea of feeding less is distressing. For these people, a low-fat diet may be the best choice, because it allows them to feed the same amount while providing fewer calories.

Other owners find it more convenient to feed a smaller volume of the same food by replacing the measuring cup they use to scoop out the food with one of a smaller size. Another factor is the number of animals in the household. The overweight cat must be denied access to other pets' food. This may require feeding it in a separate area or watching while the animals eat to prevent mooching from other pets' bowls.

Management of weight loss and control is a team effort between the veterinarian and the family. Everyone must agree on the amount and type of food given. Otherwise, the cat's diet can be sabotaged by friends or family members who don't understand the health risks involved.

Like people, some cats live to eat, while others eat to live. To prevent obesity in the first place, avoid free-feeding if food is the most important thing in your cat's life. For these cats, specified amounts at set times is the best way to go.

UNDERWEIGHT CATS

Not all weight problems stem from too much food. Some owners have the opposite problem; a cat that is too thin. Thin cats have no palpable body fat, and the ribs are visible on shorthaired cats. The thin cat's lumbar vertebrae and hip bones are easily felt. A cat that is underweight has a minimal covering of fat over its ribs, an obvious waist behind the hips and minimal abdominal fat.

If your cat is too thin, you should examine its mouth to find the reasons for this weight problem. Underweight cats may have dental problems that make it difficult or painful for them to eat. Signs include excessive salivation, drooling, and loss of appetite. Cats that eagerly approach their food, but back away or shake their heads after the first bite, may have periodontal disease. A dirty water

An emaciated cat has clearly visible ribs, a very tucked abdomen, and no fat reserves.

bowl with food in it may be another indicator that your cat is having trouble eating. Broken teeth or tartar buildup may cause infections or inflammation of the gums and tongue.

Some thin cats are ravenous eaters. Warning bells should go off if your cat eats well, but loses weight. This can indicate hyperthyroidism, or it can be an early sign of cancer or other disease. Remember, too, that lack of appetite can be a sign of illness. A cat that isn't eating may need an exam and diagnostic workup.

If its mouth is healthy and your veterinarian can find no other physical problem, try tempting your skinny cat with highly palatable canned cat foods. Before feeding these foods, however, be sure they are nutritionally complete. If they are not, give them only in small quantities, as an adjunct to a balanced wet or dry diet. Offer supplements and enticing tidbits only to cats that are finicky eaters. If your cat is eating a balanced diet on its own, don't mess with success. The following tips may help you entice your underweight cat:

- Offer more frequent meals
- Hand feed the cat
- Offer canned food

- Warm the food

- Add flavor enhancers, such as the juice from tuna or salmon cans

- Moisten the food

- Ask your veterinarian about appetite stimulants

PREVENTING PICKINESS

Old cats can become finicky, and this can lead to problems if not nipped in the bud. Resist the temptation to provide your cat only with those foods that it wants. Cats will not necessarily balance their diets. They may become addicted to a particular food to the exclusion of other things they need. This can become a serious problem if the cat develops a condition that requires a special diet. Adaptability could save your cat's life if one day it requires a special diet. A varied diet can also help prevent nutritional deficiencies that might develop when a cat eats only one type of food.

Remember that cats tend to be slow and sometimes erratic eaters. They may only nibble at their food for several days, then eat a large meal. They also tend to eat only a small amount at a time, a remnant of their ancestral past when they fed on small rodents frequently throughout the day. Cats have been shown to eat up to 16 small meals per day. Frequently changing foods just because you think the cat doesn't like it can confuse the issue. A change in the cat's appetite may reflect interest in the new food or merely an upswing in its intake.

EVALUATING CAT FOODS

Food is never a good place to economize. One of the main reasons cats are living longer is the quality of food available. When it comes to diets for geriatric cats, quality and availability of protein, vitamins, and minerals is paramount in deciding what to feed. The greater likelihood of disease in older cats makes a complete, balanced diet a must.

In making your decision, consider your cat's general health, ask your veterinarian's advice, and read labels carefully. Price and availability are valid concerns, but they should not be the only factors in your decision. When you are choosing a food, consider the following questions in your evaluation:

- Is the food complete and balanced, with appropriate levels of protein, taurine and magnesium?

- Does your cat like the food?

- Is the food digestible?

- How much energy does the food provide?

- Will the food produce an acidified urine?

- How much does the food cost?

The first thing to look for on a bag or can of food is the phrase "complete and balanced." This means that a food contains all the nutrients a cat needs at the correct levels to meet energy requirements and caloric needs. Nutrient levels are regulated by the Association of American Feed Control Officials. The AAFCO requires manufacturers to substantiate nutrient claims in one of two ways: through feeding trials or by chemical analysis, or calculations showing that the formulation meets minimum and maximum levels of nutrients established by the AAFCO.

Although the AAFCO permits manufacturers to meet the requirements on paper only, look for a food that has been tested in feeding trials. Feeding trials are the best way to determine whether a diet truly meets a cat's nutritional needs. The label must state how the food was tested. If the label states only that the food meets AAFCO Nutrient Profiles, it means that feeding trials have not necessarily been used to evaluate the diet. The statements "feeding tests," "AAFCO feeding test protocols," or "AAFCO feeding studies" indicate that feeding trials were conducted.

After nutritional quality, taste is the most important factor when evaluating food for your cat. The best food in the world won't keep your cat healthy if the cat won't eat it. On the other hand, just because a food tastes good doesn't mean it is nutritionally adequate. Your cat doesn't know and doesn't care if its diet is nutritious. It is up to you to strike a balance between what tastes good to your cat and what's good for it.

Digestibility is defined as the amount of nutrients in a food that are usable by your cat. The more digestible a food, the more nutrients are available to your cat. What isn't absorbed for use by the body is eliminated as waste. Protein quality is an important aspect of digestibility, and you can tell a lot about digestibility by reading the list of ingredients. For instance, skin, hair, feathers and connective tissues contain protein, but because the protein is of such low quality it is not digested well by cats. High-quality sources of protein include poultry, dairy products, and eggs.

The AAFCO has not set standards for testing digestibility, so procedures and results vary from manufacturer to manufacturer. Usually, however, the process involves measuring the total amount of food consumed, determining the nutrients contained in the food, measuring the amount of fecal material produced, and comparing the nutrients found in the fecal material with those found in the food.

Nutrient digestibility is calculated by subtracting the amount of the nutrient found in the stool from the total amount of the nutrient the cat ate. For instance, if a cat ate 100 grams of protein and its stool contained 15 grams of protein, the protein digestibility of the food would be 85 percent. Although digestibility information is not provided on the label, you can write or call the company for the information. Look for foods that have at least 80 percent dry-matter digestibility.

Signs of poor digestibility include flatulence, loose or large stools, and diarrhea. A highly digestible food produces smaller, firmer stools, and provides the same level of nutrients in a smaller amount of food. Thus, highly digestible foods are cost-effective because the cat doesn't eat as much. Manufacturers can measure digestibility only through feeding trials, another good reason to demand a food that has been tested this way.

A food that is high in energy and nutrients is important for growing kittens and lactating queens, but inactive older cats will gain weight on such a diet. The amount of energy available is called metabolizable energy. Knowing a food's metabolizable energy is important, because it determines how much food the cat needs to meet its energy requirements. Again, this measurement is obtained through feeding trials or by calculation, although calculation is less accurate. Some labels now indicate the suitability of a food for a specific life stage by showing the percentage of calories supplied by carbohydrates, fats, and proteins.

In addition to energy and digestibility, the urinary pH level produced by a food should be considered. If it is too high, the cat is at risk of developing lower urinary tract disease. Too low, and the cat may suffer from a condition called metabolic acidosis. Current labeling regulations do not permit information about urinary pH levels, but you can call or write the manufacturer for literature on the subject.

The cost of a food is directly related to the quality of its ingredients. In other words, you get what you pay for. A generic food may cost less, but when you factor in the necessity of feeding a greater amount of food to provide the cat's nutritional needs, as well as the veterinary bills for a less-than-healthy cat, you can see that spending a little more for a high-quality food can pay off in the long run. And because smaller amounts of high-quality foods provide better nutrition than generic products, their cost per serving may even be less than the cheaper food.

To determine a food's cost per day, jot on a calendar the price of the food on the day you bought it. When you run out, divide the cost of the food by the number of days it lasted. This method allows you to compare products with the same net weight.

Another factor in a food's cost is the manufacturer's reputation. Does the company consistently produce a high-quality product? Does it provide its address and phone number in easy-to-read lettering and readily respond to inquiries about its food? Concern for its customers, both feline and human, indicates a company that cares about making a good product.

READING THE LABEL

The label on a bag or can of cat food provides a great deal of important information—if you know how to decipher it. The law requires manufacturers to provide an ingredient list and to inform buyers of the food's name and the net weight in the package. Manufacturers must also provide a guaranteed analysis for the percentages of crude protein, crude fat, crude fiber, and moisture contained in the food. Remember that the guaranteed analysis panel provides only minimum and maximum percentages of nutrients, not exact amounts. A food can contain much less than the maximum stated on a label or much more than the minimum stated. For this reason, it cannot be used to compare one brand of food to another. Instead, ask your veterinarian or the manufacturer to help you determine the dry-matter percentage of the nutrients.

Ingredients are listed by weight in decreasing order. For instance, if the first ingredient is chicken meal, followed by brown rice, you can assume that the primary source of protein is animal-based. Note whether the same ingredient—rice, for example—is listed in a variety of forms, such as flour, flakes, middlings, and bran. This practice is called split-ingredient labeling, and it permits the manufacturer to spread out ingredients of the same type so they will appear farther down on the label. If this is the case, the food may contain more of the ingredient than is apparent at first glance.

If you buy a certain brand regularly, check the ingredient list frequently to see if the manufacturer is using a fixed formulation, which means the ingredients remain the same from batch to batch. Some manufacturers use variable formulations, in which ingredients change depending on fluctuations in market prices and availability. An unnoticed change in the formulation, while not necessarily nutritionally harmful, could cause your cat digestive upset.

Common ingredients in cat food include meat, described as the clean flesh of slaughtered cattle, swine, sheep or goats; poultry by-product meal, which is the ground, rendered,

Nutrition Notes

- *Feed your cat a food that contains high-quality protein sources such as poultry, eggs, or dairy products.*

- *Read labels carefully. Look for substantiation of nutrient claims through feeding trials.*

- *Give your cat the "hands-on" test once a month. If it is too fat, you won't be able to feel its ribs. If it is too thin, the ribs will show.*

- *If your cat is fat, reduce its weight slowly on the advice of your veterinarian.*

- *If your cat is eating well but losing weight, it should be examined by your veterinarian.*

- *Don't let your cat dictate its own diet. Canned tuna at every meal is not healthy for any cat.*

clean parts of slaughtered poultry such as necks, feet, undeveloped eggs and intestines; brewers rice, the dried, extracted residue of rice left over from the manufacture of beer; and ground corn, the entire ear without husks.

The label must state the food's nutritional adequacy or purpose; for instance, whether the food is meant for growth, maintenance or weight loss. A statement of nutritional adequacy indicates whether the food's value was determined through feeding trials or by formulation to meet AAFCO nutrient profiles. Information about digestibility and bioavailability is not required on the label. The U.S. Food and Drug Administration regulates advertising claims, ensuring that they are not false or misleading and that they can be substantiated by test results.

Look for a claim that the food provides "complete and balanced nutrition." Ideally, this claim will be bolstered by feeding trials. Companies that conduct feeding trials must sign a sworn statement certifying that AAFCO protocols were followed and that their nutrition claims are supported by test results. For information on foods certified to have met AAFCO's feeding trial requirements, call the Pet Food Institute's Nutrition Assurance Program at (800) 851-0769.

LIGHT OR SENIOR FOODS

A number of foods are formulated to help cats lose weight or to prevent them from gaining weight as they become less active. Generally, these foods are low in fat and high in fiber. Most brand name commercial foods, whether they are found in a grocery store, pet supply store or veterinary office, are good quality and will meet your older cat's nutritional needs. By consulting your veterinarian and using the guidelines set forth in this chapter, you can choose a food that will help keep your cat healthy, as well as meet your needs for cost and purchasing convenience. The following foods are commonly available in most areas of the country. Many of the companies that manufacture them offer toll-free numbers that cat owners can call for information about the foods, nutrition in general, and other pet care information, including booklets and brochures.

ANF Less Active; (800) 489-2770.

Excel Cat Senior/Lite; Pet Products Plus, 1600 Heritage Landing, Ste. 112, St. Charles, MO 63303.

Friskies Senior For Cats; (800) 772-5734. Hours: 8 am to 4 pm PST, Monday through Friday.

Hill's Science Diet Light; (800) 445-5777. Hours: 8 am to 8 pm EST, Monday through Friday.

Iams Less Active for Cats; (800) 525-4267. Hours: 8 am to 8 pm, Monday through Saturday.

Nature's Recipe Optimum Lite/Senior; (800) 843-4008.

Nutro Max Cat Lite; (800) 833-5330.

Precise Feline Light Formula; (800) 446-7148.

ProPlan Lite; (800) PROPLAN. Hours: 9 am to 4 pm CST, Monday through Friday.

Purina Cat Chow Mature; (800) 778-7462. Hours: 9 am to 4 pm CST, Monday through Friday.

VETERINARY TIP

"**Feed a complete and balanced food. Don't wait too long to take your cat to a vet if the cat stops eating, regardless of whether it is in good shape or poor shape. Older animals need to eat every day. If the eating behavior changes in any way, whether it's a big increase or decrease, that's often the only sign you have that anything is wrong.**"

—Sarah Abood, DVM, veterinary nutritionist, Ralston-Purina.

Health
Care

I am the cat of cats. I am
The everlasting cat!
Cunning, and old, and sleek as jam
The everlasting cat!
I hunt the vermin in the night—
The everlasting cat!
For I see best without the light—
The everlasting cat!—William Brighty Rands

"Your cat has diabetes," Dr. Donaldson told his client. "That's why he has been drinking so much water and making so many trips to the litter box. It also explains why he's losing weight, even though he eats so much. Fortunately, the disease can be controlled with proper diet and daily insulin injections."

"Diabetes!" Jim said. "I didn't know cats could get that."

"A lot of people don't," his veterinarian replied, "but it's quite common, especially in overweight cats."

The incidence of chronic disease in cats has increased since 1965. That's not to say that cats are less healthy today than they were 30 years ago. The more likely reason for the increase is that their owners value them more highly and are more conscientious about providing veterinary care. Therefore, veterinarians are seeing and reporting more incidences of disease.

Another reason is the advances made in feline veterinary medicine over the years. Veterinarians now have more and better diagnostic aids and treatments at their disposal. Thus, a greater number of diseases are identified and treated, resulting in an increased feline lifespan.

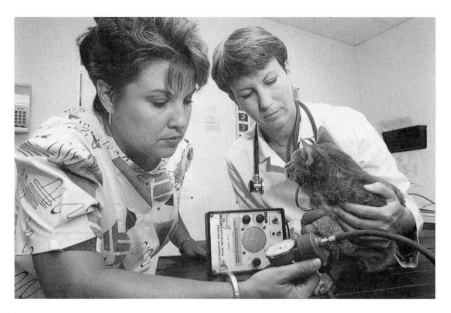

Veterinary technician Prudence Walker and Dr. Patti Snyder of the University of Florida College of Veterinary Medicine take a cat's blood pressure. (Photo by Russ Lante, UF Health Science Center)

Your cat's body, although it is smaller and shaped differently, is built along the same lines as your own. Cats have the same organs—kidneys, liver, pancreas, heart and so on—as humans, and they work in much the same way. Thus, as cats age, they are prone to many of the same conditions that affect people, including kidney disease, diabetes and cancer. By understanding the purpose and operation of your cat's organ systems and recognizing early warning signs, you can help prevent or mitigate some of these health problems.

GERIATRIC PROBLEMS

Cats are generally healthy creatures, but age brings problems to most animals. In cats, health problems can be caused by the normal deterioration of the body or by disease. Also, health problems at a young age—frequent urinary tract infections, for instance—can contribute to poor functioning of the organs in old age.

A number of conditions can affect aging cats. Of course, diagnoses can be made only by a veterinarian, but what follows is a brief overview of symptoms, methods of diagnosis, and treatment of the more common diseases affecting old cats, arranged by organ system. Each cat is an individual, so diagnosis and treatment will vary. You need to work with your veterinarian to arrive at a plan that is right for your pet. This is not a comprehensive discussion of feline medicine. Some diseases are covered in greater detail in other books. The conditions discussed here relate primarily to older cats.

PROBLEMS OF THE SKIN

Most of us don't realize it, but the skin is the body's largest organ, a protective covering that wraps the body and acts as a shield and sensor. The skin guards against invasion by bacteria and helps the body retain moisture, preventing dehydration. The hair serves as an insulator and sensor, regulating the cat's body temperature and transmitting sensations such as heat, cold, pleasure, and pain to the brain. Fright or stress can cause sudden hair shedding. You may notice this phenomenon when you take your cat to the veterinarian.

Beneath the skin lie the sebaceous glands. They secrete a substance called sebum, which gives hair an oily, protective coating and keeps it soft and supple, flexible enough to bend without breaking. The sebaceous glands are largest and most numerous in the areas a cat commonly uses to mark its territory: the lips, chin, base of the tail, and scrotum. In addition to

The scent glands are part of the skin, the body's largest external organ. Cats use their scent glands to mark territory.

their function of protecting the coat, the sebaceous glands help the cat identify its environment. When a cat rubs its face against your leg or a piece of furniture, it is marking the area as its own. As a cat ages, the glands secrete less sebum, but frequent brushing helps keep the oils distributed and the cat's coat shiny.

Age most commonly manifests itself in dry skin or fur, and cysts, warts and tumors. The body is slower to absorb and make use of nutrients, so a once shiny coat may become dull or rough. Flakiness or lumps and bumps may appear where previously there were none. Regular grooming and a good diet can help control dry skin, although the old cat may never regain the lush coat of its youth. Lumps or bumps are another matter. Any sort of lump should be examined by a veterinarian, the earlier the better. Discussed below are other skin problems that may affect old cats, including the types and signs of skin tumors.

Wounds

Because a cat's immune system weakens with age, skin irritations and wounds may heal more slowly. Although wounds in a cat of any age should be treated in a timely manner, early intervention—and prevention—are more urgent in the older cat.

Abscesses, usually the result of bite wounds, are common, especially in intact male cats that are permitted to roam outdoors. Because of the cat's fur coat, an abscess may not be immediately apparent. Signs that may indicate the presence of an abscess are pain, swelling, depression, and lack of appetite. An abscess must be drained, sometimes surgically, and a course of antibiotics is required to fight off infection.

Wounds that heal slowly or that fail to heal may indicate an underlying problem, such as an infection, poor circulation, cancer, or nutritional deficiency. Bacterial skin disease is rare, but it can occur when a cat scratches or rubs at a wound or insect bite. A cat that is taking immunosuppressive drugs (glucocorticoids) for such conditions as allergies, chronic inflammatory bowel disease, lymphosarcoma or leukemia may also be predisposed to bacterial infections.

Poor circulation limits the amount of oxygen reaching the wound, inhibiting healing. A poor diet or improper supplementation affects the healing process, too. A vitamin C deficiency, for instance, can delay healing because the body requires vitamin C to build the collagen needed to repair the skin. A daily dose of 200 milligrams of vitamin C may help. On the other hand, high doses of vitamin E can slow the healing process by retarding production of collagen. In addition to wounds, the following skin conditions may affect older cats.

Tumors

As Tom massaged Muffin's leg, he felt a tiny lump on her thigh. The cat was due for her vaccinations the next week, and he made a note to mention it to the veterinarian. When he pointed it out, Dr. Lewis was surprised that Tom had even noticed the lump because it was so small. Nevertheless, he recommended performing an aspiration biopsy. Muffin was lucky. The lump was benign, and it never recurred after removal.

As with chronic disease, the incidence of all tumors has increased in cats. About 25 percent of all the tumors that affect cats are skin tumors, and their presence can be serious. Lumps are less common in cats than in dogs, but they are more likely to be malignant when present. According to veterinarians at the University of Illinois College of Veterinary Medicine, 60 percent of the skin lumps on cats are malignant, while only 30 percent of the skin lumps on dogs are malignant. A cat with a lump should be scheduled immediately for an examination and a fine needle aspiration biopsy.

Basal cell tumors occur most commonly in middle-aged and older cats, with the likelihood highest at about 10 years of age. These tumors vary in size, usually appearing as small, firm, encapsulated lumps. They are frequently hairless and are more likely to occur singly than in groups. The good news is that basal cell tumors are usually harmless and slow-growing, but in some instances they can become ulcerated and inflamed. Surgical removal is the usual treatment.

The breeds most at risk are the domestic longhair, Angora, Siamese, and Himalayan. Because all of these cats except the Siamese have long coats, regular home examination is important so that tumors don't go unnoticed.

Patrick, a neutered male cat, had a growth removed from his right cheek. The biopsy showed that it was a mast cell tumor. The veterinarian recommended that a wider, deeper area of tissue be removed from the tumor site. She predicted that Patrick would develop similar tumors in the future and suggested that they be removed as they popped up.

Two types of cutaneous mast cell tumors affect cats: a mast cell type and a histiocytic type. Mast cell tumors are most common and represent up to 15 percent of all feline skin tumors. They occur mainly in cats older than four years, with the mean age being eight years. Sex is a factor in the development of this tumor, as male cats are twice as likely to develop mast cell tumors as female cats.

Mast cell tumors appear most commonly on the head and neck, but may occur anywhere on the body. If the tumor is solitary and compact—well-defined with clear borders—it is likely to be benign. An invasive tumor—one that has an irregular size and shape—is more common and is much more likely to be malignant. Surgical removal is the treatment of choice. If the entire tumor cannot be surgically removed, radiation therapy may be necessary. This type of tumor recurs in about one-third of the cases. Cutaneous mast cell tumors in cats are not usually malignant, nor are they likely to spread to other parts of the body.

Histiocytic tumors are found most frequently in young Siamese cats, but they are also common in older male cats. They usually clear up on their own, but an aspiration biopsy can provide the information needed to decide whether surgical removal is necessary.

A fibrosarcoma is a malignant growth common in older cats and usually found on the eyelids. This usually solitary tumor can be firm or fleshy, and its size and shape vary. If left untreated, it can spread to local lymph nodes or the lungs. It is likely to recur, even after surgical removal. If caught early in older cats, surgical removal can be effective, but usually the prognosis is guarded to poor.

When melanin-producing cells develop a tumor, the result is a black mole called a melanoma. Melanomas are rare, but when they occur in older cats, they are usually malignant, and the prognosis is poor. The mole should be surgically removed and biopsied to determine its status.

Squamous cell carcinoma occurs primarily in older cats and is a common skin tumor in cats, found especially on the eyelids, ears and nose. Cats with light pigmentation or a sparse hair coat, especially those that spend a lot of time in the sun, are prone to squamous cell carcinomas. Genetic factors may also play a role, as this condition is most common in white cats and cats with white spotting, especially if these cats have blue eyes. If your white cat spends a lot of time outdoors, applying sunscreen to its ears and nose as a preventive is often helpful.

If left untreated, squamous cell carcinoma spreads slowly to other organs. Most tumors of this type are surgically removed. If ear tips are affected, the tumors can be cosmetically removed. Photodynamic therapy with lasers has worked well in recurring cases. Prognosis depends primarily on how early the tumor is found and treated, as well as on its size.

This cat's ear tips were removed as a result of squamous cell carcinoma, a condition most likely to affect white cats.

Squamous cell carcinomas can also affect the mouth or esophagus, especially in older cats. Signs of the disease include regurgitation, weight loss, and lack of appetite. Researchers at the University of Florida College of Veterinary Medicine are testing a new drug therapy for cats with mouth cancer. Cats with this type of cancer usually have low survival times, averaging about two months, but veterinarians hope the drug will improve their quality of life.

Cutaneous lymphosarcoma is a rare skin disorder of old cats, occurring at an average age of 11 years. Signs include skin lesions with firm, raised bumps or lumps, crusty or ulcerated areas, thickened skin, or hair loss. Surgery, radiation therapy, and chemotherapy can all be used against these tumors, but the outcome is often disappointing. It is fortunate that this condition is rare, because it is usually fatal within a few months.

Although it's uncommon, some middle-aged or older cats may develop a condition called <u>paronychia</u>, an infection of the nail beds. Common causes of paronychia include trauma, contact dermatitis or seborrhea, bacteria, fungi, and tumors. Signs include swelling, discharge, odor and discomfort. Treatment involves warm water and povidone iodine soaks for the claws, a course of antibiotics, and treatment of the underlying cause.

PROBLEMS OF THE DIGESTIVE SYSTEM

Think of the digestive system as a refinery that processes raw material—food—into fuel for the body—energy. The food begins its transformation in the mouth, where it is cut into small pieces by the teeth and softened by the saliva. Enzymes in the saliva initiate the digestive process. Then the food is passed to the stomach by way of the esophagus. The stomach's powerful acids and enzymes, along with strong contractions, further break down the food.

Next, the food enters the duodenum (the first of three parts of the small intestine), where it mixes with pancreatic juices

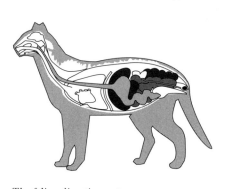

The feline digestive system.

and bile from the liver. This further reduces the food to its essential elements of proteins, fats, and carbohydrates so they can cross the intestinal wall and enter the bloodstream, which takes the nutrients throughout the body to provide energy for all body processes. The remainder moves into the jejunum and ileum, where more nutrients are absorbed, and then into the large intestine, or colon, which absorbs water and the remaining nutrients. There, fecal material is stored until it is eliminated.

Obviously, this is a complex system, and much can go wrong with it as a cat ages, from periodontal disease to diarrhea. Lack of appetite, constipation, diarrhea, and vomiting are common signs of gastrointestinal disease in old cats. In many cases, however, prevention can be as easy as selecting the proper diet and regular dental care—beginning when the cat is young. Starting with the teeth and gums, we'll look at the various parts of the digestive system to see why problems begin and how they can be prevented.

THE MOUTH

Although cats occasionally get cavities, the more important problem is periodontal disease. And just as diet and hygiene affect the dental health of humans, so do they affect feline dental health.

Diet, hygiene, and dental health go hand in hand. It's no surprise that a cat accustomed to having its teeth cleaned from an early age will have a healthier mouth and gums than a cat that has had little or no dental care. And any cat that has a problem with its mouth may very well show a change in it's pattern of eating or selection of foods. If your cat turns away from its dry food or drops bits of food when eating, these may be signs of dental problems that require veterinary examination. Surprisingly, eye discharge that doesn't respond to treatment can indicate tooth problems. An apical root abscess, a draining wound on the cheek below the eye, may be the problem.

For all these reasons, it's important to make dental care a priority by brushing a cat's teeth and rubbing its gums (see Chapter 2). If started early and continued regularly, home care can be effective in controlling plaque buildup. An ounce of prevention in kittenhood may indeed be worth a pound of cure to the old cat. In addition to cleaning your cat's teeth regularly, provide dry food, either as the cat's regular meal or as a snack. The abrasive action helps keep plaque to a minimum.

Preventive dental care can help older cats avoid the risk of anesthesia. An older cat with heavy dental tartar, severe periodontal disease, inflamed or infected gums, or even a dental root abscess will require veterinary attention necessitating the use of anesthesia. Anesthetic agents available today are infinitely safer than those used 20 years ago, and anesthetic emergencies are much less common today than they were a few decades ago, but the risks of anesthesia for extraction and treatment are real. However, the risks of not providing needed dental care are even greater, so prevention is important.

Examine your cat's mouth regularly for signs of problems. Healthy gums are firm and pink. Pigmented spots are normal. Pale gums can be a sign of anemia, internal bleeding, or other illness. Drooling, bad breath, and difficulty eating can indicate severe gingivitis, or squamous cell carcinoma under the tongue (especially in older cats) or on gums or oral mucous membranes. Other signs of severe gingivitis include red, swollen, painful gums; tooth sockets that ooze pus; and loose teeth. Gingivitis is especially common in Siamese cats.

Fortunately, gingivitis is reversible. Treatment involves sophisticated dental care, including hand or ultrasonic scaling to remove deposits above and below the gum line; surgical removal of dead or contaminated tissue; and polishing to remove remaining deposits. A course of antibiotics before and after dentistry helps prevent the infection from becoming systemic.

A professional cleaning can bring about an amazing change in a cat's demeanor. Often the cat has a better appetite, is more active, grooms itself more, and gains weight. Sometimes underneath all the tartar are teeth that are rotten and aching. Once the teeth are gone—even if all of them must be pulled— the cat feels so much better that it may show a dramatic change in personality, going from cranky to content in no time. And a lack of teeth is no impediment to a cat's ability to eat. It can even continue to eat dry food.

Oral Inflammation

Another disease that can affect cats with poor dental hygiene is stomatitis, or inflammation of the mouth lining. Like gingivitis, it is usually traceable to a diet consisting primarily of wet food, soft/moist food, or human food.

Severe dental disease affects more than the mouth. In addition to periodontal disease and dental abscesses, bacterial emboli can be carried to other organs by the blood stream. The resulting infections can lead to nephritis (kidney infection) and endocarditis (inflammation of the lining of the heart and its valves).

Like people, some cats naturally have good teeth, while others will always have problems. If you are lucky, your cat may never need to have its teeth professionally cleaned by the veterinarian. However, owners of cats with dental problems would do well to have the teeth professionally cleaned on a regular basis to prevent tartar buildup and the accompanying health problems.

VOMITING

One of the few unpleasant aspects of cat ownership is the tendency of cats to throw up at the drop of a hat. If they nibble on a plant, they throw up. If they get a hairball, they throw up. If they gobble their food, they throw up. Cat owners learn quickly to keep a ready supply of towels and carpet cleaner.

Although the above examples can be annoying, for the most part they are normal. If they happen only occasionally, they should not be a cause for concern. Vomiting of hairballs can be minimized by brushing the cat daily, administering a hairball remedy regularly, or adding a teaspoon of canned pumpkin or one-half teaspoon of bran daily to the cat's food.

Slow down cats that eat too fast by presenting the food in a different manner or placing it in a different type of container. Some cat owners find success by feeding wet cat food on a dinner plate, spreading it to the edges of the plate rather than spooning it in a pile. Others offer dry food in a single layer across the bottom of a flat dish, such as a pie plate or cookie sheet.

On the other hand, frequent vomiting for no apparent reason can be a sign of a number of disorders, including intestinal obstruction, irritable bowel syndrome, bacterial and viral diseases, hyperthyroidism, kidney or liver disease, poisoning, or upper gastrointestinal irritation. Note when vomiting occurs. If the cat throws up immediately after eating, the cause is most likely ingestion of something forbidden, such as rich food or garbage; overeating; or gastritis. If vomiting occurs more than six hours after the cat has eaten, an obstruction is more probable. The appearance, smell, and content of the vomit can also provide clues. Look for such things as the presence of blood or bile (a sticky yellow or greenish fluid), foreign material, a fecal odor, and whether the food is digested or undigested.

If your cat is vomiting and none of the usual reasons apply, remove its food and limit its access to water to avoid a cycle of drinking and vomiting. Instead, give the cat ice cubes to lick. If the cat shows no improvement in 24 hours, seems depressed, or has additional symptoms, call your veterinarian.

Vomiting Caused By Kidney and Liver Disease

Because the liver and kidneys regulate the amount of toxins in the body, any disease or injury to them can contribute to an accumulation of toxins in the body. The result may be nausea and vomiting. Another side effect of kidney or liver disease is a decreased level of potassium, resulting in muscle weakness and vomiting. Cats with kidney disease, especially older mixed breeds, should be watched closely for signs of potassium deficiency: reluctance to walk, fatigue, pain, and a tucked head. If potassium levels are low, a supplement may be necessary.

A change in diet is part of the therapy for kidney or liver disease. Providing a food with more digestible protein, at lower levels than in maintenance cat food, can relieve the burden on the kidneys and liver. However, different types of kidney and liver disease require different diagnostics and therapy. Your veterinarian will explain your options.

TUMORS

Old cats have a greater incidence of tumors of all kinds. Tumors that affect the digestive system may occur in the mouth, stomach or intestines, although intestinal tumors are rare. Tumors can cause intestinal blockage or infiltrate the intestinal wall. The result is that nutrient absorption is affected, causing chronic diarrhea and weight loss. Sometimes removal is the only treatment necessary.

When surgery is not possible, chemotherapy and radiation may help. Although cats from two to 17 years can develop intestinal tumors, the average age is 10 years. Siamese cats tend to have a high frequency of small-intestinal tumors.

Intestinal mast cell tumors are rare, but they can affect old cats. Reported cases have occurred in domestic short- and longhairs from seven to 21 years, with the average age being 13 years. These tumors, which are unlike the mast cell tumors that form in other body sites, occur in the small intestine and may spread to regional lymph nodes.

Vomiting, diarrhea, weight loss, and lack of interest in food are signs that a cat may have an intestinal mast cell tumor. Intestinal mast cell tumors frequently are malignant and require surgical removal.

DISORDERS OF THE SMALL INTESTINE

Common signs of disease in the small intestine include vomiting and diarrhea. However, although diarrhea is one of the more common signs of intestinal disease, its absence does not rule out the possibility. Weight loss, poor coat condition, dull eyes, and a lethargic attitude are other indicators of potential intestinal problems.

Diarrhea

Diarrhea, described as an increase in fecal water, is a consistent indicator of feline intestinal problems such as inflammatory bowel disease or intestinal lymphoma, or of systemic diseases such as hyperthyroidism. Unusually soft or liquid stools can also be caused by a change in diet, stress, parasites, or poisoning. Diarrhea can be a side effect of flea control insecticides or medications, such as antibiotics and cancer-fighting drugs. The most common cause of diarrhea, however, is eating indigestible or irritating items such as insects, bird feathers, or spoiled food.

Because most cats are so fastidious about using the litter box and burying their feces, diarrhea may go unnoticed unless the cat has an accident in the house. Another common sign is feces matted in the fur around the anal area, especially in longhaired cats. Although it's unpleasant, occasional diarrhea is not a cause for alarm. When it occurs, withhold food for 24 hours, then offer a bland meal of boiled rice and chicken. If it continues for two days or more, your cat should be examined by a veterinarian. If the diarrhea is bloody, or is accompanied by other signs, such as lethargy, lack of appetite or abdominal discomfort, do not wait to take in the cat. To reach a diagnosis, your veterinarian may ask questions about the frequency and duration of diarrhea; the type of diet and any recent changes; and the consistency and quantity of the stool.

Inflammatory Bowel Disease

Inflammatory bowel disease is the most common small-intestinal disorder, especially in older cats. Fortunately, it can be managed effectively if caught early.

The intestinal tract has an absorptive surface that is lined with tiny, finger-shaped villi, which help speed nutrients through the system. When this surface cannot absorb all the fluid present, diarrhea is the result. Inflammatory bowel disease occurs when the villi are invaded by inflammatory cells called eosinophils, plasmacytes, and lymphocytes. These cells "stop up" the villi, preventing nutrients from moving into the bloodstream. Signs of inflammatory bowel disease are just what you might expect: vomiting, usually of bile-stained mucus; vomiting and diarrhea; or diarrhea alone. Vomiting may occur frequently for two to four days, then settle into a routine. Appetite may either increase or decrease. The natural result is weight loss.

Endoscopic or surgical biopsy is required for a definitive diagnosis. To rule out other disorders, your veterinarian may take X rays, and run a complete blood count, a biochemical profile, a urinalysis, a fecal exam for parasites, a serum thyroxine test and a FeLV test. The causes of inflammatory bowel disease are not completely understood, but it has been associated with giardiasis and excessive numbers of bacteria.

In some instances, a food allergy may be at the root of the problem. A change to a hypoallergenic diet may bring the condition under control, especially if begun after drug therapy has been instituted. Otherwise, the condition is usually responsive to treatment. Medications such as Flagyl, an intestinal antibiotic, or prednisone, an anti-inflammatory drug, can control inflammatory bowel disease, but usually they must be given daily for the rest of the cat's life. Most cats tolerate prednisone therapy well, with few of the side effects seen in dogs and humans.

Lymphoma

Lymphoma is the most common form of bowel cancer. When it occurs in the intestine, it can be associated with some other disease such as feline leukemia virus. Early on, a cat with intestinal lymphoma may lose its appetite and seem lethargic. As the disease progresses, the cat develops chronic diarrhea and loses weight. To make a definitive diagnosis, the veterinarian will need to biopsy the small intestine. Treatment ranges from surgery to chemotherapy, depending on the type of tumor. The prognosis ranges from fair to poor, again depending on the type of tumor and how early the disease was detected. Signs of this disease can mimic those of other intestinal diseases, and many cats are already in the advanced stages of the disease by the time a veterinarian sees them. Cats that are treated early have survived for a year or more. The average age of affected cats is 10 years.

LARGE INTESTINE

Jane and Moscow had a routine. Every morning, Jane would feed Moscow, then get ready for work. But one morning, Jane noticed that Moscow had been in and out of the litter box a couple of times. That was unusual. A few minutes later, she saw that Moscow was trying to eliminate outside the litter box. The tortoiseshell cat was lying on her side, straining, and seemed distressed. Jane rushed her to the veterinarian, who diagnosed constipation, a condition common in older cats.

Constipation

Fecal blockage in cats can take three forms. Tenesmus, or straining to defecate, is usually associated with colitis, or inflammation of the colon. The cat usually produces a soft stool with mucus or blood, but hard, dry stools may also occur with colitis. Constipation is the passage of hard, dry stools. Obstipation occurs when the feces are so impacted in the colon and rectum that the cat cannot pass them. No matter what form it takes, the condition is generally referred to as constipation.

A constipated cat may have unusually delayed defecation, signalled by refusal or inability to eliminate for more than a day or two, or it can have difficulty defecating. A cat with this condition crouches or strains in the litter box, producing a hard, dark, dry stool or no stool at all. Severely constipated cats may pass liquid feces around the obstruction. They may vomit or stop eating and drinking; lose weight; and become lethargic. Constipated cats can easily become dehydrated.

What causes constipation? Frequently, it indicates a more serious underlying problem, which can be physical or emotional. A number of situations can precipitate the condition, from stress over a household change to refusal to use a dirty litter box. Constipation is not unusual in cats with pelvic fractures, bite wounds or anal tumors, who may find defecation painful. Hairballs or other foreign objects may form impactions that make it difficult for the cat to defecate.

Dehydration, often related to kidney disease or diabetes, can cause feces to be hard and dry. Constipation is a side effect of certain drugs, including diuretics, which are sometimes prescribed for heart conditions. Obesity, megacolon, and age can also be factors.

If your cat is straining to defecate, do some detective work. Have you changed litters? Is the fur around your cat's anal area matted, preventing elimination? Does the area seem tender? Is your cat alert, still eating and drinking? If none of these situations applies, it may be that your cat's digestive tract is simply not as efficient as it once was. A high fiber food or the addition of soluble fiber such as Metamucil, wheat bran, or pumpkin to the cat's regular diet can be the key to resolving the situation.

The switch to a higher fiber diet is the most important change you can make to prevent constipation and may completely solve the problem. Some cats, however, may require sedation to remove the stool and medication to stimulate defecation. Fluids may be necessary to correct dehydration.

Jane's veterinarian ran a urinalysis to rule out a urinary tract infection as the cause of straining, then gave Moscow an enema to clear the obstruction. Jane changed Moscow's food to Hill's Prescription Diet W/D to provide more fiber, and gave her Laxatone occasionally. After Moscow had two more bouts with constipation a year later, the veterinarian advised Jane to give her a daily stool softener called Lactulose, an indigestible sugar that draws fluid into the colon. Moscow has been in good health ever since.

Megacolon

This condition is similar to megaesophagus but involves the colon. It occurs most often in middle-aged or older male cats and can affect any breed. Megacolon develops when feces accumulate in the colon, stretching and enlarging it. Weakened intestinal muscles and poor motility cause retention of feces, a situation that is most uncomfortable for the cat. Once megacolon occurs, the condition is self-perpetuating, often increasing in severity and frequency before it is recognized. The more the colon stretches, the more damage that is done.

Megacolon and chronic constipation are closely linked, as it is theorized that both conditions may be caused by a defect in smooth muscle function. Megacolon often has no known cause, but it can also be secondary to other conditions such as arthritis, old pelvic fractures, strictures of the colon or, rarely, foreign bodies. Damage to the nerve supply of the colon may sometimes be a factor. Whatever the cause, the decreased colon function leads to stool retention and chronic constipation.

Signs of megacolon include constipation, straining to defecate, or taking a long time to defecate. Diagnosis is made through a medical history, palpation, and X rays. Treatment varies, depending on when the condition is diagnosed. If caught early, an attempt is made to re-establish normal fluid and electrolyte levels and empty the colon. When megacolon is caused by an underlying condition such as those mentioned above, treatment of the cause can sometimes reverse the condition. Although most cases of megacolon and chronic constipation cannot be cured, they can be controlled medically. Cats with chronic megacolon can be treated with laxatives and occasional enemas. The laxatives lubricate, stimulate intestinal motility, and help the colon retain water. Cats with megacolon may also benefit from the addition of soluble fiber, such as methyl cellulose, canned pumpkin or bran, to their food. This helps soften feces, allowing for easier elimination. Generally, however, these treatments are temporary.

If medical treatment fails, surgical correction—removal of the affected part of the colon—becomes necessary. This surgery is an acceptable alternative for healthy older cats, but others may have medical problems that make them poor candidates for surgery.

A University of Pennsylvania Veterinary Hospital study funded by the Morris Animal Foundation is examining the possibility that a smooth muscle disorder is linked to megacolon. The researchers hope to identify new gastrointestinal drugs that will stimulate colonic movement, eliminating the need for surgery.

LIVER DISEASE

The liver, the cat's largest internal organ, performs a number of functions vital to the well-being and smooth running of the cat's body. In addition to its digestive system functions of producing bile, converting sugars into glycogen and storing the glycogen for energy use, the liver manufactures a number of enzymes used to initiate chemical reactions within the body. It synthesizes hemoglobin, recycles red blood cells, and helps detoxify the body.

If liver function deteriorates, which can be a result of the aging process, the body is less able to withstand toxins. That's why it's important to feed a high-quality diet, exercise restraint in the use of flea-control products and medications, and prevent overeating. Obese cats are especially prone to a liver condition called hepatic lipidosis, which can be fatal.

Signs of liver disease can be subtle. Depression and lethargy may easily go unnoticed in an animal that sleeps most of the time anyway. More obvious signs include appetite loss, excessive thirst and urination, jaundice, abdominal distention with fluid, vomiting and diarrhea. But these may not occur until the disease has progressed. Blood tests during your cat's annual exam may provide early detection.

Liver disorders are treated by reducing the need for liver function. This requires a highly digestible diet that contains high-quality protein. In fact, cats with liver disease usually require as much as or more protein than healthy cats. The amount of sodium in the diet should be moderately restricted. It's important to control the frequency and amount of food taken in. Feeding four to six small meals per day is recommended. The smaller meals reduce the amount of nutrients requiring transformation by the liver at one time.

Hepatic Lipidosis

Tiger's owner spoiled him rotten. She fed him scrambled eggs and ham from her own plate and made sure he had an ample supply of his favorite salmon cat food. The cat became so fat that he resembled a beach ball on toothpicks.

Tiger loved food, but he loved his owner even more. When she died suddenly, Tiger went into a depression, refusing to eat. His lack of appetite led to rapid weight loss, and without force-feeding by the veterinary staff, he would have died.

Why did this happen in such a fat but seemingly healthy cat? Tiger was suffering from a condition called hepatic lipidosis.

Hepatic lipidosis occurs in obese cats on severely restricted diets. It sometimes occurs after a stressful event, such as being boarded. Too strict a diet to effect weight loss can also precipitate the condition, as can decreased appetite caused by illness.

Sometimes accompanied by diabetes or toxemia, hepatic lipidosis develops when fats accumulate within the liver cells. In addition to weight loss and lack of appetite, signs may include an enlarged liver, jaundice, and dehydration. Treatment begins with an attempt to rehydrate the cat with an intravenous, balanced electrolyte solution. Broad-spectrum antibiotics and water-soluble B vitamins help, too. Providing proper protein and caloric intake is the most important aspect of treatment. Appetite stimulants may encourage the cat to eat, but if these don't work the cat must be force-fed by mouth or by a surgically-placed gastrostomy tube.

ACUTE AND CHRONIC PANCREATITIS

Acute pancreatitis, or inflammation of the pancreas, disrupts the normal digestive process. The result is an array of what can be life-threatening problems, including disrupted blood circulation, cell death, and lowered blood pressure. A cat with pancreatitis may lack its usual appetite, vomit, lose weight, become lethargic or depressed, or suffer diarrhea or jaundice. Unfortunately, cats with pancreatitis can sink into shock and die before it is realized anything is seriously wrong. The good news is that pancreatitis is rare in cats, far less common than in dogs. However, an old cat may be more susceptible to pancreatitis because of a decrease in digestive function. Old cats may also be less able to recover from such a serious illness.

A diagnosis of pancreatitis requires a medical history, complete blood count, serum chemistry analysis, and X rays or ultrasound. When pancreatitis is caught in time, treatment involves reducing the workload of the pancreas by withholding food; administering fluids and electrolytes, plasma or whole blood; and giving drugs to reduce pain. In severe cases, surgery may be required to remove dead pancreatic tissue.

Chronic pancreatic inflammation can destroy cells that produce insulin and enzymes, resulting in diabetes or pancreatic exocrine insufficiency (PEI), a deficiency of digestive enzymes and fluids. Although PEI is rare in cats, its likelihood increases with age. A cat with this condition loses weight rapidly despite eating well, and produces soft, light-colored stools. PEI is treated by changing the diet to a low-fiber, easily digestible food and feeding replacement pancreatic enzymes in powder form.

CARDIOVASCULAR SYSTEM

If the digestive system is the body's refinery, the cardiovascular system, comprising the heart, blood vessels, blood and spleen, is its pump. The heart beats 120 to 240 times per minute to circulate blood throughout the cat's body, sending it first to the lungs for oxygen and then throughout the body by way of the blood vessels. The blood carries carbon dioxide to the lungs and metabolic wastes to the kidneys for removal, and helps maintain body temperature. Blood components each perform a specific task. The red blood cells carry fuel—oxygen and nutrients—to all body organs and muscles. White blood cells ward off disease by destroying invading germs. The spleen destroys used blood cells, holds a reserve of red blood cells and produces lymphocytes, which play a role in immune function.

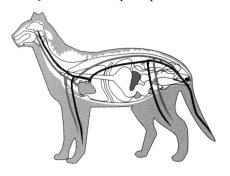

The feline cardiovascular system.

Heart function decreases with age. To compensate, the blood vessels constrict and the kidneys retain fluid and sodium. This helps restore cardiac output, but it also puts a heavier load on the system, leading to further deterioration. Congestive heart failure occurs when the heart muscles weaken, reducing the heart's ability to pump blood. This leads to failure of the left ventricle, resulting in an accumulation of excess fluid in the lungs, a condition called pulmonary edema.

Although heart disease is not as common in cats as it is in dogs and people, signs of this condition should not be ignored. A cat with heart disease may tire easily or have difficulty breathing because fluid has accumulated in the chest. It may cough frequently, become depressed or weak, or lose weight. Some cats with heart disease tend to lie flat on the breastbone and move from that position reluctantly. In severe cases, bluish-gray gums or tongue indicate insufficient oxygen in the blood. If your cat shows any of these signs, take it to your veterinarian.

Heart disease usually develops in middle age, when a cat is six to eight years old. Middle-aged male cats and certain breeds are more likely to develop cardiomyopathies. Obesity can be a contributing factor in development of congestive heart failure.

CONGESTIVE HEART FAILURE

Congestive heart failure occurs when one of the heart's lower chambers, or ventricles, begins to fail. The heart has four chambers, with an upper chamber (atrium) and lower chamber (ventricle) on each side. Heart failure may occur on the left side or the right side. Signs of left-sided heart failure include difficulty breathing and lack of appetite. The air sacs, or alveoli, in the lungs fill with fluid. Cats with right-sided heart failure may accumulate fluid in the abdomen or suffer decreased liver and gastrointestinal function, compromising their ability to digest and absorb nutrients. Right-sided heart failure is much less common than left-sided heart failure.

Diet is one of the keys to managing congestive heart failure. The goal is to reduce water retention by restricting sodium intake. Usually, a commercially prepared low-sodium diet is prescribed. Cats on such diets may need taurine supplements to prevent depletion of this essential amino acid in the cardiac muscle. In addition, rest and sodium restriction help decrease the heart's workload. Medications can be used to improve cardiac function and reduce pulmonary congestion.

HYPERTROPHIC CARDIOMYOPATHY

This condition is the most common form of acquired (as opposed to congenital) heart disease in cats. Primarily it affects young to middle-aged (less than five or six years old) male cats, especially Persian and Maine Coon cats. But veterinary reports show that cats of all breeds, as young as eight months and as old as 16 years, have developed it.

The cause of hypertrophic cardiomyopathy is unknown, but it occurs when the left ventricular wall, papillary muscles and septum become enlarged or thickened, causing the left side of the heart chamber to become smaller and less pliant. This prevents the heart from expanding adequately to receive blood. A cat with this form of heart disease may be lethargic, with labored or noisy breathing, and a poor appetite. Arterial blood clots can cause lameness or paralysis of hind legs.

If your veterinarian suspects cardiomyopathy, she may use such diagnostic aids as echocardiography, electrocardiography or X rays. Echocardiography, for instance, allows the veterinarian to see what's going on inside the heart. It can measure the thickness of the heart walls, and shows the chamber size, the heart's ability to contract, and how well the valves are functioning. Other diagnostic tests include blood counts, packed cell volume, and percent of hemoglobin. It may be necessary to rule out hyperthyroid heart disease and systemic hypertension by determining resting serum T4 concentration and serial arterial blood pressures.

Diuretics help your cat eliminate sodium and water, but in the process the cat can lose such water-soluble nutrients as B vitamins, potassium, calcium, chloride, and magnesium. These nutrients must be replaced by the diet or with a supplement. Your veterinarian can advise you on how best to proceed. Most geriatric cats diagnosed with hypertrophic cardiomyopathy live another one to two years with treatment.

DILATED CARDIOMYOPATHY

This heart condition occurs when all four chambers of the heart become dilated and no longer contract effectively. This means the heart cannot pump the blood that passes through it. The result is lung or liver congestion, and a decrease in the blood's ability to permeate tissues.

Thanks to research in the 1980s at the University of California at Davis, dilated cardiomyopathy was linked to taurine deficiency. Cat food manufacturers began supplementing their products with taurine, and the condition is now rare. When it does occur, it is most common in middle-aged and older cats, especially Siamese, Abyssinian, and Burmese. If the condition is not treated, a cat with dilated cardiomyopathy will develop congestive heart failure.

Other cardiovascular disorders that may affect geriatric cats include cardiac arrhythmias, chronic valvular disease, pericardial effusion, hyperthyroidism, hypertension, and arterial thromboembolism. The last condition is common in geriatric cats with any form of heart disease that results in enlargement of the heart's upper chambers. Treatment is often disappointing; even when it is successful, the condition recurs frequently. Any cat with signs of respiratory difficulty, weakness, or weight loss should be seen by your veterinarian.

PROBLEMS OF THE RESPIRATORY SYSTEM

Your cat's breathing is an involuntary action controlled by centers in the medulla oblongata, or brain stem, the most primitive area of the brain. Although breathing is the most obvious function of the respiratory system, it also plays a role in protecting the body from an onslaught of unseen particles in the air.

The respiratory system consists of the nose, turbinates, sinuses, pharynx and larynx—the upper respiratory tract—and the trachea, bronchi and lungs—the lower respiratory tract. The nose serves as the first line of defense against invading microorganisms. As air enters the nasal passages, dust, pollen and microbes are trapped in mucous secretions and then moved to the pharynx, where they are eliminated. Air is then moistened and warmed as it passes over the turbinate bones, which are covered by thin mucous membranes inside the na-

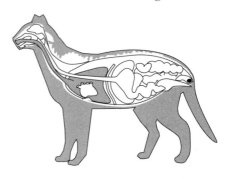

The feline respiratory system.

sal chambers. The warmed air passes over the part of the nasal lining called the olfactory mucosa. The olfactory nerves conduct scents to the brain for interpretation. This sensory organ plays a vital role in the cat's appetite, behavior, and protection. Cats use their noses to identify food, friends and prey, as well as to investigate unfamiliar items or people.

The epiglottis prevents food and water from entering the larynx and trachea, but if a cat eats or drinks too quickly, the food may go down the wrong pipe. The result is violent coughing or, in serious cases, aspiration pneumonia.

Respiratory disease offers one of the greatest challenges a veterinarian can face. Because the respiratory tract can host a variety of infectious organisms, the veterinarian may be faced with successfully anticipating and managing a number of primary and secondary infections. Diseases of the respiratory system can have several causes. The most likely respiratory problems in old cats are infectious upper respiratory infections. Viral and bacterial upper respiratory infections, such as feline herpesvirus and chlamydia, primarily affect kittens, but older cats are not immune to them. An old cat's weaker immune system is less able to fight off infections, so it's important to keep vaccinations current. If your cat does catch a cold, fluid therapy and nutritional support are critical. And although antibiotics have no effect on viruses, they can fight secondary bacterial opportunists that may take advantage of your cat's weakened condition.

Other respiratory problems are aspiration pneumonia and pulmonary edema. Aspiration pneumonia occurs when food or liquids go down the trachea instead of the esophagus. It occurs most frequently in cats that are unconscious, seizuring, or being force fed. It can also be caused by esophageal disorders, obstructions, or persistent vomiting.

Heart failure, pneumonia or kidney disease are some of the conditions that can cause pulmonary edema, an accumulation of excess fluid in the lungs. Cats with this condition find it difficult to breathe. They wheeze and breathe rapidly, with their mouths open. Your veterinarian may prescribe drugs to eliminate the fluid and improve the cat's breathing. There are many other conditions that can cause respiratory difficulties in older cats. In any case of difficult or noisy breathing, you should take your cat to the veterinarian.

Signs of lower respiratory problems include coughing, wheezing, panting, or changes in the rate, rhythm or effort of breathing. Sneezing, nasal discharge and watery eyes may indicate upper respiratory infections. Trauma, such as being hit by a car or receiving a blow to the chest, can injure the lungs or cause a diaphragmatic hernia, causing respiratory difficulty. An emergency situation is indicated when a cat has a bluish tongue or lips, or is breathing heavily and with difficulty for no apparent reason. Get it to your veterinarian immediately.

PROBLEMS OF THE URINARY SYSTEM

The urinary system is the body's septic system. Consisting of the kidneys, ureters, bladder, and urethra, it removes wastes and regulates the chemical and water components of blood.

Urine passes from the kidneys through the ureters to the bladder. When the bladder is full, the urine is eliminated through the urethra and out by way of the vulva in females, the penis in males. Age and disease can cause the urinary system to deteriorate, leading to serious health problems. Most cats with chronic renal disease are diagnosed between the ages of 10 and 15 years.

A number of signs can indicate urinary problems. Consult your veterinarian if your cat is unusually thirsty, accompanied by excessive urination, or if it drinks and urinates less than usual. Other signs that should raise a red flag are lack of appetite; weight loss; back pain, indicated by a hunched position; frequent urination of small amounts; bloody urine; mouth sores; bad breath or an ammonia-like odor to the breath; lethargy; occasional vomiting or diarrhea; and a dull coat, broken hairs or excessive shedding. A cat with any of these signs should be examined by a veterinarian. Kidney disease is especially common in old cats, and the sooner it is diagnosed, the better a cat's chance of survival.

KIDNEY DISEASE

The kidneys filter out and eliminate toxins from the body; regulate body fluids, electrolytes and minerals; and produce various hormones and other chemicals. If the kidneys fail, uremia occurs as toxic metabolic wastes accumulate in the blood stream, eventually poisoning your cat.

Kidney disease may occur at any age, but it is most common in cats seven years or older. It may or may not be reversible, depending on the cause, the amount of damage and the cat's response to therapy. Kidney failure, which is the most common cause of death in old cats, occurs when about 70 percent of the kidney tissue is no longer functional. The most common form of this disease in older cats is chronic interstitial nephritis, which results in scarred, shrunken kidneys.

If diagnosed early, however, cats with chronic renal failure can have a good quality of life for months or even years. Subtle, early signs of kidney disease include a slight level of dehydration and a slight increase in urination and subsequent thirst. These cats often have an unkempt appearance. Eventually, the cat will display a noticeable increase in volume of urine. Compensatory water consumption increases with some cats, that may even jump into the sink or bathtub to drink. It's as if

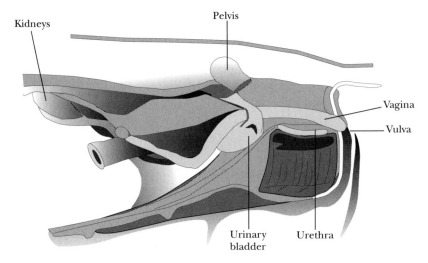

The urinary system of a female cat.

they are drinking water that doesn't satisfy them. Increased urination and thirst is a "chicken and egg" problem. Increased thirst stimulates urination, and vice versa.

It is important that the veterinarian help determine which came first. In the case of chronic interstitial nephritis, the decreased kidney function causes increased urination and compensatory water consumption to prevent dehydration. Other common signs of kidney disease include dehydration, bad breath, mouth ulcers, and occasional vomiting. Unfortunately, these signs often do not occur until after much of the kidney is injured or destroyed.

Blood tests measuring creatinine and blood urea nitrogen (BUN) are good indicators of kidney function. Elevation of these substances means the kidneys are not adequately filtering wastes from blood. Your veterinarian may take X rays or do ultrasound to see changes in the size, shape, or position of the kidneys. A biopsy can help provide an accurate assessment of damage and allow a more accurate prognosis.

Cats can survive with only one kidney, and kidney transplants done at some universities and private practices have been successful in cats. Of course, transplants are not widely available and are very expensive, so early detection and treatment are preferable. Because signs are subtle and may go unnoticed, annual screening is recommended for cats, beginning at 7 to 10 years of age. Screening is also important for cats of any age with unusual volumes of urine and increased thirst.

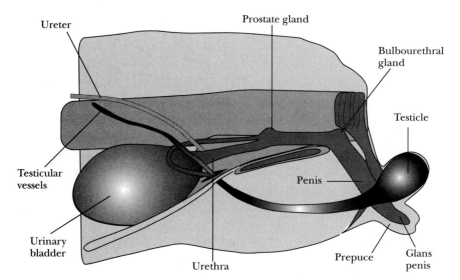

Ureter

Prostate gland

Bulbourethral gland

Testicle

Testicular vessels

Penis

Urinary bladder

Urethra

Prepuce

Glans penis

The male urinary system.

Treating Kidney Disease

The primary goal in managing chronic interstitial nephritis is to provide the cat with plenty of water. The effect is to make up for quality of urine with quantity. To encourage a cat to drink, place several water dishes around the house or add flavor enhancers such as milk, broth or clam juice. Fluid intake can also be supplemented with subcutaneous fluids, a procedure that is easily done at home with proper instruction. Providing a treat along with the fluid administration will make the cat more likely to cooperate. (This strategy works well with injections for diabetic cats, too.) The increased water intake can cause the body to lose water-soluble vitamins, so a vitamin supplement may be in order.

To ensure that the kidneys are not overworked, a commercially prepared medical diet may be prescribed, one that is high in digestible fats and carbohydrates, but low in phosphorus and protein. The diet of a cat with chronic renal failure should contain only 20 percent to 22 percent of calories as protein—enough to allow for tissue repair and turnover of enzymes. What protein there is should be of high biological value. The reduced-protein diet produces fewer waste products for the kidneys to eliminate. Nutritional management can reduce signs of uremia; help prevent deficiencies and excesses of fluids, electrolytes, minerals and acid-base; and delay progression of chronic renal failure.

It's also important to reduce stress in the life of a cat with chronic renal failure. These cats should not be permitted to roam outdoors unless they are supervised or confined in an enclosure.

Conditions Related to Kidney Disease

Anemia is one side effect of kidney disease. One of the jobs of the kidneys is to stimulate the bone marrow to produce more red blood cells. When there is a chronic kidney problem, anemia is often a result. Anemia can noticeably slow a cat down, but veterinarians can improve the condition with injections of erythropoietin, a substance the kidney produces to stimulate the production of red blood cells. Erythropoietin is not a cure-all and it must be used carefully, but it can dramatically improve the quality of life of a cat with kidney disease. When the injections are successful, owners often say that their cats are like kittens again. However, this is symptomatic rather than curative therapy. The underlying problems must still be addressed.

Kidney failure and hyperthyroidism are commonly found in older cats. If your cat is diagnosed with either disease, it may well be suffering from or susceptible to the other. Your veterinarian can advise you on the steps you should take to diagnose and treat these conditions.

Cats with chronic renal failure may also suffer from systemic hypertension, which is diagnosed by measuring blood pressure. This condition is usually treated with oral medication and moderately reducing the amount of sodium in the diet. Retinal hemorrhages are associated with chronic renal disease, but they have been known to improve if systemic hypertension can be controlled.

Another condition associated with kidney failure is hypokalemia, or low blood potassium, which may play a role in the progression of chronic renal failure. A primary indicator of hypokalemia is generalized muscle weakness. Cats with this condition have difficulty walking. Researchers believe that hypokalemia may be caused by an acidifying diet that is low in magnesium. Fortunately, treatment is easy. Oral administration of potassium usually provides results in one to five days.

Urinary Tract Disease

Feline urinary syndrome (FUS), or feline lower urinary tract disease (FLUTD), as it is now more accurately known, is not necessarily a disease of old cats. But cats that are overweight or inactive, especially if they are male, are more likely to have urinary tract problems. The percentage of cats exhibiting these factors increases with age. However, FLUTD is primarily a disease of young cats, with most cases diagnosed in cats two to six years old.

Signs and Diagnosis

A female cat with FLUTD may urinate frequently, leak urine while at rest, urinate outside the litter box, or frequently lick her urogenital area. Male cats are more likely to develop obstructions, indicated by frequent posturing without urinating, lethargy, dehydration and loss of appetite. An obstruction can rapidly become fatal if not detected and treated. Diagnosis of FLUTD requires a physical exam and a urinalysis. Routine blood tests and serum biochemical tests may be necessary to rule out other conditions. FLUTD has a high recurrence rate. Once a cat develops it, the likelihood that it will crop up again is about 40 percent.

Prevention and Treatment

Highly digestible cat foods, both dry and canned, produce high urine volume and low amounts of magnesium excreted in the urine. This is important because high urine volume appears to reduce the incidence of FLUTD, although this effect is not entirely understood. A high-fat, high-calorie diet may also be helpful.

Findings by veterinary researchers at Ohio State University Veterinary Hospital offer both good news and bad news. In a report in the July 1995 issue of the *Cornell University Animal Health Newsletter,* the researchers say that currently available cat foods no longer appear to be a common cause of lower urinary tract disease in cats.

Problems once associated with the production of high-alkaline urine and the development of some urinary tract stones (struvite urolithiasis) are now uncommon. They warn, however, that urinary tract diseases have not gone the way of the dinosaurs. No one knows the effect that changing the feline diet to contain less magnesium and to produce a more acidic urine will play in the long run. Some veterinarians are now seeing an increase in calcium oxalate stones, which form in acidic urine. Veterinarians may find that their feline patients face new urinary tract problems in the future.

What Is Excessive Urination?

Indications that a cat is urinating more than usual are changes in the amount of urine produced, its color, and the frequency of urination. Keep tabs on the situation with regular scooping of the litter box. It is normal to find a round spot up to three or four inches where the cat has urinated. Clumping litter may produce a baseball-size clump. A wet spot or clump larger than that is probably something to worry about, especially if litter is extremely wet. Of course, in multi-cat households, it may be necessary to catch a particular cat in the act to judge the amount it is urinating. A constant need to refill the water bowl is another sign. Hot weather can be one reason for excessive thirst, but if the weather can't be blamed, consider whether a health problem may be the cause. This cycle of excessive urination and thirst is called PUPD, or polyuria/polydipsia.

There is a difference between PUPD and incontinence. Incontinence is described as the inability to hold urine in the bladder normally. The cat usually dribbles urine or releases small amounts of urine while it is at rest. An incontinent cat is not deliberately missing the litter box and should not be punished for what it can't control. Sometimes incontinence can be controlled with medication. Consequently, it is important that cats with urinary incontinence be examined by your veterinarian.

PROBLEMS OF THE ENDOCRINE SYSTEM

The endocrine system has often been compared to the thermostat in a home. It secretes hormones that serve as regulators of bodily functions, or metabolism. Among the endocrine organs that are of special importance to the cat are the pancreas and the thyroid gland.

In addition to digestive enzymes, the pancreas secretes insulin, a hormone that is essential for the metabolism of carbohydrates. The thyroid gland produces thyroxine, a hormone that affects many body tissues and cellular processes. When something goes wrong with either of

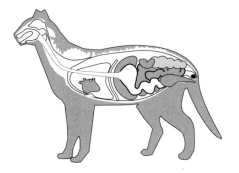

The feline endocrine system.

these organs, the result can be serious. Older cats are particularly prone to two endocrine system malfunctions: diabetes and hyperthyroidism.

DIABETES

This disease occurs when islet cells in the pancreas fail to secrete enough insulin, a hormone that enables cells to absorb glucose, which the body needs for energy. The body, confused by the apparent lack of glucose, begins to metabolize fat stores. The result is weight loss and starvation, even though the cat may be eating ravenously. Blood sugar levels increase rapidly. Eventually, the kidneys are unable to handle the amount of glucose in the blood, and they begin to eliminate it from the body through the urine.

Two common signs of diabetes are excessive urination, caused by the presence of glucose in the urine, and a compensatory increase in water consumption. The more the cat urinates, the more it must drink to prevent dehydration. Weight loss is another warning sign, although it can be subtle since it usually occurs gradually. Blood and urine tests to measure the levels of glucose, as well as certain enzymes and chemicals, are used to diagnose the condition.

Cats of any age, breed or sex can develop diabetes, but it is most common in middle-aged or old cats that are overweight, especially males. In many cases the cause of diabetes is unknown, but it can be associated with the use of such drugs as glucocorticoids and progestins, especially in overweight cats. Always ask about a drug's risks and any signs of side effects before administering it.

Each morning, Jerry awakes to the demanding meows of his diabetic cat. He follows the impatient cat to the kitchen, where he prepares a syringe of insulin. Peter waits for the injection in the back of his neck, then dances around while Jerry fills his food dish. His rumbling purr sounds as he eats. When he has finished, Jerry fills the bowl again and sets a timer that will open the feeder in eight hours.

The treatment goal for a diabetic cat is three-pronged: to maintain an acceptable level of blood glucose, to prevent ketone formation (a toxic byproduct of metabolized fat), and to decrease or eliminate signs of the disease. Diet and insulin therapy are the keys to achieving this goal. The amount of food and insulin the cat receives must be strictly regulated.

Diabetic cats are usually fed a weight-reduction diet that contains high levels of protein and low levels of fat and carbohydrates. Since both fats and carbohydrates depend on insulin for their removal from circulation, their blood concentration affects the amount of insulin required. Fiber is another important element in the diet of the diabetic cat. High levels of fiber aid in weight loss, slow the absorption of sugar from the intestinal tract, and decrease swings in blood glucose levels after meals.

Meals must be timed to coincide with peak insulin release. Generally, cats that receive one injection each day receive three meals of equal size. Some cats are given two injections daily, and they are usually fed four meals of equal size. Feeding several small meals each day helps control fluctuations in blood glucose. In cases where it is not possible to feed these meals at the appropriate times, the glucose level can be controlled by feeding two meals of equal size. Usually, this means feeding half the daily amount of food with the morning insulin injection and providing the rest several hours later, depending on the type of insulin used.

Old cats that are used to snacking on dry food throughout the day may be unwilling to change their habits. Rather than stressing these cats by forcing them to adhere to the new meal schedule, you may wish to set a timed feeder that will open midway between the two scheduled feedings and provide a small amount of dry food. A cat that is hooked on semi-moist food is out of luck, though. Because of its high sugar content, diabetic cats should not eat semi-moist food.

A number of types of insulin are available for use in the cat, but there are no set guidelines for which type is best, how much to use, or how frequently to administer it. Each cat is an individual and will require a custom treatment plan. Depending on your lifestyle and the cat's condition, your veterinarian may recommend a single daily injection of a long-acting insulin or twice-daily injections of an intermediate-acting insulin.

Although Peter is doing well now, Jerry and his veterinarian originally feared the cat would not survive. Without regular testing, it can be difficult to determine the appropriate amount of insulin a cat needs, but Peter was so unnerved by the frequent veterinary visits or hospitalization that the blood tests were not an accurate reflection of his condition. Finally, the veterinarian advised Jerry to keep his cat at home and rely on Peter's clinical signs and urine sugar tests to guide him. With his good observation skills and several months of trial and error, Jerry was finally able to bring Peter's diabetes under control. Five years later, Peter is in good health.

A diabetic cat receiving appropriate insulin therapy should be healthy and active with a good appetite, no longer losing weight or drinking and urinating excessively. If urine tests are given daily, they should be negative or low in glucose for most of each day. If blood glucose is measured, ideal concentrations should remain between 100 and 200 milligrams per deciliter (mg/dl). Ideally, the blood and urine glucose levels should be measured by the veterinarian. However, some cats are too severely stressed by veterinary visits for lab results to be reliable. In these cases, close observation and urine monitoring by the owner can help the veterinarian alter the dosage appropriately. In difficult cases, it is better to be conservative in administration of insulin.

People who are familiar with diabetes in humans may be concerned about side effects of the disease in their cats. Fortunately, diabetic cats rarely suffer from the problems that affect people. Nor do they develop cataracts as frequently as diabetic dogs. When cataracts do occur, they tend to progress more slowly. Other problems that may result from diabetes include bad teeth, weak nails, and urinary tract infections. Often, these problems can be improved with a change in the cat's treatment regimen.

If your cat continues to lose weight and drink and urinate excessively, review its regimen. The problem could be outdated insulin, incorrect administration of injections, insulin that doesn't last long enough, insulin overdose, or insulin resistance. Your veterinarian can help you determine the problem and how to solve it.

Hypoglycemia

His owners were running late, but they wanted to stop by the house and check on Peter, their diabetic cat, before they went out for the evening. When they got home, Peter was nowhere to be found. Finally, they looked in the garage, where they found him lying on his side, limp and unable to move. They ran for some honey and placed it on the back of his tongue, stroking his throat until he swallowed. They alerted the emergency clinic and drove as quickly as they could in the rush-hour traffic. By the time they arrived, Peter was reviving, but the veterinarian on duty advised keeping him there in an incubator for the night. Because his cells weren't producing any energy, the incubator would help the hypoglycemic cat maintain a constant body temperature.

Hypoglycemia occurs when the cat receives too much insulin and is also related to the amount of food the cat receives. Too little food and too much insulin can be a fatal combination. The amount of insulin given is related to the amount of food consumed and the level of physical and psychic activity. For example, emotions such as excitement or fear combined with unusual exertion can affect insulin activity, as in the case of a cat that escapes outdoors and is chased by a dog. In Peter's case, the move to a new home had made him too nervous to eat his usual amount of food. It is important that a diabetic cat's routine stay as consistent as possible.

Signs of hypoglycemia are weakness, lack of energy, shaking, and convulsions. In the early stages, a cat with low blood sugar may appear glassy-eyed and confused, moving slowly and with difficulty. If you find your cat in such a condition, rub Karo syrup or honey on the oral mucous membranes or give orange juice, wrap the cat warmly to prevent shock, and rush it to the veterinarian.

HYPERTHYROIDISM

"I bet this is another hyperthyroid cat," the veterinary technician said as she placed the cat on the exam table. "Why do you think so?" the veterinarian asked. "She's old and thin," the vet tech replied, "and her owner says she has been unusually nervous. She's eating more than usual, too."

The thyroid gland, located in the neck, secretes hormones (T4 and T3) that help regulate the body's metabolism, stimulating cells to produce energy and controlling the body temperature. When thyroid hormone levels become too high, usually in cats with tumorous thyroid glands, the result is hyperthyroidism.

The incidence of hyperthyroidism has increased over the past 20 years. It is one of the most frequently diagnosed disorders in small-animal practices, and it is the most common endocrine disorder in middle-aged and old cats. Although most cats diagnosed with hyperthyroidism are more than 10 years old, with the average age being 13 years, this condition can be seen in younger cats.

The cause of hyperthyroidism is unknown, but according to a report by the Morris Animal Foundation, preliminary studies by researchers at the University of Georgia, University of California at Davis, and the Animal Medical Center indicate that some cats may be retaining certain chemicals that have the potential to stimulate thyroid growth. If this is the case, they hope to determine whether these compounds originate in food or in the environment. If diet is the culprit, changes in cat food formulations may prevent the disease in the future, just as the increase in taurine levels reduced the incidence of dilated cardiomyopathy in the 1980s.

Signs of Hyperthyroidism

A cat with hyperthyroidism eats ravenously, yet doesn't gain weight. It may seem active or agitated, and it may have a soft stool. Often, the coat is unkempt, and the fur sheds or mats more than usual. One interesting side effect is rapid nail growth. Some hyperthyroid cats have gastrointestinal problems such as vomiting, diarrhea and hairballs; others show excessive thirst and urination. A rapid heartbeat is common. Cats with hyperthyroidism don't tolerate stressful situations well. Sometimes, though, the signs of hyperthyroidism can be misleading. Because the cat is active and has a good appetite, owners often don't recognize that there's a problem until the disease has progressed and signs become more severe.

Diagnosing Hyperthyroidism

Routine tests that help your veterinarian diagnose hyperthyroidism are a complete blood count, a serum biochemical panel, urinalysis, an electrocardiogram, chest X rays, and thyroid function tests. Hyperthyroidism can have multisystemic effects.

The electrocardiogram and chest X rays are necessary because the increased heart rate and blood volume associated with hyperthyroidism can cause hypertrophic cardiomyopathy and congestive heart failure. Disorders that may mimic hyperthyroidism include diabetes, kidney failure, cardiac disease, liver insufficiency, hyperadrenocorticism and neoplasia (tumors). For instance, diabetes, kidney failure, liver disease, and neoplasia can depress a cat's serum T4 concentrations. The result is that a cat with mild hyperthyroidism could exhibit a serum T4 concentration in the normal range.

Treating Hyperthyroidism

Left untreated, a cat with hyperthyroidism will literally starve, and its heart will fail. Fortunately, the disease can be treated, especially if detected in its early stages. Treatment may take one of three forms: surgery, medication, or radioactive iodine.

Surgery is the most difficult of the three treatments. It involves removing the abnormal lobe or lobes of the thyroid gland. Because surgery can affect the parathyroid glands, which regulate calcium, it is often safest to remove only one lobe. Removing only one lobe leaves the opposite side's parathyroid untouched. The other thyroid lobe can be removed later, after the first side's parathyroid gland has stabilized. Fortunately, in many cases only one thyroid lobe is affected, so the cat needs only one surgery to be cured.

When the thyroid gland is removed to treat hyperthyroidism, one common complication is a decrease of calcium in the blood due to hypoparathyroidism.

If your cat has recently had thyroid surgery, be on the lookout for a loss of appetite, weakness or muscle tremors. Seek treatment immediately if you notice these signs. Your veterinarian will prescribe dosages of calcium and vitamin D. Failure to treat this condition can result in the cat's death.

Medication cannot cure hyperthyroidism, but it can control it and in most cases it is easy to administer. The drug works by destroying the thyroid hormone as it is being produced. If your veterinarian recommends medical therapy, the medication must continue for the rest of the cat's life. The drawback of drug therapy is that if the cat doesn't get the medication, the thyroid level goes back up. Therefore, long-term use of medication requires the ability to effectively medicate the cat as well as periodic blood tests, especially during the first three months of treatment, to evaluate the cat's condition.

Medication is not for every cat. Potential side effects of antithyroid drugs commonly include nausea and vomiting. Blood and skin disorders sometimes develop, but these are rare. Because the hyperthyroid cat is already underweight, vomiting can make matters worse. Medication is, however, the least expensive treatment, so many owners want to try it first before subjecting their cats—and their wallets—to radioactive iodine therapy or surgery. In most cases, medication ends up being a stopgap measure until the cat can receive radioactive iodine therapy or surgery.

Radioactive iodine therapy works by destroying the thyroid gland while leaving other tissues unharmed. This treatment, which is by far the best for this condition, is safe and effective, but its main disadvantage is that it is not readily available. The Animal Medical Center in New York City and Woodbridge Animal Hospital in Irvine, California, are two of the few nonuniversity facilities that offer the procedure.

Radioactive iodine therapy has its drawbacks. Cats that undergo this treatment are required to stay at the treatment facility because they are producing radioactive waste, which must be disposed of properly. The amount of time a cat is required to stay in radiation isolation varies from state to state, depending on each state's radiation exposure standards. For instance, in California most cats remain at the facility for about a week, whereas in Missouri cats must be kept in isolation for about three weeks.

PROBLEMS OF THE REPRODUCTIVE SYSTEM

Tuffy was a wanderer. He liked to prowl the neighborhood, searching out receptive female cats and fighting other toms to protect his territory. One morning, however, he didn't come home. The kids searched for several days, but didn't find him. Their father didn't have the heart to tell them he had found Tuffy dead, hit by a car on his nocturnal ramblings.

Because they are hormone-driven, the reproductive organs play a major role in a cat's behavior as well as its health. Under their direction, the intact cat sprays, roams, fights, and yowls its desire throughout the neighborhood. Males and females alike are ruled by the instinct to reproduce. Although this instinct is a natural one, the cat's environment has changed in a way that makes uncontrolled reproduction undesirable. Whereas once Nature and disease kept the cat population in check, today good food, indoor living and regular vaccinations mean that more cats survive for more years than ever before.

The number of cats born each year is far greater than the number of good homes available. The result is that millions of cats die in shelters or on the streets each year. Overpopulation is not technically a health problem, but it kills more cats in this country than any disease.

Overpopulation is not the only disease of the reproductive organs. Intact female cats also suffer mammary tumors and pyometra, a serious infection of the uterus. Both of these conditions—as well as the population and behavior problems that result from surging hormones—can be prevented by spaying or neutering the cat before it reaches sexual maturity.

MAMMARY TUMORS

As Lori rubbed Cleo's chest, she noticed a lump where one had never been before. Concerned, she called her veterinarian, who advised her to bring Cleo in for an examination. The lump appeared to be a mammary tumor, the veterinarian said, and he recommended surgery as soon as possible to remove it. Fortunately for Lori and Cleo, the lump was benign, and the big black-and-white cat was soon ruling the household again.

■

Patricia wasn't so lucky. Her seven-year-old Siamese, an intact female, died of metastatic breast cancer.

The mammary glands are the third most common site of cancer in cats (after blood cell cancers and skin tumors). Mammary tumors occur less frequently in cats than in dogs, but 80 percent to 90 percent of feline mammary tumors are malignant, and they often spread to the lymph nodes, liver and lungs. Cats most likely to develop mammary tumors are intact queens or females spayed late in life. The average age of occurrence in cats is 11 years, so owners of geriatric cats should be diligent in searching for lumps. Siamese cats have a high risk of developing mammary tumors, with an earlier age of onset than other breeds.

Fortunately for all cats, spaying at an early age, especially before first estrus, greatly reduces the risk of mammary tumor development. If a lump does develop, chest X rays and a biopsy will help your veterinarian determine the best course of action. Usually, this means surgical removal or chemotherapy. The smaller the tumor, the greater the survival rate, so early detection is important.

PYOMETRA

Seven-year-old Misha, a Maine Coon, lived a pampered life. Her owner, Mark, kept her indoors, made sure she received regular veterinary checkups and fed her a high-quality food. Although she had never been bred, Misha was unspayed because Mark feared the risks of anesthesia and surgery. Normally, Misha was a healthy cat, but she had been depressed and uninterested in eating for a couple of days. When Mark came home from work, he examined Misha, only to discover that her abdomen was unusually firm and that a smelly, pus-filled discharge was draining from her vulva. A trip to the veterinarian resulted in a diagnosis of pyometra.

This uterine infection affects female cats that have not been spayed. It is most common in cats older than five years that have never borne a litter. Pyometra begins during a cat's heat cycle, when bacteria enter the uterus through the open cervix. After the heat cycle, the cervix closes, trapping the bacteria within. They multiply quickly, forming pus and filling the uterus. By the time the infection is diagnosed, ovariohysterectomy—removal of the uterus and ovaries—is often the only way to save the cat's life.

A young cat that is not destined for breeding should be spayed before its first heat. An older cat that is no longer being bred should also be spayed to prevent the chance of pyometra. Although surgery has some risks, it is better to do it when the cat is young or healthy than when it is weak from infection and less able to withstand the stresses of anesthesia and surgery.

FELINE EYE DISORDERS

The eyes are said to be the windows to the soul. Cat owners may find this description particularly apt. A cat's eyes are perhaps its most powerful sense and one of its most beautiful features.

The eyes also display one of the most visible signs of aging. Nuclear sclerosis, a condition in which the center, or nucleus, of the lens becomes a hazy gray, is the most common lens disorder in old cats. It usually does not develop until late in the cat's life. Often confused with cataracts, it occurs when the central area of the lens becomes dense and compacted compared to the outer area. The pupil appears blue or gray. Fortunately, vision is not impaired to any serious degree, and no treatment is necessary.

CATARACTS

Another eye condition associated with old age is opacity of the lens, or cataracts. Cataracts are not as common in cats as in dogs, and they tend to develop at a later age. When they occur, they are usually caused by inflammations, cellular debris, trauma, or hemorrhage within the eye. Senile cataracts develop in old age, sometimes in tandem with nuclear sclerosis. Cats with diabetes may develop cataracts, although

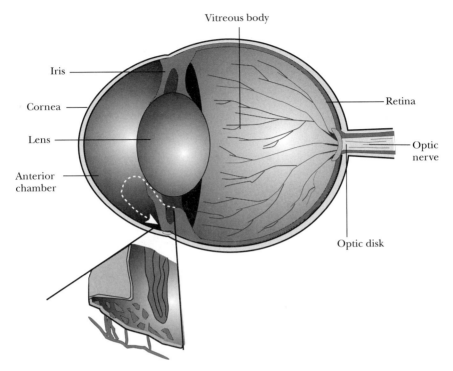

The parts of the feline eye.

this is rare. If inflammation is not the cause, surgery can have good results.

GLAUCOMA

Glaucoma is defined as an increase in pressure within the eye. Its signs are subtle and usually don't become noticeable until the disease has progressed. Often, this means that the cat is not brought in for treatment until little can be done for it. A cat with glaucoma may have dilated pupils and a cloudy cornea. The eyeball may look red and enlarged. Although pain is not always evident, it can be manifested in sleepiness, depression, irritability, tearing, pawing at the eye and reduced playfulness.

Glaucoma, which can take one of two forms, can cause blindness if not recognized and treated immediately. Few cats are diagnosed with primary glaucoma, although some Persians, Siamese and domestic shorthairs appear to be genetically predisposed to the condition. Secondary glaucoma is seen a little more often. It is usually associated with inflammation, but other causes include trauma to the eye and cancer. Also

When Should Your Cat See the Veterinarian?

The following signs are often seen in geriatric cats. They may or may not indicate a serious problem, but usually some sort of veterinary attention is required. It is not possible to list all signs and all possible diagnoses. If you have any questions about your cat's health, call your veterinarian.

● **Acting tired or sluggish:** *Lethargy is a common sign of many diseases.*

● **Constipation or diarrhea that lasts for more than two days:** *Severe constipation can leave a cat unable to eliminate bodywastes. Diarrhea can be indicative of a number of conditions. If either condition does not improve within 48 hours, take your cat to the veterinarian. If the diarrhea is bloody, take the cat in sooner.*

● **Dehydration:** *This can be caused by excessive vomiting or diarrhea, excessive urination, and failure to eat or drink. Signs include dry, tacky gums, and skin that does not quickly return to place after being pinched.*

(continued)

associated with glaucoma are feline leukemia virus, feline immunodeficiency virus, feline infectious peritonitis and toxoplasmosis, diseases that can alter the eye's fluid dynamics.

Diagnosing glaucoma requires a thorough eye exam, including measurement of intraocular pressure and examination of the retina and optic nerve. If caught in time, the eye may be saved with medical therapy or, in the case of secondary glaucoma, treatment of the underlying cause. In some cases, noninvasive diode laser treatment helps decrease fluid buildup in the eye. If the eye cannot be saved, removal is the best course, because glaucoma can cause intense, continuous pain. This is not as drastic as it sounds, and the cat will feel a lot better.

TUMORS

Eye tumors are not common in cats, but eyelid and conjunctival tumors occur more frequently, especially in white cats with nonpigmented eyelid margins. These cats may suffer from squamous cell carcinomas of the eyelid, conjunctiva and nictitating membrane. Such tumors appear as white, roughened, irregular masses or as pink, red or nonhealing areas. They are usually malignant and difficult to treat. Depending on the type of tumor, its size and location, treatment may involve surgical removal, radiation therapy or cryotherapy.

Primary intraocular tumors, such as melanoma of the iris or ciliary body, also occur and tend to spread to other parts of the body. These tumors may be benign or malignant, but in either case if they grow too large they can result in loss of the eye. Again, diode laser treatment may be effective in stopping tumor growth.

A cat with eye problems may need to be examined by a veterinary ophthalmologist, who is specially trained to diagnose and treat eye diseases and can provide the appropriate examinations and tests needed to identify serious eye problems, as well as the appropriate therapy.

HELPING THE CAT ADAPT

Often cats adjust easily to blindness, so if treatment is not possible or is unsuccessful, the cat will usually function well. Behaviorist William Campbell offers the following suggestion for helping a blind cat learn its way around the house and avoid bumping into furniture or walls. Apply a scented polish to upright obstacles such as chair and table legs, door jambs, and television sets. Apply a polish with a different scent to horizontal hazards such as low walls, table edges and steps. The cat will soon learn to identify obstacles by their scents so it can go around them.

Walking up to or touching a blind cat without notice can startle it. Avoid being bitten or scratched by speaking the cat's name first. Remind children and other guests not to run up to or pet the cat without warning.

HEARING PROBLEMS

Simba's owners were on vacation for two weeks, and she had a live-in petsitter to keep her company. The white cat spent her days following her

● **Difficulty urinating:** *This can indicate cystitis or, especially in males, urinary tract obstruction. Urinary obstruction can cause death within 24 hours, so if you notice this, seek veterinary advice immediately.*

● **Dragging hindquarters or scooting the rear on the floor:** *Kidney disease, diabetes, cardiomyopathy and anal obstructions can all cause a cat to drag its hindquarters, as can a spinal or pelvic injury. A cat that scoots its rear on the floor may have impacted anal glands.*

● **Drooling:** *Excessive salivation can indicate gingivitis, oral squamous cell carcinoma, poisoning, or a viral infection.*

● **Enlarged abdomen:** *This may be caused by a mammary tumor, heart or liver disease, peritonitis (inflammation of the abdominal lining) or pyometra (uterine infection). Obesity, of course, is another reason for an enlarged abdomen.*

● **Excessive thirst or urination:** *Diabetes, hyperthyroidism, and kidney disease can all cause a cat to drink more than usual or to seek water from unusual places, such as the toilet, sink or bathtub.*

(continued)

(continued)

When Should Your Cat See the Veterinarian?

- **Eyes that are cloudy or red; squinting; ocular discharge:** To avoid permanent damage, have the eyes checked. These signs may indicate keratitis, or corneal inflammation; anterior uveitis; and cataracts.

- **Gasping or shortness of breath:** This can be a sign of heart disease or respiratory disease.

- **Increased sensitivity:** Depending on the area where the cat is sensitive, this can indicate neck or back problems, an internal infection or injury, an abscess or allergic dermatitis.

- **Loss of appetite for more than one day:** Lack of interest in food can indicate a number of problems, from dental disease to cancer. If your cat likes to eat but suddenly loses interest in its food, it may be ill.

- **Lumps:** Tumors occur less frequently in cats than in dogs, but they are more likely to be malignant. A soft, hot, or painful swelling is probably an abscess. Any lump on your cat should be examined by a veterinarian.

usual routine: eating, sleeping, playing, sleeping, eating, sleeping. But on the day her owners returned, she was waiting in the window by the front door several minutes before their car turned into the driveway. "It's as if she knew you were coming," the petsitter said.

Cats have far better hearing, up to 60 kilocycles, than humans, whose upper auditory range is only 20 kilocycles. As cats age, however, their hearing ability may decrease. If your cat is older than 13 years, it may be among the 10 percent to 15 percent of cats that suffer gradual hearing loss. The tiny bones in the middle ear become less able to transmit the vibrations produced by the tympanic membrane, and the cochlear nerves deteriorate. Fortunately, this is rarely a problem, because most cats can compensate by relying on their other senses.

If hearing loss is suspected, try a couple of simple tests. Speak loudly to the cat when it's asleep, or stand behind it and jingle keys or make some other loud noise. If the cat doesn't respond, its hearing is probably affected. To compensate, give the cat another cue it can pick up instead. Vibrations and high-pitched sounds may become a new means of communication. Try stamping on the floor, blowing a dog whistle, or flashing a light to get the cat's attention. Don't startle the cat by touching it unexpectedly from behind. Always let the cat see you before trying to pet it or pick it up. Advise friends or visiting children of the best way to approach the cat. If the cat can't hear the can opener anymore, take his food to him or show him the dish and then place it in the normal spot.

Deaf cats usually get along well in a household despite their disability. In many cases, they compensate so well that their owners are unaware of the hearing loss. However, it's important to remember that deaf cats permitted outdoors are unable to hear approaching cars or other dangers. They should be kept indoors or allowed out only in confined areas.

DISEASES OF THE EAR

A number of conditions can affect a cat's ears—hematomas, ringworm, ear mites, and yeast or bacterial infections—but these are not specific to the old cat and can be prevented with general good care. Certain antibiotics—most commonly streptomycin and gentamicin—can damage the cochlea's sensory nerve cells. These drugs are safe at the recommended dosages, but hearing loss can result from an overdose or from long-term use.

White cats exposed to a great deal of sunlight may develop squamous cell carcinoma on their ear tips. At the first sign of scaly, scabby ear tips, schedule your cat for a veterinary exam. If caught early, this cancer can be cured by surgically removing the ear tips. If you have a white cat that spends time outdoors, consider applying sunscreen to its ears to protect them from the sun's harmful rays.

An ear condition that can affect middle-aged and older cats is a tumor of the ceruminous gland, which

● *Red or swollen gums:* *These are indicators of gingivitis and periodontitis, common feline dental problems. Gingivitis can also be a side effect of feline immunodeficiency virus, feline leukemia virus, kidney or liver failure, respiratory disease, and diabetes mellitus.*

● *Repeated vomiting, gagging, sneezing, or coughing: These actions can be signs of megaesophagus, obstruction, respiratory disease, heart disease, or aspiration pneumonia. All are serious conditions that require veterinary treatment. Excessive vomiting can cause dehydration.*

● *Rough, dull coat: Poor coat condition can be a sign of a number of problems, including dietary insufficiency, kidney disease, hyperthyroidism and various types of dermatitis.*

● *Vulvar discharge: This may indicate pyometra, a serious infection of the uterus. Pyometra occurs only in female cats that have not been spayed.*

● *Weight loss despite ravenous appetite: Diabetes, hyperthyroidism, and chronic pancreatic insufficiency can all cause a cat to lose weight, even if it is eating well. Weight loss almost always has significant medical implications.*

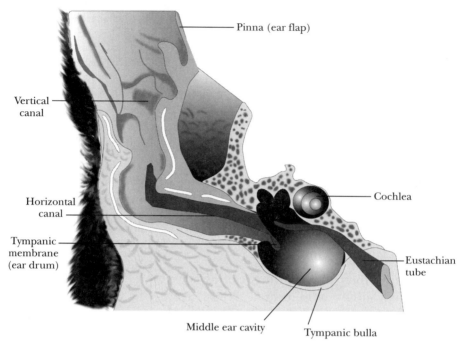

The internal and external features of the feline ear.

produces the wax found in the ear canal. These tumors may be benign or malignant. Treatment depends on location and surgical removal is usually successful.

PROBLEMS OF THE MUSCULOSKELETAL SYSTEM

Pandora and her owner were both surprised the first time the cat leaped for the window across the stairs—and missed. Pandora had been making the four-foot jump for years, with never a misstep. This time, she was a little short and dropped down into the stairwell. Fortunately, only her pride was hurt, but her owner feared that as she aged she wouldn't always be so lucky.

A cat's ability to leap tall bookcases in a single bound or to twist pretzel-like while grooming a hard-to-reach spot is unparalleled. The feline musculoskeletal system is a miracle of engineering: Of its 244 bones, nearly 70 are found in the spine and tail. Feline joints are unusually mobile, thanks to cartilage that permits the bones to slide together easily. Attached to the bones, via tendons, ligaments and cartilage, are muscles

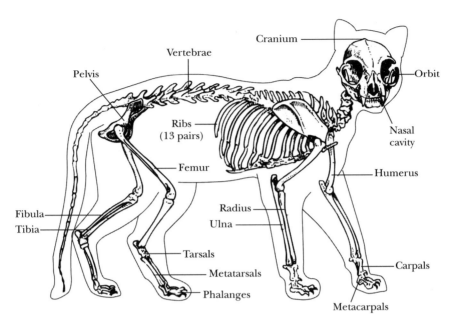

The feline skeletal System.

which make movement possible. Together the bones, muscles, and joints give the cat its famous flexibility.

Although cats suffer fewer musculoskeletal problems than dogs and humans, muscles, joints and vertebral discs degenerate with age. The most common feline musculoskeletal problem is loss of muscle tone, especially in the legs. Your cat may become stiff or lame, or its muscles may quiver from exertion. Although arthritis is rare in cats, trauma, infection and disease can take their toll. Muscle injuries can lead to inflammation and permanent loss of function. Bite wounds, abscesses, and severe periodontal disease can cause bone infections. Old age and obesity are culprits, too. Cartilage cushions joints, and when it deteriorates the result is primary osteoarthritis, or degenerative joint disease. Cats are well-known for their ability to hide pain or discomfort, but if you know what to look for you can help your cat be more comfortable.

MUSCULOSKELETAL DISORDERS

There are two types of joint disease: inflammatory and noninflammatory. Noninflammatory joint disease can be caused by such things as degenerative, metabolic or dietary factors; trauma; poorly formed joints; or tumor formation. Inflammatory joint disease is generally caused by infectious agents such as bacteria or fungi, or by autoimmune disease. Both inflammatory and noninflammatory joint disease can lead to arthritis, which is defined as inflammation of the joint. Because cats often suffer injury to the joints, noninflammatory joint disease is most common. Cats that are hit by cars or hurt in falls are especially prone to arthritis, which develops when the injury does not heal properly.

Inflammatory joint disease is linked to diseases such as chronic progressive polyarthritis, feline leukemia virus and systemic lupus erythematosus. Other causes include bacterial infections from bite wounds—one of the most common causes of septic arthritis—and certain viruses. Chronic progressive polyarthritis—which is often associated with feline leukemia virus—is an immunodeficiency disease that can take two forms.

The most common form occurs in young male cats between the ages of one and five years. The other form usually affects older cats and has been reported in cats as old as 16 years. It is characterized by swollen, painful joints and eventually results in crippling joint deformities. The disease can be slowed with glucocorticoid drugs, either alone or in combination with cytotoxic drugs. If treatment begins early enough, long-term remission may be possible.

Systemic lupus erythematosus is rare in cats, but when it occurs the signs include lameness, stiffness and swollen joints. Oral prednisone usually permits long-term control.

Arthritis caused by a bite wound can, of course, occur at any age. It usually results in a warm, swollen, painful joint. Generally, it can be cured with early treatment of the infection, which involves draining the pus from the joint, cleaning the area, and administering antibiotics. If not caught early, bone infections can take a long time to heal.

Immunoarthritis, possibly triggered by certain viruses, causes healthy joints to come under attack from the body's own immune system. There is no treatment for this condition, although researchers are experimenting with gold injections and immunosuppressive drugs to block inflammatory reactions.

Osteoarthritis is often associated with aging in dogs and humans, but it is uncommon in cats. When it occurs, it is often related to extreme old age or to stress on bone and tissue caused by obesity or abnormal joint construction. The result is arthritic inflammation. If the condition is relieved by surgery or weight loss, the arthritis may be cured.

If your cat shows signs of any form of arthritis, never try to treat it at home with aspirin, acetaminophen (Tylenol or Advil) or ibuprofen (Motrin). Anti-inflammatory drugs should be given to cats only under veterinary supervision. Because they don't metabolize them well, these drugs, especially acetaminophen, can be harmful or fatal to cats. Instead, your veterinarian may prescribe corticosteroids, such as prednisolone and prednisone.

Unfortunately, these synthetic anti-inflammatory drugs can have such unwanted side effects as excessive thirst and urination, an increased appetite, and weight gain. The side effects of long-term use include cataracts, diabetes, high blood pressure, kidney disease, and osteoporosis. If corticosteroids are prescribed, the cat must be monitored closely for signs of problems. Fortunately, cats seem better able to tolerate corticosteroids than dogs or humans.

Lameness is the most common sign of any type of joint disease. Cats are normally such graceful animals that any hint of lameness or other difficulty of movement should raise a red flag. Although occurrence is rare, some cat breeds are predisposed to developing orthopedic disorders such as patellar luxation, a condition in which the kneecap slides in and out of place, causing the cat to limp and to be reluctant to jump. Patellar luxation can occur in conjunction with hip dysplasia, also rare, in which poorly formed hip joints cause the cat to limp or to walk abnormally and to be reluctant to jump.

Although patellar luxation and hip dysplasia may have existed from an early age, the cat often does not show signs until it begins to age. X rays are necessary for a definitive

What Constitutes an Emergency?

Because cats are good at hiding illness, it can be difficult to know when to take them to the veterinarian. If your cat shows any of the following signs, take it to the veterinarian immediately. A delay in treatment can make it difficult or impossible to successfully treat your cat.

- *Acute persistent sneezing—may indicate a foreign body*
- *Heavy bleeding*
- *Marked difficulty breathing*
- *Eye injury*
- *Fractures*
- *Pain*
- *Paralysis*
- *Poor responsiveness*
- *Urinary obstruction—straining or inability to urinate; attempt to urinate outside the litter box*

diagnosis. Depending on the severity of the condition, surgery may be necessary, but mild cases can be controlled medically.

Breeds in which patellar luxation and hip dysplasia have been diagnosed include the Abyssinian, Chartreux, Devon Rex, Maine Coon and Persian. The Chartreux, Maine Coon and Persian tend to be large or chunky in build, so it is especially important to control the weight of these cats to help prevent aggravating these two disorders.

Osteosarcoma (Bone Cancer)

Ninety percent of the bone cancer cases diagnosed are attributable to osteosarcoma, making it the most common type of bone cancer in cats. Most common in middle-aged and older cats, osteosarcoma usually affects the long bones. The bones of affected cats are often weakened by the disease and may fracture easily.

It is sometimes difficult to tell whether a broken bone was caused by trauma or cancer, but a pathogenic fracture —one caused by cancer—heals slowly, if at all. Other signs of bone cancer include pain, lameness, or bony enlargement. Although the thought may be repugnant to cat owners, the best treatment is amputation. Cats can learn to get along well on only three legs, and—unlike the case with dogs and humans—the feline prognosis for long-term survival of long bone cancers is good: The survival rate is up to five years.

Veterinarians are also finding success with a new treatment called limb-sparing surgery, which can be performed if a tumor has not invaded too far into the bone. The process involves removing the affected segment of bone and transplanting a piece of bone from a cadaver animal into the cancer patient. The transplanted bone provides structural support for the limb while the healthy bone remodels the transplanted piece. Sometimes radiation therapy is helpful in controlling the growth of tumors.

A cat with a musculoskeletal disorder may have difficulty jumping up to a favorite spot or finding a comfortable position while sleeping. Be sure to provide a warm, soft, easy-to-reach bed that is indoors and away from drafts. If the arthritis is caused by obesity, a weight-loss diet may be necessary. For other forms of arthritis, use of heat can be therapeutic, as can veterinary acupuncture and chiropractic treatment. Discourage your cat from making high or dangerous jumps by blocking the area or booby trapping it with upside down mousetraps.

CENTRAL NERVOUS SYSTEM

Wanda stepped away from the stove to get the butter out of the refrigerator. As she set her foot down, she realized it had connected not with the floor but with Chessie's tail. The small black-and-white cat let out a yowl and took off into the dining room to repair her dignity. In the space of a split second, the cat's sensory cells had registered pain and transmitted the sensation from the neurons to the brain. All of Chessie's reactions—yowling, running away, and licking herself afterward—were made possible by the direction of the central nervous system, which stimulated the appropriate muscle fibers to enable the actions.

Your cat's central nervous system is its operations center. Without it, the cat would be unable to arch its back, jump up on the kitchen counter, or twitch its tail. In addition to controlling voluntary actions such as walking and jumping, the central nervous system directs such involuntary actions as breathing and heartbeat. Balance, behavior, movement, and instincts such as hunger and sexual drive, are all controlled by the central nervous system, as are the senses of hearing, sight, taste and smell. The central nervous system is made up of the brain, spinal cord, and peripheral nerves.

The basic operating unit of the central nervous system is the neuron, or nerve cell. The nerves connect the central nervous system to the rest of the body: the heart, the muscles, and the skin. The central nervous system has two main types of neurons: sensory and motor. Sensory nerves pass messages to the brain from such sensory organs as the nose and skin, while the motor nerves send messages from the brain to the organs and muscles.

Neurons are tiny but important. Without them, the body could not carry out the brain's directives. Neurons work by transmitting electrical impulses to and from the cell bodies in much the same way as a telephone system, connecting the brain to other parts of the body. Making up each neuron is a cell body. Projecting from the cell body is an axon, which conducts impulses away from the cell body. Protruding from the nerve cell and the axon are fine, branchlike tentacles called dendrites, which conduct impulses toward another cell body. Nerve cells use dendrites to communicate their messages, and the point at which the dendrites meet is called a synapse. When a nerve cell "fires" an electrical impulse, it passes down the axon to the synapse and releases a chemical called a neurotransmitter. The neurotransmitter passes across the synapse to activate the next nerve cell. When it reaches its destination, the end organ reacts to whatever stimulus has been received.

If the neuron is the basic operating unit, the brain is the chief operating officer. It controls the central nervous system by interpreting information received and passing messages along the spinal cord to the nerves (the peripheral nervous system). When something goes wrong with the central nervous system, all bodily functions can be affected. Brain disorders can affect various parts of the body, depending on the area of the brain affected. For instance, if the brain stem is injured, appetite, sleep patterns or behavior may change. An injury to the occipital lobe can affect vision. Among the conditions affecting the central nervous system that can strike older cats are meningioma and feline ischemic encephalopathy.

DISEASES OF THE CENTRAL NERVOUS SYSTEM
Meningioma

An old cat may develop a nervous system tumor called a meningioma. This type of tumor is usually benign, but depending on its location, pressure from the tumor can cause seizures, paralysis, personality changes, depression and circling. An affected cat may forget its litter box training, wander and yowl, or not recognize its house and family. Diagnosis may require blood tests, urinalysis, a cerebrospinal fluid tap, X rays, a CT scan, or an MRI. Treatment depends on how severely the meningioma is affecting the cat's behavior. Surgical removal is sometimes possible. The majority of cats that develop meningiomas are more than ten years old.

Feline Ischemic Encephalopathy

Vestibular disorders, which affect balance, are common in old cats. One such disorder is feline ischemic encephalopathy. Its cause is unknown, but it can occur suddenly when not enough blood gets to the brain, similar to a stroke in humans. Strangely enough, this condition occurs most frequently in the eastern United States, with most reported cases occurring during the summer months, especially in August. Perhaps it is heat-related. The cat may circle or have a seizure, show lack of coordination, or become depressed. Usually the chances for recovery are not good, but some cat owners have had success with supportive therapy: anticonvulsants, intravenous fluids and physical therapy. Occasionally the condition may clear up in a few days, but it can leave lasting behavioral changes, including aggression, as well as visual impairment or other neurologic dysfunction, such as seizures.

Other Diseases

The central nervous system can also be affected by high levels of insecticides containing organophosphates, such as dursban or malathion. Some flea control products for use on cats and in the home contain these chemicals, and they should be used sparingly, if at all, on or around old cats. Signs of organophosphate toxicity include constricted pupils, drooling, anxiety, respiratory difficulty, twitching, and vomiting. Organophosphate toxicity can be fatal, so immediate veterinary treatment is necessary. Carbamates, pyrethrins and rotenone can also cause problems if used in excess, although death rarely occurs with rapid, effective therapy.

Common Lab Tests

Biopsy—This is the surgical removal and examination of tissue, cell, or fluid samples. A biopsy may be taken if cancer or infection is suspected. Sometimes cells are removed by applying suction with a very thin needle and syringe. This nearly pain-free procedure is called a fine-needle aspiration biopsy and does not require anesthesia.

Blood Tests—A wide array of blood tests is available to determine the presence of antibodies, infections, or viruses. Blood tests can also be used to evaluate kidney, liver, and pancreas function. Examples of common blood tests include BUN and complete blood count.

Blood Urea Nitrogen (BUN)—This is a blood test that measures the amount of protein waste (urea) excreted by the kidneys. An elevated BUN level can indicate kidney disease.

(continued)

Common Lab Tests

Chemistry Panel— *This is a group of tests used to evaluate levels of proteins, enzymes and metabolic by-products such as calcium, potassium, sodium and phosphorus in blood plasma. It lets veterinarians know how the body organs are functioning.*

Complete Blood Count (CBC)—*This measures levels of red blood cells, white blood cells, and platelets. It is used to determine the presence of infection or disease, or a deficiency of red blood cells or platelets.*

Electrocardiography—*This measures the heart's electrical activity. It is used to determine type of heart disease, evaluate arrhythmias, and determine appropriate treatment.*

(continued)

PERIPHERAL NERVOUS SYSTEM

Besides the central nervous system, there are conditions that affect the peripheral nervous system (cranial nerves, spinal nerves and autonomic nerves), including diabetic polyneuropathy, dysautonomia, and myasthenia gravis. Of these, the one most likely to affect the old cat is <u>diabetic polyneuropathy</u>. This condition develops when diabetes goes unrecognized and untreated. It manifests itself in dragging hindquarters, with the cat standing and walking with its hocks flat on the floor. Without treatment, the front legs can become affected, too. When the diabetes is brought under control, the strength in the legs usually returns.

Another peripheral nerve disorder can occur when the neck or middle ear is injured. If the cranial nerve that controls pupil size and eyelid muscles is damaged—for instance, by an ear infection, tumor or trauma—the result can be constricted pupils, a droopy eyelid on the affected side of the face, or a protruding third eyelid. It is often difficult to identify the primary problem, but this condition, called <u>Horner's syndrome</u>, is fairly common, and treatment is usually possible.

The spinal cord, which links the brain to the rest of the body, is subject to disease, too. A damaged disc places pressure on the spinal cord, causing <u>intervertebral disc disease</u>. Fortunately, this condition is much more rare in cats than in dogs. Injury, such as the impact from a car, can damage or sever the spinal cord itself. The extent of injury depends on the type of trauma and where the damage occurs. Too much vitamin A, usually the result of a diet high in liver, can also affect the spinal cord. It causes new bone formation in the spine, compressing it, a situation that causes severe pain and even paralysis.

Other neurological disorders include meningitis and encephalitis, both of which may occur when viruses or bacteria invade the central nervous system. Signs include chronic nasal discharges, weight loss, and coughing. Depression may set in, followed by seizures, circling and incoordination. These conditions are not specific to old cats, and researchers have found no age, breed or sex preference.

INFECTIOUS DISEASES

The most dangerous time of life for a cat is from birth to two years. That is when it is most likely to fall prey to an infectious disease. If they can make it through kittenhood, however, cats usually enjoy a healthy and trouble-free middle age. But with old age comes a decrease in the immune system's ability to protect against disease. Old cats have a high risk of illness from respiratory diseases, and viral infections are the most common cause of death in cats of any age. Feline immunodeficiency virus and feline leukemia virus are just two of the infectious diseases that can kill cats. Other infectious diseases are upper respiratory infections, such as feline viral rhinotracheitis, chlamydia and calicivirus, and feline infectious peritonitis.

To fight the viral onslaught, cat owners have a potent weapon: regular vaccinations. Vaccines may not entirely prevent infection, but they can protect against severe disease. There are vaccinations for rabies, feline rhinotracheitis (FVR), feline calicivirus (FCV), feline panleukopenia,

Endoscopy—This is a means of examining the interior of hollow organs or body cavities such as the urethra, intestine, or trachea. The long, thin endoscope is fitted with a flexible light source that allows the veterinarian to examine tissues or insert instruments to remove biopsy samples. It is frequently used to diagnose gastrointestinal problems.

Radiographs— More commonly known as X rays, these are images produced on a sensitive surface by a form of radiation called an X ray. Radiographs are used to evaluate musculoskeletal problems and to detect heart disease, lung disease, and tumors.

Skin Scraping— This is the removal of a thin layer of skin for microscopic examination. This test may be used to determine the presence of parasites, such as mange mites or ear mites.

T4 (thyroxine)— This is part of a chemistry panel that determines the level of thyroid hormone circulating in the blood.

(continued)

Common Lab Tests

Ultrasound—This is the examination of internal body structures by aiming ultrasonic wave pulses at the body's tissues and recording their echoes. The resulting image is displayed on a screen. It may be used to evaluate heart function, detect lymphosarcoma, intestinal tumors and abscesses, perform ultrasound-guided biopsy, and diagnose pancreatitis. This noninvasive test requires no anesthesia unless a biopsy is being performed.

Urinalysis—This is used to determine the presence of abnormal amounts of certain substances, abnormal cells, or bacteria that might indicate a urinary tract infection. This is often necessary to diagnose liver, kidney, and endocrine dysfunctions.

feline leukemia virus (FeLV), and feline infectious peritonitis (FIP).

Unfortunately, some infectious diseases such as feline immunodeficiency virus (FIV) and feline infectious anemia (FIA) cannot be prevented with vaccinations. FIV is similar to human immunodeficiency virus, but it is not a zoonosis; in other words, it cannot be transmitted to humans or to other animal species. It is transmitted from cat to cat through saliva, usually bite wounds, so cats with FIV should be isolated from other cats and should not be permitted to roam outdoors, where they can spread their disease. Signs associated with FIV include chronic respiratory and gastrointestinal infections, periodontal disease, and skin infections. These symptoms can be treated as necessary.

FELINE LEUKEMIA VIRUS (FELV)

Unknown until about 30 years ago, feline leukemia virus and its associated diseases can cause blood cell cancer and lymphosarcoma, as well as impair a cat's ability to resist infection. Feline leukemia virus may result in cancerous or noncancerous disease. Veterinarians estimate that it contributes to 33 percent of feline cancer deaths yearly.

However, according to University of Illinois veterinarians, the incidence of lymphomas in cats has decreased, thanks to the introduction of feline leukemia vaccine in 1985. The vaccine can be given at nine weeks of age and older. As with other infectious diseases, vaccination is especially important for old cats, especially those that go outside, since their immune systems can weaken with age. The most frequent noncancerous response to FeLV is suppression of the immune system, leading to chronic infections.

The virus is present in saliva, urine and feces, and is transmitted from cat to cat by such casual contact as licking, biting, and sneezing. Contaminated food bowls and litter pans can be a source of infection, so cats with FeLV should be kept away from uninfected cats. The disease can also be transmitted in mother's milk or through the womb to unborn kittens. FeLV is most likely to attack cats that are very young, very old, stressed, or sick. It is also more common in multi-cat households or catteries, and in cats that are allowed to roam, especially males, which show a higher rate of FeLV infection than females.

Signs of FeLV include depression, fever, loss of appetite, and swollen glands in the neck or abdomen. Recurring illness, skin and mouth sores, and anemia, indicated by pale gums, should also raise a red flag. Cats with this disease often develop tumors of the lymph nodes, kidneys, and intestines. Although blood tests for the presence of FeLV are not 100 percent accurate, their availability has greatly enhanced the ability to diagnose this disease.

Although the outlook isn't great, a diagnosis of FeLV isn't necessarily a death sentence. A positive test means a cat has been exposed to the virus, but if the cat is healthy and has a strong immune system its body may reject the virus. This occurs in about 40 percent of cats. Another 30 percent neither reject the virus nor develop infection. Called "latent carriers," they can be a source of infection for other cats. Chemotherapy may permit a short-term remission in the other 30 percent, but eventually they develop persistent infections that result in disease and death.

FELINE INFECTIOUS ANEMIA

Feline infectious anemia, or Haemobartonellosis, is caused by a parasite that fastens onto red blood cells, in the process damaging them so that they become vulnerable to attack by the immune system. The loss of the energy-carrying red blood cells results in severe anemia. Cats spread FIA when blood is drawn during fights. The cat with FIA is pale and weak, sometimes feverish, and lacks an appetite. This malarialike condition can usually be treated with antibiotics.

In multi-cat households, decrease the incidence of infectious disease by reducing stress, quarantining new cats, and storing food in watertight, verminproof containers. Proper nutrition is important, too. It can slow the age-associated decline in immune function.

CANCER

The word cancer strikes fear into the hearts of most people. A diagnosis of cancer was once a death sentence, but today medical advances have improved diagnosis and treatment, making survival more common. The advent of computed tomography (CT) and magnetic resonance imaging (MRI) units in diagnostics helps veterinarians prepare more detailed work-ups, leading to definitive diagnoses. New medical therapies are yielding more complete remissions, and good quality of life is often possible.

Cancer is defined as the uncontrolled growth of cells, occurring when there is a malfunction of the mechanisms that regulate tissue growth and replacement. Why cancer develops is unknown, but age-related cancers may be related to a buildup of carcinogens in the body, certain viruses such as the feline leukemia virus, or an impaired immune system. Cancer can strike all areas of the body, from blood to bones to skin. Old cats are more likely to develop cancer, especially lymphoid or skin tumors.

More than 50 percent of all cats and dogs older than 10 years will get cancer. The most common cancers in cats develop in the gastrointestinal tract, the skin—including the mammary glands—and the immune system.

Diagnosing Cancer

There is no specific test for cancer. The word cancer is a generic term for many forms of the disease. When a cat that is losing weight or otherwise not doing well has blood tests that come back normal, the next logical step is to consider a diagnosis of cancer. Any unexplained weight loss should trigger evaluation of the gastrointestinal tract, liver, pancreas, lymph nodes, and bone marrow for signs of cancer. Confirming a diagnosis of cancer is not always easy. Chest and abdominal X rays can give the veterinarian an idea of what's going on internally, although they aren't always definitive. Ultrasound is another good diagnostic tool. If there is an indication that the problem lies in the gastrointestinal tract, endoscopy can be helpful.

Other types of cancer are visible on the skin or palpable when the cat is examined. When a mass or lump is found on an animal, a biopsy is taken to determine if the lump is malignant (cancerous) or benign (noncancerous). The size of the tumor is important. Generally, cats with small tumors survive longer than those with large tumors, so early detection is important.

Treating Cancer

Depending on the type of cancer, several options for treatment are available, often used in combination. These include surgery, radiation therapy, and chemotherapy. Immunotherapy is another promising treatment. Because some therapies work better than others on certain forms of cancer, an accurate diagnosis is required.

Tumors, which are large masses of cells, can be difficult to fight because the immune system may not see them as "foreign." Immunotherapy is another promising treatment. Because the immune system doesn't appear to be doing its job of recognizing and combating the abnormal cells, more aggressive therapies such as surgical excision, radiation, and chemotherapy are required to eliminate these out-of-control cells.

Surgery may be as simple as removing a small benign tumor or as drastic as amputating a limb. Radiation has potential side effects such as dry, scaly skin, and hair loss, but overall, animals respond better to radiation than humans.

Chemotherapy is most commonly used to treat generalized, rapidly spreading cancer. In some cases, chemotherapy may be used to prevent a cancer from spreading to other parts of the body. Other benefits of chemotherapy include the ability to slow a rapidly progressing disease that cannot be treated with surgery or radiation, and to increase the length of time the cat remains disease-free after surgery or radiation. A recent innovation in chemotherapy is the use of a timed-release gel that is injected directly into a tumor. The procedure permits a lower drug dosage and minimizes adverse reactions.

Is Chemotherapy Right for Your Cat?

Chemotherapy is a valuable weapon in the veterinarian's arsenal, but it isn't appropriate for every type of cancer, nor for every cat owner. You and your veterinarian should discuss the following questions when determining whether to use chemotherapy.

- Is the tumor a type that is responsive to chemotherapy?

- Are the potential side effects of chemotherapy acceptable? The rate of side effects from chemotherapy is low in animals, only 15 percent, compared to 75 percent for humans. Cats do not usually suffer the same debilitating side effects of chemotherapy as human cancer patients, but in some instances chemotherapy can suppress the body's immune function, predisposing the cat to infection, or it can cause nausea or lack of appetite. These side effects are temporary and can be lessened or eliminated by decreasing the amount of the initial dose.

- Is the treatment regimen practical? Can the cat receive chemotherapy on an outpatient basis on a convenient schedule, or must it be hospitalized for a long period? Most chemotherapy drugs must be given intravenously by a veterinarian, but some can be given orally by the owner at home.

- Is the expense acceptable? Costs for chemotherapy can range from $300 to $1,000 per year, depending on the type of tumor, the drugs used, and the veterinary and laboratory fees. Compared to the human costs for chemotherapy, this is not very much, but most people have in-surance coverage for such medical treatments. Pet health insurance is available, but it is not yet wide-spread. If you do not have pet health insurance, you may be able to work out a payment plan with your veterinarian.

If the answer to all these questions is yes, it is probably a good idea to go ahead with chemotherapy. It can improve your cat's quality of life and extend the amount of time you have with your pet. In all cases, the treatment goal should be to improve the cat's quality of life rather than to keep it alive at all costs.

In addition to medical or surgical treatment, nutritional support can be important. Some researchers have found that cats with cancer respond well to canned foods that are highly digestible and high in fat with little fiber, such as pediatric, growth or concentration diets, which are energy-dense and palatable. Diet does not affect the final outcome of the disease, but it can improve longevity and temporarily improve quality of life.

FINDING A SPECIALIST

Sometimes a cat needs more help than a general-practice veterinarian can provide. Diagnosis or treatment of a complex condition may require specialized equipment, techniques, or knowledge. If this is the case, your veterinarian will refer you to a board-certified specialist. Specialists receive extensive post-graduate training in their fields through internships and residencies, which typically last three to four years. Before they can practice a particular specialty, they must pass a credential review and rigorous examinations. Once they meet all the requirements, they are admitted as diplomates of the college for their specialty.

The practice of a board-certified specialist is usually limited to the area of his or her expertise. Veterinarians may specialize in anesthesiology, behavior, cardiology, dentistry, dermatology, emergency and critical care, feline practice, internal medicine, neurology, nutrition, oncology (cancer), ophthalmology, pathology, radiology, reproduction, surgery, and toxicology.

Specialty Organizations:

● *American Veterinary Dental College, Sandra Manfra Marretta, DVM, Secretary, University of Illinois, College of Veterinary Medicine, 1008 W. Hazelwood Dr., Urbana, IL 61801; (217) 333-5300.*

● *American College of Veterinary Dermatology, Craig E. Griffin, DVM, Animal Dermatology Clinic, 5610 Kearny Mesa, Ste. B., San Diego, CA; (619) 560-9393.*

● *American College of Veterinary Internal Medicine (specialties in internal medicine, cardiology, neurology and oncology), June Johnson, Executive Director, 7175 W. Jefferson Ave., Ste. 2125, Lakewood, CO 80235-2320; (800) 245-9081.*

(**continued**)

One of the newest specialties is feline practice. At this writing, only 22 veterinarians in the United States and Canada had qualified for this specialty (they're listed in the Appendix). In the future, as more veterinarians specialize in the field of feline studies, this certification may be something cat owners will look for when choosing a clinic.

Specialty Organizations:

● *American College of Veterinary Ophthalmologists, Mary B. Glaze, DVM, Louisiana State University, Veterinary Clinical Sciences, Baton Rouge, LA 70803; (504) 346-3333.*

● *American College of Veterinary Surgeons, Alan Lipowitz, DVM, Executive Secretary, University of Minnesota, College of Veterinary Medicine, 1352 Boyd Ave., St. Paul, MN 55108; (612) 625-7249.*

Referrals from other veterinarians make up most of a specialist's clientele. The referring veterinarian transfers the cat's records, including laboratory and diagnostic test results, to the specialist. This helps reduce costs by avoiding repeat testing. Usually, the referring veterinarian is kept informed of the progress of the cat's case and will receive a final report of its diagnosis, treatment, and care.

To find a veterinarian with a particular specialty, obtain a referral or contact the organizations listed in the box. A nearby school of veterinary medicine is also a good resource.

HEALTH RESEARCH

Without veterinary research into the health problems of cats, we wouldn't have many of the advances that help us keep them healthy and long-lived. Studies by veterinarians have brought us new vaccinations, treatments for disease, and advances in diagnostic equipment and testing. Many of these research projects were funded by two organizations with a special interest in animal health: the Morris Animal Foundation and the Winn Feline Foundation.

The Morris Animal Foundation, a nonprofit organization founded in 1948, has no connection with Morris the cat, as many people believe. It was begun by two men with a special interest in pet welfare: Dr. Mark L. Morris, who developed the first medical diets for dogs, and Morris Frank, owner of America's first Seeing Eye guide dog. The Morris Animal Foundation's purpose was to "underwrite research into diseases threatening the health and lives of America's companion animal population."

Today, the organization funds humane veterinary research that benefits cats, dogs, zoo animals, and wildlife. It has been instrumental in developing feline vaccines and improving the understanding of feline diseases. In 1995, feline studies funded by the Morris Animal Foundation included research on the effects of dietary fats in the progression of kidney disease and on substances that may be potential triggers of hyperthyroidism. The Morris Animal Foundation is located at 45 Inverness Dr. E., Englewood, CO 80112-5480; (303) 790-2345 or (800) 243-2345.

The Winn Feline Foundation is a nonprofit organization devoted to the support of health-related studies benefiting cats. Projects are selected for funding by a board consisting of veterinary medical experts from academia and private practice, physicians, cat owners, and cat breeders. All donations are used for the direct support of research funded by the Winn Foundation, which is currently supporting research into the feline immune system, early altering, feline infectious peritonitis, insulin-resistant diabetes, and constipation, as well as development of a model prediction method that will help give veterinarians and cat owners a better idea of a cat's chances of survival for a given illness. The Winn Feline Foundation is located at 1805 Atlantic Ave., P.O. Box 1005, Manasquan, NJ 08736-0805; (908) 528-9797.

VETERINARY TIP

"Be aware that things change as your cat gets older. Seek the help of your veterinarian when you first notice things, not when the cat is skin and bones, further along the road of deterioration."

—*Tom Elston, DVM, T.H.E. Cat Hospital, Irvine, California.*

Alternative Therapies

"Natural forces are the healers of disease."
—Hippocrates

The arsenal against disease used by the traditional veterinarian contains vaccinations, antibiotics, diagnostic aids and surgical techniques that have been developed especially for animals or adapted from human medicine. Without these advances, cats would not enjoy as long a lifespan as they do. But in addition to drugs and surgery, there are a number of treatments that rely on natural elements such as herbs or on such physical manipulation of the body as massage, chiropractic or acupuncture. These age-old practices are now frequently used to treat animals, and older cats often benefit from the judicious combination of natural and medical treatments.

Many people prefer alternative methods because they believe they are less invasive than surgery and have fewer side effects than drugs. Veterinarians who use such approaches are often called holistic practitioners. They have received the same training as veterinarians who use more traditional methods, but they have acquired additional knowledge about the use of acupuncture, herbs, and homeopathy.

Holistic therapies encourage evaluation of the pet's complete circumstances—diet, relationships, and physical condition—in order to reach a diagnosis. This "whole cat" viewpoint allows the veterinarian to determine the best method for solving the problem. Ideally, of course, a veterinarian makes use of all types of therapies.

There is no doubt that alternative therapies can be used to treat a number of conditions. Used in conjunction with traditional veterinary medicine, they can provide relief from skin problems, digestive disturbances, kidney disorders and liver disease. Acupuncture and homeopathy can decrease the side effects of drugs for cats that are undergoing chemotherapy or taking medication for hyperthyroidism. As with any approach, an accurate diagnosis should be reached before treatment begins. Alternatives must be fully and honestly discussed, and any treatment, whether medical or alternative, must begin early in the disease process to be effective.

Examples of holistic practices are acupuncture, chiropractic, herbology, homeopathy, massage, naturopathy and Tellington TTouch. A veterinarian may incorporate some of these methods into a traditional practice, or specialize in one or more such disciplines. Not all holistic therapies require a veterinary degree, although in many states these therapies must be administered under the supervision of a veterinarian. With training, however, anyone can perform massage or Tellington TTouch on a pet. Some alternative therapies and their uses are described below.

ACUPUNCTURE

The Chinese developed acupuncture thousands of years ago. They believe that the body contains meridians, channels through which energy flows. When the circulation of this energy is impaired, its normal function or movement can be restored through acupuncture. The acupuncturist can redirect the body's energy by using needles, finger pressure, heat sources or other methods to manipulate certain areas along the meridians, called acupoints. In modern terms, when the energy is flowing correctly, it supplies proper information to the cells and the body heals itself.

Acupuncture can be compared to the magnetic keys now given to guests at many hotels. If the correct magnetic information is encoded on the strip, the hotel door will open. If acupuncture needles are inserted in the correct place, the body's computer is reset to start the healing process.

It has not been explained why acupuncture works, although Western researchers believe it relieves pain by increasing endorphin production and blocking the transmission of pain signals from the spinal cord to the brain. The insertion of the needles at predetermined points releases endorphins and other neuropeptides from the hypothalamus in the brain. These neurotransmitters regulate important body functions.

Researchers have also noted an increase in white blood cells and blood circulation in the areas being manipulated. It has been found that acupoints are home to microtubules containing tiny nerves and blood vessels. It may be that stimulating these areas helps heal or prevent disease.

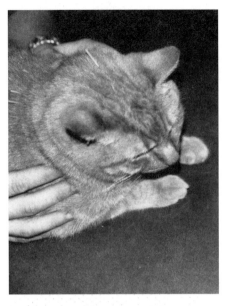

When acupuncture was introduced in the West it was ridiculed by the medical establishment, but today it is generally a respected form of treatment. Some people claim that the proof of acupuncture's

This cat is receiving an acupuncture treatment. You can see a needle on its head and near its neck.

effectiveness is in its results with animals, who can have no preconceived notions about its efficacy.

Acupuncture is often used in conjunction with traditional veterinary medicine, such as antibiotics. Veterinary acupuncturists have used this ancient therapy to treat a number of conditions, including allergies, arthritis, constipation, diabetes, kidney disorders and liver disease. Like other holistic practitioners, they recommend preventive care and a total approach to health that includes diet, herbs, and massage.

Most veterinary acupuncturists have completed a training and certification program under the auspices of the International Veterinary Acupuncture Society. To find a veterinary acupuncturist in your area, contact the IVAS, listed at the end of this chapter.

With training, owners can use acupressure, the manipulation of the meridians with finger pressure, to help old cats feel more comfortable. Conditions that can benefit from acupressure include arthritis, digestive disorders, and muscle strains. For example, working the tip of the ear by gently squeezing it is good for stomach problems. A holistic veterinarian or acupuncture practitioner can teach you the proper techniques.

CHIROPRACTIC

The theory behind chiropractic is similar to that for acupuncture. Chiropractic was developed in the 19th Century based on the belief that nerve energy flowed through the spinal column. If the spinal column became misaligned, the energy would be blocked. Practitioners believe that restoring correct alignment requires careful manipulation of the vertebrae. Today, chiropractic is described as musculoskeletal manipulation to restore normal mobility or function to joints and surrounding tissues. The action on the body is fast but gentle.

Like acupuncture, it is not entirely understood why chiropractic works. The theory is that vertebral misalignments cause problems elsewhere in the body. Chiropractors believe these problems can be corrected by spinal manipulation. Chiropractic has been used to treat a number of problems, from digestive upsets to arthritis. According to a report in a veterinary publication, one cat regained its eyesight after chiropractic treatment relieved pressure on its spinal cord. To find a veterinary chiropractor, contact the American Veterinary Chiropractic Association, listed at the end of this chapter.

HERBOLOGY

Since ancient times, people have used herbs and flowers to treat illness. The tradition continues today, with scientists searching rain forests and other wild places for new plants with healing powers. Among the drugs and chemicals derived from plants that are used on cats and humans are digitalis (foxglove), which is used to treat some heart conditions, and pyrethrins (chrysanthemums), found in many flea-control products.

Fresh and dried herbs have been used to treat a number of conditions, including kidney and bladder disease, skin problems and diarrhea. Like other alternative techniques, it is not exactly clear why or how herbs work, but according to Allen M. Schoen, DVM, researchers have found that herbal remedies contain four active chemical components that may be involved in the healing process. Two of these include polysaccharides, which act as sedatives and pain relievers, and flavonoids, which boost the immune system.

Just because something is natural does not mean it is safe. Medicinal herbs are quite powerful and can be toxic if misused. They should never be administered except under veterinary supervision. For home use, herbs are safest and most effective for conditions requiring external treatments, such as flea infestation or skin problems. Before dosing your cat with any herbal concoction, internally or externally, consult a qualified holistic veterinarian.

HOMEOPATHY

Another 19th Century development, homeopathy is based on what is called the "law of similars." The underlying principle of homeopathy is that "like cures like." This theory suggests that the cure for a particular disease lies in whatever medication produces similar symptoms in a healthy person. Essentially, homeopathy is the application of very diluted substances that, if given in excess, would mimic the same symptoms for which they are being given. For instance, one group of researchers discovered that bee venom given to a healthy person caused the production of dark, concentrated urine that burned during urination. They found that homeopathic administration of bee venom to patients with cystitis relieved the symptoms in many cases. Furthermore, homeopathic remedies are diluted to almost nothing before being administered. It is believed that the smaller the dose, the more powerful the effect.

Like other holistic practitioners, the homeopathic veterinarian is interested in the big picture. Before prescribing a medication, he or she questions the owner closely about the cat's lifestyle, diet and behavior. Only when the environment is analyzed will a homeopathic preparation be administered.

Homeopathy can be used to treat such conditions as diabetes, hyperthyroidism and urinary disorders. In addition to homeopathic medications, the practitioner may use tissue salts or flower essences to stimulate the body. As well as treating medical problems, homeopathic remedies are believed to affect behavior problems and emotional distress. However, in his book Natural Health for Pets, Richard H. Pitcairn, DVM, recommends against combining homeopathy with acupuncture or oriental medicine, saying that they can interfere with each other. To find a homeopathic veterinarian, contact the

American Holistic Veterinary Medical Association, listed at the end of this chapter.

MASSAGE

Hardly anyone can resist the relaxing sensation of a good massage—not even a cat, an animal that in most cases is already naturally relaxed. The stress-reducing benefits of massage are well-known, and it is a technique that is especially appropriate for use in older cats, whose bodies are not as lithe and limber as they were in kittenhood.

Massage can be relaxing for both cat and owner.

Massage is the manipulation of tissues by rubbing or stroking with the hands. Massage can speed recovery from injury or illness and improve the flexibility and mobility of older cats. A daily massage can be used either to energize or to relax a cat. Just a few minutes of bodywork daily can release muscular tension and keep tissues supple.

Massage doesn't just feel good. The medical effects of massage are numerous. It stimulates blood circulation, especially to the limbs. As a result, oxygen flow to the tissues is increased, more nutrients become available, and metabolic wastes are more easily flushed from the system. Skeletal muscles relax when massaged, reducing pain and muscle spasms. The back pain associated with kidney disease can be alleviated by massage.

But massage isn't appropriate for every ache and pain. Cats with fractured, sprained or swollen limbs, ruptured vertebral disks, or cancer should not be massaged. Nor is massage advisable for cats that are feverish, in shock, or suffering from heatstroke. In these situations, massage won't help and can easily make matters worse by delaying more appropriate therapy.

Regular massage is a good way to become familiar with your cat's body so you will be more likely to notice any changes. By using your hands as a diagnostic tool and doing bodywork weekly or even more frequently, you will pick up changes such as lumps, bumps or other anomalies. Another benefit is that regular massage accustoms your cat to being handled, a definite advantage when veterinary care is needed. Used in conjunction with traditional medicine or homeopathic remedies, massage or other forms of bodywork can improve the quality of your cat's life.

MASSAGE TECHNIQUES

Most people can't afford a massage therapist for themselves weekly, let alone for their cats, but you can easily massage your cat at home. After a couple of sessions with a massage therapist, you should be able to massage your cat effectively using some basic strokes. Effleurage is a slow, light stroking with an open palm and fingers. Make small circles over the skin with light to medium pressure fingertip massage. For deeper muscle massage, slowly roll and knead the skin with your open palm or between your fingers and thumb. This technique is called petrissage. To energize your cat, use two or three fingers to give fast, smooth strokes—one or two per second—in the direction the hair grows. Finish the session with very light, slow open-palm strokes along the entire body, starting at the nose and moving to the tail.

With old cats, very light massage is best. Heavy stroking can be painful or uncomfortable. Rather than stroking a cat idly, use your fingers to move the skin around in big circles. This action stimulates the neurological system in a different way than linear stroking. It is soothing and relaxing and helps stimulate circulation. This circular form of petting is more comfortable for animals with arthritis and helps keep them healthier longer. Often, it is more acceptable to cats than linear stroking and can even change how a cat relates to people. Cats that normally dislike petting may react positively to this form of touch.

Your cat may at first be touchy about where you massage it. Cats often dislike having their feet handled or their stomachs touched. Having these areas exposed or handled gives the cat a feeling of vulnerability. Start slow and don't force the issue. As the cat learns to enjoy the massage, it will be more willing to let you spend time on these sensitive areas.

Two requirements for successful massage are an open, quiet mind and proper breathing. Don't try to massage your cat while you're watching *NYPD Blue*. If you are tense or distracted, your mood will be communicated to your cat. For the two of you to get the most out of the massage, your mind must be aware of the cat's body and its reactions. Related to this is proper breathing. Breathing is not something that we have to think about doing; it's an involuntary action. However, when we are tense or panicked, our breathing quickens or becomes shallow, and we may even hold our breath. On the other hand, when we are calm and relaxed, we can think and communicate clearly. Proper breathing imparts a calmer state of mind to the cat.

How long should a massage last? It should last as long as the cat enjoys it. There is no set formula for how to massage a cat or how long a massage should last. Massage techniques can be modified depending on the situation. Each cat is an individual, with its own likes and dislikes. Some cats are unused to touch or have never before been touched in ways that were comfortable to them. For these cats, a two-minute massage is perfectly acceptable. More is not necessarily better. If you're having difficulty touching your cat, wait until it is resting in a favorite spot.

Begin by simply breathing quietly, without touching the cat. Breathing imparts a sense of calm. Next, touch the cat very lightly in a circular motion. If the cat likes the touch, walk away and then give the cat a treat. Try it again the next day for a slightly longer period. Another technique is to wrap the cat in a towel and massage it through the towel. Give praise when the cat allows you to massage it for even a short time. By taking the fear out of the situation, you can break the habitual pattern of dislike of touch. Your cat will let you know which moves it likes and dislikes and when it's tired of being massaged. You may have an intent and a plan you want to carry out, but you're not leading the dance, at least when you are working with old cats or dealing with health problems. As your cat becomes used to the pleasurable sensation, it may stay around for more and will soon be asking for a massage.

With your hands, you can work wonders. Regular massage is empowering. It enables you to become more aware of your cat and to listen to it with understanding. Although animals can't communicate verbally with people, their bodies can be very eloquent.

NATUROPATHY

This therapy is defined as a system of treatment of disease that avoids drugs and surgery. It emphasizes the use of natural agents, such as air, water and sunshine, as well as physical manipulation and electrical treatment. Baths, fasting, and massage are among the techniques used by naturopaths.

Naturopathy has been used to control constipation, arthritis and liver disorders, among others. To find a naturopathic veterinarian, contact the American Holistic Veterinary Medical Association, listed at the end of this chapter.

TELLINGTON TTOUCH

The Tellington TTouch is often mistaken for a form of massage. This method of therapeutic touch can best be described as systematic stroking using the hands or a wand. It differs from massage in that it involves moving the skin rather than rubbing it. The intent of massage is to affect the musculoskeletal system, whereas the intent of TTouch is to reorganize the nervous system and activate cell function.

The TTouch was developed by animal trainer Linda Tellington-Jones, who began evolving the exercises for use with horses while studying the Feldenkrais method of functional integration, which uses physical techniques to help people awaken new brain cells and activate unused neural pathways. Tellington-Jones believed the techniques could be adapted not only to help train animals, but also to treat such physical and behavioral problems as shock and resistance to veterinary examination, and to speed recovery from illness or injury.

The use of the Tellington TTouch, massage and other forms of bodywork helps keep people in touch with their animals, perhaps in a new and deeper way. In effect, it is an opening of a wider channel of communication.

Using descriptive names, such as Clouded Leopard, Lying Leopard, and Tarantulas Pulling the Plow, Tellington-Jones describes the 15 circular hand positions and movements that make up the system and explains how they can be used to help various animals, including geriatric cats. The TTouch can benefit cats that are antisocial and relax cats that dislike car travel or veterinary visits.

Techniques especially recommended for old cats include the basic movement, called Clouded Leopard; Lying Leopard, which creates a feeling of warmth and support; Tarantulas Pulling the Plow, a pleasant, stimulating sensation; and, for cats with poor appetites or those that don't get much exercise, Belly Lifts followed by the Snail's Pace. If a cat has respiratory or heart problems, TTouch works around the chest area and nasal area can help. In an emergency situation, ear work on the way to the veterinary clinic can help a cat in shock and restabilize the body. Light mouth work—gentle circles on the gums using the lips—or eye work can be soothing for a cat with cancer or one that is dying. For more information on TTouch methods or to find a practitioner in your area, write to the address at the end of this chapter.

Despite the leaps made in veterinary technology and knowledge over the past 30 years, many mysteries remain. Although we may not understand exactly how or why they work, these drug-free, noninvasive techniques have a place in modern veterinary medicine. Used in conjunction with traditional methods, alternative therapies can play an important role in making the geriatric cat's life healthier and more comfortable.

RESOURCES

Organizations

International Veterinary *Acupuncture* Society, Meredith L. Snader, VMD, 2140 Conestoga Rd., Chester Springs, PA 19425; (610) 827-7245. For a referral to a veterinary acupuncturist in your area, send a self-addressed stamped envelope with your name, address and phone number.

East-West Animal Care Center, Training Program in Traditional *Chinese Medicine*, Cheryl Schwartz, DVM, 1201 E. 12th St., Oakland, CA 94606; (510) 534-3924.

American Veterinary *Chiropractic* Association, Sharon Willoughby, DVM, DC, P.O. Box 249, Port Byron, IL 61275; (309) 523-3995. For a referral to a veterinary chiropractor in your area, send a self-addressed stamped envelope with your name, address and phone number.

American *Holistic* Veterinary Medical Association, Carvel G. Tiekert, DVM, 2214 Old Emmorton Rd., Bel Air, MD 21014. For a referral to a holistic veterinarian in your area, send a self-addressed stamped envelope with your name, address and phone number.

Academy of Veterinary *Homeopathy*, Richard Pitcairn, DVM, Ph.D., 1283 Lincoln St., Eugene, OR 97410. For a referral to a veterinary homeopath in your area, send a self-addressed stamped envelope with your name, address and phone number.

National Center for *Homeopathy*, 801 N. Fairfax St., Ste. 306, Alexandria, VA 22314; (703) 548-7790. For a referral to a veterinary homeopath in your area, send a self-addressed stamped envelope with your name, address and phone number.

TTeam Training USA, Linda Tellington-Jones, P.O. Box 3793, Santa Fe, NM 87501-0793; (800) 854-TEAM (phone) or (505) 455-7233 (fax).

BOOKS

The Healing Touch: The Proven Massage Program for Cats and Dogs. Michael W. Fox, Ph.D., D.Sc. Newmarket Press, New York, NY; 1990.

Dr. Pitcairn's Complete Guide to Natural Health for Dogs & Cats. Richard H. Pitcairn, DVM, Ph.D., and Susan Hubble Pitcairn. Rodale Press Inc., 1995.

Love, Miracles and Animal Healing. Allen M. Schoen, DVM, and Pam Proctor. Simon and Schuster, 1995.

The Tellington TTouch. Linda Tellington-Jones with Sybil Taylor. Penguin Books, 1992.

VETERINARY TIP

"Diet and water supply are most important. A change of diet can make a big difference in a cat's behavior. Some pet foods have sugar in them, and cats react to that just like kids do."

—John Limehouse, DVM, Limehouse Veterinary Clinic of Holistic Medicine, Toluca Lake, California.

Home 9
Care, First Aid, *and* *Hospitalization*

> *"The cat has a nervous ear*
> *That turns this way and that.*
> *And what the cat may hear*
> *Is known but to the cat."*—David Morton

As a cat gets older, the probability becomes greater that it will require some form of medical care at home. From giving a pill to administering an injection, the ability to provide home health care is an important adjunct to regular veterinary care. By working as a team, you and your veterinarian can ensure that your cat receives appropriate treatment. Don't wait until your cat is sick to learn how to give a pill or take its temperature. If you already know what is required, you will be less likely to panic in a stressful situation.

GIVING MEDICATION

The odds are good that an aging cat will require medication at some time in its life. The more skilled you are at administering medications, the more cooperative your cat will be. Ease of administration will also decrease the stress your cat may feel at having a pill thrust down its throat or drops placed in its ears. The following tips will help you both survive the ordeal. Remember to be calm and patient. Offer a treat or petting after giving medication so the cat associates its medicine with something pleasant.

GIVING PILLS

Have someone hold your cat while you give the pill, or hold the cat firmly between your knees while kneeling on the floor.

When giving any kind of medication, it sometimes helps to wrap the cat in a towel so it can't move. Also available from pet supply stores or catalogs are bags that immobilize the cat, leaving only its head sticking out. In some cases, it may be easier to place the cat on a table or counter rather than on the floor.

With the pill in your right hand, gently open the cat's jaws with the first and middle fingers of your left hand. Place the pill far back on the tongue, then close the cat's mouth and hold it closed while stroking the throat. Another technique if you are right-handed is to hold the cat's head in your left hand. Tip the cat's head back until it is looking straight up. Holding the pill between the thumb and forefinger of your right hand, open the mouth with the middle finger of your right hand. Drop the pill into the back of the mouth and push it over the tongue with the index finger of your right hand. Close the mouth and rub or blow into your cat's nose to make it lick and thus induce swallowing. Some pills have an unpleasant flavor, so try to avoid breaking them apart. If you are left-handed, just reverse these directions.

If you are unable to give your cat a pill using the above methods, disguise the attempt by wrapping the pill in something tasty: a soft cat treat, cream cheese, liver sausage or peanut butter, for instance. Unless a cat is extremely bright or picky, the pill will go down without the cat even knowing it. Pills can also be crushed and mixed with water, honey, or syrup. They can then be administered with a needleless syringe or licked up by the cat. Before using any of these methods, check with your veterinarian to make sure they won't affect the efficacy of the medication.

Cats can be tricky. They are not above holding pills in their mouths and spitting them out when you aren't looking. To ensure that medication is effective, it's important to perfect your pill-giving technique so the cat receives the entire amount prescribed at the appropriate times each day. *Never* stop giving medication until it is all gone, even if the cat appears to be well.

EAR DROPS

Putting drops into a cat's ears can be tricky, because if the cat shakes its head, most of the medication is sure to go flying. To avoid this, hold the cat between your knees as described above, and gently but firmly hold the ear. Tilt the head slightly to the opposite side. Administer the required amount of medication; then gently fold the ear down or together and massage the cartilage at the base of the ear. The massaging action gets the medication into the ear, ensuring that less of it is lost when the cat shakes its head. Unless its ears are unusually painful, the cat will enjoy the massage.

EYE DROPS

The same precautions apply for eye drops as for ear drops. Prepare the eye dropper before restraining your cat. Holding the dropper in your right hand (reverse this if you are left-handed), tilt your cat's head upward and place the drops in the inner corner of the eye, directly on the eyeball, without touching the eye with the tip of the applicator. Be sure you are holding the cat firmly so it doesn't shake its head, causing you to poke it in the eye. Distribute the medication evenly by opening and closing the eyelids.

LIQUID MEDICATIONS

Fill a medicine dropper with the appropriate

Try to hold the mouth closed around the dropper as you give liquid medication.

amount of medication. Restrain your cat as described above. Tilting the head upward, open the mouth and aim the eye dropper at the cheek pouch. Holding the mouth closed around the dropper, squeeze out the medication. The cat's automatic swallowing reflex will kick in as the liquid reaches the back of its mouth. Another good technique is to rub or blow into the cat's nose to make it lick, thus initiating the swallowing reflex.

GIVING INJECTIONS

If your cat develops diabetes and requires insulin injections, don't despair. Even the most needle-phobic owner can learn to fill a syringe and inject a cat. Your veterinarian will help you practice—usually by injecting an orange—until you feel comfortable with the procedure. The sharp, thin needles are virtually painless.

Insulin injections are given subcutaneously, meaning under the skin. The most common injection site is under the loose skin at the back of the neck or between the shoulder blades. By providing a treat along with the injection, or feeding a meal afterward, you can ensure the cat's cooperation. He may even remind you if you forget.

The ability to give an injection may also come in handy if your cat develops kidney disease. The primary goal in managing kidney disease is to provide the cat with plenty of water. This includes supplementing fluid intake by regularly injecting the cat with lactated Ringers, Ringers, dextrose or sodium chloride solutions, a procedure easily done at home. Like an insulin shot, the fluid solution is injected under the skin at the back of the neck. Before the body absorbs the fluid, the cat may look as if it is wearing shoulder pads.

As with insulin injections, your veterinarian will show you how to set up the fluids and place the needle. At first, it can be difficult getting the needle through the skin, but it becomes easier with practice. Giving fluids takes only a few minutes once or twice a day or several times a week, depending on the cat's condition. Owners who give their cats subcutaneous fluids usually establish a routine that most cats quickly learn to accept and expect.

Choose a specific area, such as the kitchen, bathroom or utility room, in which to give the fluids. This teaches the cat to associate the treatment with the place so it will be prepared for it and more relaxed. One couple placed a nonskid rubber pad covered with a towel on top of their washing machine, which was the right height for standing and working with their cats. At first the procedure required two people—one to hold the cat and one to insert the needle and give the fluids. Eventually, however, the cats became accustomed to the routine and now only one person is required for the twice-daily procedure.

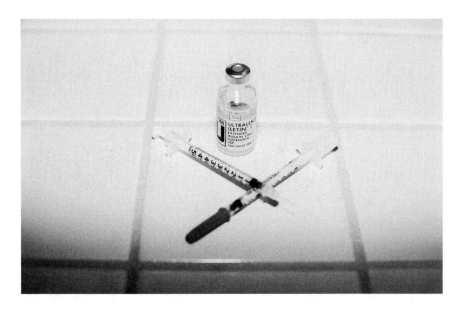

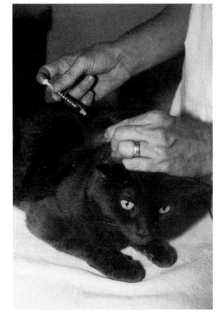

Knowing how to give an injection can come in very handy. Ask your veterinarian to show you how to familiarize yourself with the equipment; get the medicine into the needle; and safely and effectively give the injection.

One owner turned the nightly treatment into quality time with her cat that both enjoyed. She would prepare the fluids and then sit on the bed with the cat between her legs, facing her feet. A session of brushing, stroking and conversation followed until the cat relaxed. Then the owner inserted the needle to deliver the fluids into the loose skin at the back of the cat's neck. She continued petting and talking to the cat, using its name frequently, until all the fluids were administered.

"It was our private quiet time, and as she needed the fluids more and more often, I began to talk with her about the olden days and adventures we had had together. I think she knew what I was doing, and it helped me to let go when the time came."

Supplementing fluid can prolong a cat's life, and quality of life is not sacrificed. It may seem like a difficult or unpleasant procedure for the squeamish, but it can quickly become a special time of bonding with an older cat.

APPLYING OINTMENTS

Generally, ointments are applied to a cat's eyes or ears. To medicate eyes, hold the cat's head steady and gently pull down on the lower lid, exposing the inner eyelid. Apply the ointment to the inside lower lid, being careful to avoid directly touching the eyeball. You may also pull back the upper lid and place the ointment on the white of the eye. After application, close the cat's eyelids to distribute the medication. Don't let ointments sit out in the sun. The heat can spoil their effectiveness.

To apply ointments to ears, follow the directions for ear drops on page 168.

USING HUMAN MEDICATIONS

Although cats have the same organ systems as people, physiologically they differ in many ways, including their sensitivity to drugs and medications that people take without a second thought. For instance, nonsteroidal anti-inflammatory drugs such as ibuprofen, acetaminophen and phenylbutazone are toxic to cats and should never be given. Aspirin should be given only under veterinary supervision.

Common medications your veterinarian may recommend using are dramamine for car sickness, hydrogen peroxide to induce vomiting, and Kaopectate for diarrhea. Give these drugs to your cat only under veterinary supervision, and ask your veterinarian what dosage is correct for your cat. Do not give any medications without asking your veterinarian's advice.

WHAT YOU SHOULD KNOW ABOUT GIVING MEDICATIONS

Each cat is an individual, and what works well in one cat may affect another very differently. Cats react to drugs differently than humans do, and some drugs that are safe for humans are toxic to cats. Age and condition are factors, too. Adverse drug reactions are more common in very young and very old cats, as well as in obese cats or those that are very thin.

When a drug is given can also play a role in its effect. For instance, some medications are best given on a full stomach, while others are neutralized by food. Must a particular medication be given along with other drugs or in a certain sequence? Also, be sure you understand whether the drug is to be given orally (by mouth) or topically (on the skin), and how frequently it should be administered. Ask your veterinarian to write everything down if you aren't sure you will remember correctly.

The right drugs can save a cat's life, but they should never be given blindly. Of course, your veterinarian knows why the drug's action is appropriate, but it's important for you to be aware of a drug's actions, too. Ask what the medication's effect will be; when to start giving it; how soon it will take effect; how long the drug should be given; and whether the medication must be refrigerated or requires other special storage.

DRUGS AND THEIR APPLICATIONS

Most drugs are capable of causing side effects under the wrong circumstances. Always ask your veterinarian about the risk and likelihood of potential side effects before you give your cat any drug. In most cases side effects are rare, but it doesn't hurt to know what they are. That way, you can make an informed decision about whether to administer the medication, and you can spot problems early. The following are some common medications that may be prescribed for older cats.

Diazepam (Valium) may be used as a tranquilizer, appetite stimulant, or for control of urine marking/spraying. It can sometimes have a reverse effect of excitement or aggression.

Megestrol acetate (Ovaban or Megace) is a progesterone—a type of female hormone—sometimes used as a behavior modifier for cats that spray. It can cause side effects that mimic diabetes (excessive thirst and urination) and can even induce diabetes in some cats, especially those that are overweight or obese. Discuss these possibilities with your veterinarian before giving this drug.

Methimazole (Tapazole) is given for hyperthyroidism. Potential side effects include lack of appetite and vomiting.

Lactulose is a stool softener often prescribed for constipated cats. It can cause abdominal discomfort, vomiting, diarrhea, and loss of appetite.

Metronidazole (Flagyl) is an antibiotic that is usually given for irritable bowel disease. Side effects can include loss of appetite, and vomiting.

Prednisone is an anti-inflammatory that is sometimes given for arthritic conditions and allergic dermatitis. Possible side effects include excessive thirst and urination and, rarely, diabetes. These side effects are less common in cats than in dogs.

Diltiazem (Cardizem) is a calcium channel blocker usually given for hypertrophic cardiomyopathy. Potential side effects include abnormally low blood pressure, decreased appetite, and slow heart action.

Enalopril (Enacord) is an ACE inhibitor used to treat several types of cardiac insufficiencies.

Furosemide (Lasix) is a diuretic that is used for congestive heart failure and acute renal failure. Potential side effects include dehydration and hypokalemia.

Propranolol (Inderal) is usually given for hypertrophic cardiomyopathy. Potential side effects include abnormally low blood pressure, slow heart action, and worsening congestive heart failure.

EFFECTIVE FLEA CONTROL

Although not strictly medications, flea control products contain chemicals that can affect your cat's health. Remember that your old cat is more susceptible to poisons than it was in its youth; its body is less able to tolerate large amounts of toxins.

Keeping a cat indoors is the easiest way to prevent flea infestation, but if your cat goes outside or is exposed to fleas by other pets, you may need to use flea control products to rid your cat of these pesky bloodsuckers. Pet supply stores, grocery stores and veterinary offices abound with shampoos, dips, sprays, powders, mousses and collars to fight fleas. Use flea control products with care, and follow the directions on the label. Note whether the product is safe for kittens and old cats, and *never* use products formulated only for dogs.

Over the years, manufacturers have worked to develop less toxic products, and in many instances they have succeeded. There is still no magic bullet that will zap fleas forever, but a number of new products rely on ingredients that affect only the flea, not the cat. Methoprene, an insect growth regulator, prevents young fleas from developing and reproducing. Lufenuron, the active ingredient in the recently developed flea control pill (program), interferes with the egg's ability to hatch. Borates, which are found in powder-based carpet formulas, kill adult fleas, eggs and larvae by removing the moisture from their bodies. Pyrethrin-based products, derived from chrysanthemum flowers, are thought to be safer than those containing carbamates and organophosphates.

Two new products available from veterinarians are fipronil (Frontline) and imidacloprid (Advantage). Fipronil is a spray that kills fleas on contact and is effective for one month on cats. Imidacloprid is a solution that is applied monthly between a cat's shoulder blades. It also kills fleas on contact. Both products have a wide margin of safety. Many "natural" products, usually containing vitamins or herbal ingredients, are also on the market, but their effectiveness is not predictable.

Whatever product you use, always read the label and follow the directions, especially regarding frequency and strength of application. One owner nearly killed her cat by applying a treatment too frequently.

Never use a product on your cat that is made for dogs only, and never apply more than the recommended amount. More is *not* better. Too much of anything can be harmful. Even natural products should be used with caution. Pennyroyal oil, for instance, is toxic to cats and can be fatal. Citrus oil is also toxic and potentially fatal. Most manufacturers are aware of this and do not use these herbal oils in their products, but it doesn't hurt to keep an eye out for them on product labels and to avoid their use around the home. Do not confuse d-limonene, a citrus oil product, with citrus oil itself. D-limonene has been found to be safe for use on cats.

When treating your home and pet for fleas, be careful not to mix types of products or use several at one time, except under veterinary supervision. These products often have an additive effect. Used individually, a collar, shampoo, dip, powder or house treatment may be safe, but if all are used on the same day the collective effect can be deadly. Excessive salivation and nervous tremors are early warning signs of chemical poisoning and may be followed by collapse, convulsions, and coma. Neuromuscular weakness, along with lab test results that indicate a low serum cholinesterase level, may be a sign of organophosphate toxicity.

If you use an exterminator service, determine beforehand whether the company's product is safe for use in pet-owning households. Ask for written information about the ingredients and confirm their safety with your veterinarian. Remove your cats from the home while it is being treated, and do not bring them back until after the recommended time period. Remember that outdoor cats can easily become poisoned by licking their paws after walking through a treated yard. If you or your neighbors are having your lawns treated, keep your cats indoors or otherwise confined until the lawn is dry.

TAKING A CAT'S TEMPERATURE

A cat that seems unwell but has no apparent signs of illness may have a fever. Take its temperature before calling the veterinarian. To take the cat's temperature, shake the mercury down below 98 degrees Fahrenheit and lubricate a rectal thermometer with petroleum jelly, K-Y jelly, or vegetable oil. With the cat lying flat, lift the tail and gently insert the thermometer one and a half inches into the cat's rectum. Be sure to restrain the cat so it can't escape. It may help to have someone else hold the cat while the thermometer is being inserted. Remove the thermometer after one to three minutes.

A cat's normal temperature is 101.5 degrees Fahrenheit, with an acceptable variance of one degree higher or lower. Call your veterinarian if the temperature is below 100 degrees Fahrenheit, or if it is 103 degrees Fahrenheit or higher.

HOW TO GET A URINE SAMPLE

A urine sample may be needed to diagnose a bladder or kidney infection or diabetes. Owners of diabetic cats sometimes do routine urine testing at home to determine the level of glucose and ketones. In most instances it is best if the sample is obtained by the veterinarian, but if for some reason you need to gather it, one of the following methods should work. Empty and clean the litter box. Rinse it thoroughly to remove any cleaning residue. Place a few thin strips of newspaper inside and wait for the cat to urinate. After urination, tip the box so the urine runs into a corner. You can remove a sample with an eyedropper or a small paper cup. Placing plastic wrap or aluminum foil over the top of the litter also works well. Certain litter boxes are designed to make it easy to collect urine. The two-part boxes have a collection tray at the bottom and permanent granules in the top section. Once you are successful, be sure to refrigerate the sample if you aren't taking it directly to the veterinarian.

FIRST AID FOR YOUR CAT

When a cat is injured, the best thing to do is to rush it to the veterinarian, but sometimes immediate help is needed to save its life. Knowing when and how to apply first aid can be vital. Emergency situations include bleeding, burns, choking, fractures, poisoning, and shock. By keeping calm and using the following techniques, you can stabilize your cat until it can receive further treatment.

BLEEDING

If your cat has an open wound that is spouting bright-red blood, an artery is involved. A stream of dark-red blood indicates that a vein is involved. In either case, apply and maintain direct pressure, using a gauze pad or other clean cloth.

Secure the pad or have someone hold it in place, and get immediate veterinary help.

A tourniquet is not as effective as direct pressure, and improper use of a tourniquet can damage the limb. Never apply a tourniquet unless bleeding cannot be controlled by direct pressure. If a wound on a leg or the tail requires a tourniquet, apply the tourniquet between the wound and the body, directly above the wound, and tie a half knot. Then place a pencil or stick on top and complete the knot. Twist the stick slowly until bleeding stops. Release the tourniquet every five minutes to permit blood flow. To make a tourniquet, you can use anything with some length to it, such as a necktie, shoelace or pantyhose. You should be able to fit a finger beneath the tourniquet when it is in place. Again, seek immediate veterinary help. Tourniquets can do more harm than good if used incorrectly and should be used only as a last resort.

Bleeding from a scratch or scrape, while less serious, still requires treatment. Clean the wound with 3 percent hydrogen peroxide, and apply antibiotic ointment after the bleeding stops. This type of wound is not life-threatening, but to rule out damage under the skin, ask your veterinarian to take a look. Cuts or injuries to the ear, foot pad, or penis should be taken seriously. Such injuries can become life-threatening if not tended to, because bleeding is difficult to control in these areas. Treat them by applying pressure as described above, and seek veterinary attention.

BURNS

A cat's curiosity can lead it to investigate just about anything, including a hot stove or the flames in a fireplace. If your cat burns its paws or fur, bathe the affected area with cool water or apply a cool compress. If the burn is over a large area of the cat's body, cover the burn with a thick layer of gauze or cloth (avoid using cotton balls or cotton batting, as it will stick to the damaged skin), wrap the cat in a blanket to prevent shock, and get immediate veterinary help. Never apply ice, butter, or ointment of any kind to a burn.

Chemical burns can be caused by such substances as battery acid or some toilet bowl cleaners. Treat a chemical burn the same way you would a thermal burn, but wear rubber gloves to protect your hands. Seek immediate veterinary treatment.

If your cat has reached old age, it probably isn't going to start chewing on electrical cords all of a sudden, but accidents happen. A cat that has suffered electrical burns may have burns around the corners of its mouth or on the tongue and palate. It may convulse or lose consciousness. Respiration can slow to fewer than 10 breaths per minute. Severe electrical shock may make the heart stop beating. *Before* touching the cat, switch off the electrical source. Then check to see whether the cat is breathing and if its heart is beating. If it is, get the cat to a veterinarian for treatment. If it isn't, you will need to perform cardiopulmonary resuscitation, described below. Do not perform CPR unless you are sure the cat's heart has stopped. Otherwise, you could cause more damage.

CHOKING

Here again, curiosity can kill the cat. Fish bones, sewing needles, and tinsel are just a few of the things a cat might swallow that could cause it to choke. If you see your cat coughing, gagging or pawing at its mouth, press the thumb and forefingers of one hand into the cat's upper cheeks to force the mouth open, and look for the obstruction. If the item is something other than string or yarn, gently try to remove it with your fingers or a pair of long-nosed pliers. If removal isn't possible, perform the Heimlich maneuver by placing the cat on its side and pushing sharply on its rib cage three or four times with the flat of your hand. Repeat until the obstruction is dislodged. Once the object is removed, or if you cannot remove it, seek veterinary help immediately.

What's Normal

● *Body temperature—* *A cat's normal body temperature ranges from 100.5 degrees Fahrenheit to 102.5 degrees Fahrenheit. Anything consistently above or below that range is cause for concern.*

● *Pulse—A cat's normal pulse rate has a range of 120 to 200 beats per minute. To find the pulse, lightly hold your finger on the femoral artery, found on the cat's inner thigh where the leg meets the body. If you have difficulty finding the pulse there, an easier way is to count the cat's heartbeats. Hold your hand over the chest between the legs and count the number of beats for 15 seconds. Multiply that number by four, and you will get approximately the number of beats per minute.*

(continued)

What's Normal

● **Respiratory rate**—A cat's respiratory rate—the number of times it inhales and exhales in one minute—can range from 30 breaths to 100 breaths, depending on its state. A cat at rest will have a lower respiratory rate than one that has just exerted itself or is frightened or excited. To determine your cat's respiratory rate, count the number of times its chest moves in and out in 15 seconds, then multiply that figure by four. Respiration should be relaxed and easy, not too shallow and not too difficult.

Never try to pull string, thread, or yarn out of a cat's throat once it has been swallowed. If one end is in the mouth and the other end is in the intestines, the fiber can cut through the intestinal walls, a potentially fatal situation. Take the cat immediately to the veterinarian for removal.

FRACTURES

There are two types of broken bones: simple fractures and compound fractures. A compound fracture is one in which the bone sticks out through the skin. No matter which type of break it has suffered, try to keep the cat as still as possible. A simple fracture can turn into a compound fracture if the leg flops around too much. Treat the cat for shock (explained later), place it in a cushioned carrier or box, and seek immediate veterinary attention.

If the cat has suffered a spinal injury, indicated by paralysis, stiff, rigid, limp legs, or the head thrust backward, try to move it as little and as carefully as possible. Improvise a stretcher using a board or rigid piece of cardboard large enough to support the cat's back. A blanket pulled taut will do in a pinch. Slide the cat onto the stretcher rather than lifting it. Try to keep the back, head, and forelegs stable during the ride to the veterinary hospital.

If your cat's lower jaw is hanging open and the cat is drooling, it may have fractured its jaw. Tie a scarf or bandage underneath the chin, fastening it behind the ears, and get the cat to a veterinarian.

A cat with a skull fracture may have a bloody nose or be dizzy or unconscious. Gently control any bleeding, and seek immediate veterinary help.

FROSTBITE

The cats most prone to frostbite are those that are very young, very old, or sick. The extremities—the footpads, tail and ear tips—are most likely to be affected. Signs of frostbite are skin that becomes pale, then reddens and becomes hot and painful to the touch; swelling; and peeling of external skin layers. Take the frostbitten cat to a warm place immediately, but thaw out frostbitten areas slowly. Don't compound the damage by massaging the skin or applying hot compresses. Instead, use warm, moist towels and change them frequently. When the skin regains its normal color, stop warming it. Conserve its body heat and prevent shock by wrapping the cat in a blanket. Seek veterinary treatment as soon as possible.

POISONING

Poisoning can be internal or external. Because they groom themselves orally, cats tend to be exposed to many more poisons than dogs or other animals. They may lick their coats after being sprayed or dipped with a flea control product, or lick their feet after walking through a yard that has been treated with pesticides, herbicides or fertilizers. Consumption of or exposure to household products, rat poisons, or yard treatments are all ways cats can become accidentally poisoned.

Cats that eat seasonal plants, such as Easter lilies, can also become poisoned. The Easter lily can cause kidney failure in cats, especially if the cat already has kidney problems, as many older cats do. If the problem is not diagnosed and treated promptly, death can be quick. Other plants that are toxic to cats include azaleas, caladium, dumbcane, English ivy (berries and leaves), ficus (leaves), holly, mistletoe (berries), oleander and philodendron. Bulbs such as amaryllis, daffodil, iris, and tulip are also poisonous.

If, despite your best efforts, your cat ingests or comes in contact with poisonous plants or substances, it may drool, vomit, convulse, develop diarrhea or collapse. Other signs of poisoning include muscle weakness or irritation of the eyes, mouth, or skin.

If the poison is external, don rubber gloves and wash it off with warm water. If you know or suspect that your cat has ingested poison, do not induce vomiting. Instead, give activated charcoal tablets to help absorb the poison and take the cat to your veterinarian immediately, as well as the package containing the suspected poison and any vomitus. If a veterinarian is not available but you can identify the substance, call the National Animal Poison Control Center for advice. The phone number for the NAPCC is listed at the end of this chapter.

Physiologically, cats are very different from dogs and other species, and they metabolize poisons differently. The feline system is less able to transform toxic compounds into inactive substances that can be quickly eliminated in the urine. The cat's small size is also a factor. Rapid, expert advice is vital. Remember that an old cat's internal organs are less able to process toxins in the body, so it is urgent that it receive quick treatment for any type of poisoning. Supportive care, including plenty of food and water to maintain urine production, is critical for survival. Delayed reactions are another possibility. Cats may show signs of nerve damage weeks after exposure. This is another instance when a diary can come in handy. Without a regular written record, the cat's exposure to toxins may be overlooked.

SHOCK

A cat that has been hit by a car or suffered some other trauma may go into shock, a potentially fatal condition in which the body is unable to maintain adequate blood pressure. Other causes of shock include blood loss, severe fluid loss from vomiting or diarrhea, and poisoning. Signs of shock include a weak, rapid pulse; dry gums and lips that are pale or gray; shallow, rapid breathing; a low body temperature; and weakness or lethargy. Control bleeding if necessary; otherwise, keep the cat still, and gently wrap it in a blanket to keep it warm. Seek veterinary treatment immediately.

ARTIFICIAL RESPIRATION AND CARDIOPULMONARY RESUSCITATION

Your knowledge of artificial respiration and cardiopulmonary resuscitation, or CPR, could save your cat's life. Use artificial respiration—mouth-to-nose—or chest compression when your cat is having difficulty breathing or if breathing has stopped. CPR, a combination of external heart massage and artificial respiration, should be performed only when both the heart and breathing have stopped.

It's not easy to perform CPR on a cat and it's not always successful, but sometimes it is a cat's only chance. This procedure can be used in cases of trauma, drowning, or respiratory arrest. To give mouth-to-nose respiration, follow steps A and B below. To give chest compression, follow step C. For CPR, follow all three steps.

Because irreversible brain damage occurs three to four minutes after the heart stops, CPR should be initiated immediately. Early establishment of an airway and breathing is essential to long-term survival. A simple acronym—ABC, standing for Airway, Breathing, and Circulation—can help you remember the steps to take. First, determine whether the cat is breathing by observing whether the chest is rising and falling or feeling for air flow from the nose and mouth. If the cat is not breathing, place it on its right side on a firm, level surface, and remove its collar.

"A" is for airway. Clear the airway by opening the mouth and removing any food, vomit, or foreign objects. Try to avoid being bitten. Then pull the tongue forward and cup your hand around the mouth to hold it closed.

"B" is for breathing. Place your lips around the nose tightly and blow as if inflating a balloon. Blow steadily into the cat's nose for three seconds. When the chest expands, wait a moment for the air to come back out. Do this approximately 15 times per minute, or once every four seconds. Do not perform artificial respiration unless the cat's breathing is very shallow or has stopped altogether. This technique is called forced respiration and should be used if chest compression fails or if the chest is punctured. Continue mouth-to-nose respiration until the cat is breathing on its own, then seek immediate veterinary attention.

"C" is for circulation. Determine whether the cat has a pulse by checking the carotid (neck) or femoral (upper hind leg) arteries. If there is no pulse and the cat is not breathing, begin CPR. Compress the lower half of the chest just behind the foreleg where it meets the body, quickly compressing it one to two inches 60 to 80 times per minute. After five compressions, perform artificial respiration for one breath, then repeat compression. (If you have a helper, one person should perform mouth-to-nose respiration while the other massages the heart.) Alternate until spontaneous breathing and heart-beat return, then seek immediate veterinary help.

STOCKING A FIRST-AID KIT

You can buy ready-made first aid kits, which often include a first-aid book, or you can put one together yourself, usually from items that you already have at home. Be sure to include your veterinarian's phone number, as well as the phone number of and directions to a nearby emergency clinic. Label the kit and keep it in a specific place, making sure everyone knows where it is. Don't forget to replace items when you run low. Some items that you might not keep in your kit but that could be useful include: sanitary napkins to help stem blood flow, needle-nose pliers to remove obstructions from the mouth or throat, and towels. A typical first-aid kit contains the following items:

- Activated charcoal (available at drug stores) for absorbing poisons
- Adhesive tape to secure bandages
- Antibacterial ointment or powder for cleaning wounds
- Blunt-tipped scissors to trim away hair from wounds and cut bandaging material
- Children's medicine spoon to administer liquid medications
- Cotton balls
- Cotton swabs
- Gauze pads and rolls to make bandages
- Hairball remedy
- 3 percent hydrogen peroxide to clean wounds
- Kaopectate (ask your veterinarian what amount is appropriate to control your cat's diarrhea)
- K-Y jelly or petroleum jelly to lubricate a thermometer
- Milk of Magnesia

- Needleless syringe for giving liquid medications
- Plaster splint for broken limbs
- Plastic eyedropper to administer liquid medications or eye drops
- Rectal thermometer
- Rubbing alcohol
- Syrup of ipecac to induce vomiting
- Tweezers

ANESTHESIA AND SURGERY

Janice's veterinarian recommended that they do a geriatric profile for 11-year-old Missy before cleaning her teeth. The blood tests would indicate any problems that might be exacerbated by anesthesia, and the information would serve as a baseline if Missy became ill later in her life.

As a cat ages, its ability to tolerate anesthesia and surgery lessens. Age, stress and pre-existing conditions such as heart disease, kidney disease or thyroid disease can affect how the cat will react to the anesthetic. Although today's anesthetics are much safer than those of the past, veterinarians tend to be conservative and treat all older cats as high-risk, even if they are undergoing anesthesia for a simple procedure such as a dental cleaning. If your aging cat requires anesthesia, whether for teeth cleaning or major surgery, your veterinarian will likely run a blood panel first to check for such conditions as hyperthyroidism, or kidney or liver problems. The information from the blood panel helps the veterinarian tailor the anesthetic regime to the patient. For instance, cats with these diseases may recover more slowly from anesthesia than healthy cats. In addition, certain anesthetics require good liver and kidney function for elimination.

Fortunately, with the use of preanesthetics, old or temperamental cats, or those with heart disease, can better tolerate anesthesia. Veterinarians today can tailor anesthetic agents to each cat's particular situation. Anesthetics have been developed that limit the negative effects on the cardiac system and the liver and that permit a quicker recovery time. With careful monitoring, old cats can safely undergo anesthesia. Remember that although general anesthesia poses a significant risk to your cat, the condition being treated poses an even greater risk to the cat's health.

There are things your veterinarian should know about your cat before anesthetizing it. Just as a history is important in making a diagnosis, it is also important in determining which anesthesia to use and how much to administer. Changes in eating habits, the cat's reaction to being handled or restrained, and any previous reactions to medications or anesthesia can affect the choice of anesthesia. Other relevant information is whether the cat is on any medications, whether it has a history of seizures or breathing problems, and whether it has shown a recent change in activity level, such as tiring more easily than usual. Be prepared to provide as much of this type of information as possible to ensure your cat's safety under anesthesia.

Your veterinarian will instruct you to withhold food and water the night before surgery. If food is in the stomach when anesthesia is induced, the cat may vomit and inhale the food into its airway. The result can be aspiration pneumonia or even suffocation and death. Since your cat will likely be hungry, take precautions to ensure that it doesn't get into the garbage or some other food source.

HOSPITALIZATION

Another aspect of medical care is the prospect that your cat will require veterinary care away from home. At some point, your old cat may face hospitalization or surgery requiring anesthesia. Cats tend to be homebodies, and a stay in the pet hospital, no matter how good the care, can be stressful. Comfort and routine are important factors in their ability to recover.

> *Buster's owners were going away for the holidays. They feared that the stress of travel would send the nine-year-old diabetic cat's blood sugar soaring, so they decided to board him with his veterinarian. Buster would be sure to receive the best of care by the knowledgeable staff. However, upon returning, they discovered that Buster*

was at death's door due to the stress of hospitalization. It took all the veterinarian's skill and devoted nursing at home to bring him back to health. The next time Buster's owners went on a trip, they hired a pet sitter who was a veterinary technician to come in and give the cat his injections and ensure that he ate his meals on time. A happy, healthy cat greeted them two weeks later.

AVOIDING STRESS DURING HOSPITALIZATION

Because cats are such creatures of habit, especially as they age, any change in routine may lead to a refusal to eat, drink or eliminate. Diagnostic procedures, such as blood testing or X rays, can cause anxiety. Whenever possible, older cats should be cared for at home or by a pet-sitter. When hospitalization can't be avoided, you can take steps to help your cat feel more comfortable. Each cat is an individual and will react differently to being hospitalized. Some are real troopers and work hard to get better, while others are extremely stressed by being away from home. Your veterinarian can work with you to make the experience less traumatic.

To lower its anxiety level, a hospitalized cat should be kept quiet and warm and receive gentle handling. A covered cage may make it feel more secure. Keeping its routine similar to home care can also help. If the cat is used to being fed or groomed at a particular time each day, let the hospital staff know so its schedule can be maintained as closely as possible. If possible, provide the same litter and diet the cat uses at home. Some clinics provide a soothing atmosphere by leaving a light on or playing soft music.

One way to ease a cat's reaction to hospitalization is to provide partial home care: dropping the cat off at the veterinary clinic first thing in the morning for treatments all day, then taking it home at night and returning with it the following day. On the other hand, frequent trips in a car could be more stressful to some cats than a week's stay at the clinic.

Another stress-reduction tactic is care at a cats-only clinic or at a hospital with a separate ward for cats. Being housed in the same room as a barking beagle can raise the blood pressure of any self-respecting cat. The relatively quieter atmosphere of a clinic or ward dedicated to cats can ease the pangs of separation from the familiar.

Summing Up

● *Accustoming your cat to being handled will make it easier to administer medication when the cat is ill.*

● *Administer human medications only under veterinary supervision. Ask your veterinarian what the appropriate dosage for your cat is.*

● *Apply flea-control products sparingly. Be sure they are formulated only for cats and that they are safe to use on old or very young cats.*

● *Keep a first aid kit on hand and know how to use it. The ability to recognize and deal with common injuries could save your cat's life.*

● *Be creative if your cat must be hospitalized. If depression sets in, recovery can take longer. Work with your veterinarian to provide a relatively stress-free environment while the cat is hospitalized.*

● *Consider protecting your cat's health and your wallet by purchasing pet health insurance or joining a pet HMO if one is offered by your veterinarian.*

A room with a view can also lighten a cat's depression. Some clinics offer their feline patients a setting in which they can do a little bird-watching. Watching the fish in an aquarium is known to be soothing to humans, and it no doubt brightens a cat's day, although perhaps not in the same way. Following the darting movements of fish can hold a cat's interest in an otherwise confined situation.

For hard-core cases, the freedom to move around once in a while in a larger area such as an exam room can be all that is needed to put them in a better frame of mind. A little catnip sometimes helps, too.

The cats that are the greatest challenge are those that are aggressive. They don't know or don't care that the veterinarian and staff are trying to help. Veterinarians who see aggressive cats regularly know that these patients are really sick when they are brought in and are willing to be handled. Often, one of the first signs of recovery is when the cats regain their aggressive natures.

STIMULATING APPETITE

The combination of constipation, a cold, and lack of appetite put Moscow in the hospital. Because she wouldn't eat, the veterinarian had to tube-feed her.

Often the first response of a cat that is hospitalized is to go on a hunger strike. The stress of being in a strange place, or just the fact that it doesn't feel well, can make a cat lose its appetite. Some veterinarians encourage owners to come in and feed their cats themselves, going on the theory that cats are more likely to eat for their owners than for strangers. Because a sick cat can go downhill quickly, ensuring that it eats well is of paramount importance. Unless the cat can keep its strength up, the road to recovery will be rocky.

When Jane was finally able to take Moscow home, she fed her a special diet for sick cats. She heated the food to enhance its smell, and she offered Moscow all kinds of tempting delicacies to entice her to eat. She could tell Moscow was hungry, so she put the food on her finger and rubbed it onto the roof of the cat's mouth until she swallowed. When Moscow returned to their usual routine and began grooming herself again, Jane knew she was feeling better.

Persuading a sick cat to eat can try the patience and ingenuity of the most devoted owner. Your resourcefulness and persistence can be the key to your cat's recovery. Don't hesitate to enlist your veterinarian's help, though, if your cat is unwilling or unable to eat. Rapid weight loss can only make your cat's condition worse. Your veterinarian can prescribe an appetite stimulant or keep the cat in the office for the day for tube feeding or intravenous administration of nutrients.

PET INSURANCE AND VETERINARY HMOS

Americans spend about $10 billion per year on pet health care costs. Although the cost of veterinary care and hospitalization is far below that of human medical care, it can still be a drain on the family pocketbook, especially if it is frequent or unexpected. Emergency hospitalization or surgery can cost hundreds of dollars or more, depending on the care required. The older a cat gets, the more likely it is to need veterinary care or hospitalization.

Fortunately, owners don't have to bear the burden alone. Pet health insurance and, in some locations, veterinary HMOs, can help lower the costs involved and ensure that owners don't have to decide to euthanize Fluffy because the cost of care is beyond their reach. Although fewer than 2 percent of the cats and dogs in the United States are covered by pet insurance, it's something to consider, especially in households with several pets or older pets.

In this country, only one company currently offers pet insurance. Underwritten by National Casualty Company, Veterinary Pet Insurance is available in 38 states and the District of Columbia. The company's policies cover a number of feline ills, ranging from ear infections, cuts and skin rashes to chemotherapy, broken bones, heart disease and major surgery.

Five plans are available with varying deductibles and coverage. Premiums start at $59 annually and increase with the cat's age, but there is no age limit for coverage. Depending on the plan selected, benefits can be as high as $4,000 per incident or $12,000 per policy term. Special rates and payment plans are available for multi-pet households. VPI does not cover preventive care, such as vaccinations or annual exams, but it can be a lifesaver for the cat that is hit by a car or develops a serious illness. Prescriptions, lab fees, and X rays may also be covered. Figures from VPI show that the treatment cost per incident of cancer is up by 62 percent since 1986. With cancer being a leading cause of death in cats and dogs, and the cost of a diagnostic tool such as a CT scan being $300 to $700, an insurance policy can be a smart investment for owners of old cats.

Cats insured with VPI receive a stainless steel identification tag engraved with the policy number and VPI's toll-free number. A good Samaritan who finds an ill or injured cat wearing one of these tags can rest assured that the animal's veterinary care will be covered—if, of course, the policy is up-to-date. The information on the tag can also be used to locate the cat's owner.

A portion of VPI's proceeds is donated to the American Humane Association, and the company offers a 30-day money-back guarantee after purchase. For more information, talk to your veterinarian or contact VPI. The company's address and phone number are listed at the end of this chapter.

HMOs, or health maintenance organizations, have been common in human medicine for some years now, but they are just beginning to make an appearance in veterinary medicine and are still relatively rare. Unlike pet insurance, which is great for covering catastrophic incidents but doesn't provide preventive care, HMOs cover such services as office visits, vaccinations, flea control, and testing for feline leukemia virus and feline immunodeficiency virus.

In the few veterinary HMOs or wellness plans available, the client usually pays a one-time membership fee, a monthly payment and sometimes a copayment for services rendered.

Usually, several plans are available, depending on the owner's finances and the cat's age and needs. The package for a healthy cat that is 2 to 8 years old will differ from that for a 17-year-old cat with kidney disease. For example, a plan designed for adult cats at Banfield Pet Hospital and Health Center in Portland, Oregon, covers two physical exams per year; all vaccinations and a vaccine warranty; testing for feline leukemia virus and feline immunodeficiency virus; a yearly fecal exam for intestinal parasites; and counseling on nutrition and flea control. The per-cat cost for this Primary Care plan is a one-time membership fee of $59.82 and a monthly fee of $9.84. As a cat ages, clients at this clinic might move up to what is called the Optimum Care plan. This plan covers everything offered in the Primary Care plan, plus annual chest X rays, complete blood counts, deworming, biannual electrocardiograms, eye exams, annual dental cleaning and any necessary extractions, organ function screening and urinalysis. In addition, clients receive a 20 percent discount on all other products and services. The cost for this plan is a one-time membership fee of $199.82 and a monthly fee of $35.84. Two other plans are offered with rates and services that fall between these two.

As chain veterinary clinics spread across the country, look for them to offer more wellness plans and HMOs. PetsMart locations in California, Florida, Illinois, Maryland, Oregon, Virginia, and Washington already offer similar plans. In Hawaii, cat owners can join the Hawaii Pet Care Alliance, which allows them to choose among four participating veterinary clinics on the island of Oahu.

RESOURCES

National Animal Poison Control Center. This hotline, based at the College of Veterinary Medicine at the University of Illinois at Urbana-Champaign, receives 33,000 calls per year, many of them regarding cats. It is staffed around-the-clock by veterinary professionals and provides assistance to both veterinar-ians and pet owners. The hotline can be accessed by calling a toll-free number—(800) 548-2423, or a toll number—(900) 680-0000.

If you call the toll-free number, the charge for the service can only be billed to a credit card. There is a set fee for the consultation, with follow-up calls at no extra charge. The toll-free number is best used for crisis calls. Calls to the 900 number are charged to the caller's phone bill. The fee for calls to this number is lower, and it is best used for questions that are not urgent, such as whether a particular plant is poisonous.

Hawaii Pet Care Alliance, 711 Kapiolani Blvd., Ste. 100, Honolulu, HI 96813; (808) 591-4907.

Veterinary Pet Insurance, 4175 E. La Palma Ave., Ste. 100, Anaheim, CA 92807; (714) 996-2311 or (800) USA-PETS ([800] 872-7387). Available in 39 states.

VetsMart, 12375 S.W. Walker Rd., Beaverton, OR 97005; (503) 644-1100. Check your local telephone listings for one in your area. Wellness plans are available in seven states.

VETERINARY TIP

"Doing lab tests periodically in elderly cats is important to detect early disease, such as kidney failure, which is then more effectively managed."

—Diana Webster, DVM, Kansas City, Missouri

When 10
to *Let Go*

*It has been the providence of Nature
to give this creature nine lives.—Pipay*

Despite all our care and love, the day must come when our cats reach the end of their ninth life. No one can ever be truly prepared for that day, but knowing what to expect can help ease the decision-making process as well as the grief.

The owner of an aged cat must begin to face the issues of quality of life, euthanasia, and even whether there is life after death. Philosophers and theologians have wrestled with these issues for centuries but have come to no definitive conclusions. Each decision is an individual one that must be tailored to the owner, the owner's circumstances, and the cat itself. In the dance of life and death, there are no right or wrong steps for caring owners.

More practical decisions also face the cat owner. Where should Fluffy be euthanized: at the veterinary clinic or at home? Should the owner be present? What should be done with Fluffy's body: disposal by the veterinarian, burial, or cremation? Where should Fluffy be buried: at home or at a pet cemetery?

A statue of St. Francis of Assisi presides over a pet cemetery.

Finally, the owner must deal with the loss itself. The grief may seem overwhelming, and this sometimes comes as a surprise. "I didn't cry this much when my mother died," the bereaved cat owner says. "It can't be normal to feel this way." It is both normal and healthy to grieve, and today, support groups and hotlines abound to help pet owners come to terms with the pain.

Many factors can influence the decisions made regarding the care and death of an old cat. Each factor must be weighed against the cat's well-being. Despite the lack of absolute answers, there is no dearth of resources to help cat owners make the decisions that are right for them and their cats.

QUALITY OF LIFE

Pepper was 22 years old. In his salad days, he had been king of the household: Even the dogs deferred to him when he wanted a particular sleeping spot. But that was long ago. Now Pepper rarely moves from his favorite sleeping spot. When he does move, he isn't always fast enough to make it to the litter box. His appetite isn't the same either. Although his owner tempts him with warmed Turkey-Liver Delight, he takes only a few bites before turning away.

■

Kinks was 14. The bone cancer in her leg would kill her if something wasn't done quickly. Her best chance, the veterinarian said, was with amputation.

■

Taylor's lymphoma was spreading throughout his body. Neither surgery nor chemotherapy could stop it. His breathing was labored, and he was hunched over. He paid little attention to his worried owner.

Not every illness, even in an old cat, need be fatal. Even cancers can be excised or brought into remission. However, the cure must sometimes come at a cost. A cat with cancer may require chemotherapy treatment or amputation of a limb. A cat with inoperable cataracts will live, but it will be unable to see. Whether the cats in these situations live or die depends on their owners' perceptions of what a cat needs to have a good life.

The decision to retain the status quo, go ahead with treatment, or to euthanize a cat is not always clearcut. The words "quality of life" have different meanings for different people. To a human, loss of sight or amputation of a limb may seem unbearable. A cat, on the other hand, can adjust quite well to these handicaps, shifting to greater use of its other senses to get along. Rather than anthropomorphizing, investing the cat with your own feelings, try to base your decision on facts instead of perceptions.

For instance, anyone who has experienced chemotherapy or known someone who has undergone this treatment might find it difficult to agree to the same treatment for a beloved cat. Visions of the cat throwing up and losing all its hair would inhibit most such owners. As a group, however, cats tolerate chemotherapy much better than people, although it's difficult to know if an individual cat will respond well to the treatment.

The benefit of chemotherapy is that it helps bring a cancerous cat back to normal for a time. This grace period permits an opportunity to spend more time with the cat and adjust to the knowledge that it will not live forever. The question then becomes whether it is ethical to prolong the cat's life. A good counselor can help you determine your feelings and evaluate the cat's chances. Call a pet-loss hotline for advice or ask your veterinarian to refer you to a local grief counselor. Some veterinary hospitals, such as New York City's Animal Medical Center, which pioneered grief counseling for pet owners, provide such counseling on the premises.

Try not to rush your decision. Take a hard look at the prognosis offered by the veterinarian. Ask whether the condition can be cured or if it can be slowed down. Can your cat be made comfortable or is there no hope? Your cat's personality and your ability to provide care are important factors, too.

This is another area where counseling can be helpful. One of the benefits of counseling is the advice of a third party who may be able to see things more clearly and help ask the right questions. Clarity and communication can go out the window when a concerned owner is listening to a pet's prognosis. For instance, an owner may say, "The vet says Chessie only has a fifty-fifty chance."

Once their condition is stabilized, diabetic cats can get along well with proper care. Consistency is the key; this 15-year-old cat receives injections and meals on a regular schedule. (Courtesy of Pat & David Urie)

"Fifty-fifty what?" the counselor asks. "Fifty-fifty she'll survive the surgery? Fifty-fifty she'll survive long enough to come home? Fifty-fifty that she'll survive for another year?"

The cat's age and health status must be considered, too. One owner of a 19-year-old cat with several health problems has made the decision not to go to any dramatic or heroic methods to save the cat should she become seriously ill. Her veterinarian has advised her that the cat probably would not survive much anesthesia anyway. On the other hand, the owner of a 15-year-old cat with diabetes believes that the effort of regulating the cat's condition with insulin injections and diet is likely to bring her several more years of companionship with the cat. Each situation is unique and must be judged on its own merits.

Once such questions are raised and the answers determined, you are better able to make a decision regarding a pet's treatment or euthanasia. Other factors include quality of life, the meaning of suffering, ability to provide care and quality time, and, although we may not like to consider it, the cost involved. A counselor can help you wrestle with difficult questions: How much money is too much? What is quality of life? What is suffering? Will your lifestyle allow you to provide needed care?

For instance, two cats with identical medical situations could receive very different treatment depending on their owners' circumstances. The writer who is home all day is better able to provide care or medication on a strict schedule than the salesperson who lives alone and must travel frequently. Such factors can mean the difference between life and death for a seriously ill cat. Money plays a role in the decision, too. Although the salesperson isn't home during the day, she may be able to afford regular home care for the cat.

WHEN IS LIFE DIMINISHED?

Even tougher than providing the care needed is determining a cat's quality of life and whether it is suffering. Again, it's important not to anthropomorphize in this situation. For instance, just because a cat can't see too well anymore and spends its day sleeping in the sun, getting up only to amble over to its food dish or the litter box, doesn't mean its quality of life isn't good. Ask yourself whether your cat is doing things that it has always enjoyed doing. Is it sitting in the sun? Does it come to the door when you come home? Is it glad to see you? Does it get in your lap?

The day will come, however, when the cat stops doing these things and nothing more can be done to keep it comfortable. The cat no longer wishes to be near you or even hides from you. Then you must make a decision regarding euthanasia. Knowing when to let go can sometimes be difficult. Like most predators, cats are unwilling to show weakness of any kind. "But he's still purring" is the refrain heard by many veterinarians when discussing euthanasia. The reality, however, is that cats purr not just when they are happy, but also when they are stressed or in discomfort. It takes an observant, caring owner to see past the purr to the physical signs of pain. It is even more difficult to assess quality of life. In the end, no one knows your cat better than you do.

THE DECISION TO EUTHANIZE

The time comes when it is no longer appropriate, or even possible, to keep a cat alive. Its pain is unrelieved or its condition is incurable; for instance, the kidneys no longer function, leading to a slow death by uremic poisoning, or the lungs are filled with fluid, making every breath difficult. The cat shows no desire for food or water, and it loses interest in its surroundings. It spends the majority of its time in a deep sleep and eliminates in or near its bed. A cat in this condition is letting you know that it is no longer interested in life. This is when you can make the greatest sacrifice, give the greatest gift of kindness: an easy death in a loving atmosphere.

Being prepared for this decision is important. Planning for a pet's death is something no one wants to face, but although it's difficult, it can make the actual event easier to face. Knowing the options available helps ease the confusion and pain.

A cat may be euthanized at the veterinary office or, in some cases, at the home. The veterinary office is where most cats are euthanized. Euthanasia is a quick, easy, painless death. The veterinarian prepares an IV injection of a concentrated anesthetic. The amount injected brings unconsciousness in 10 to 20 seconds, and the cat simply never wakes up. You can ask the veterinarian to tranquilize the cat before giving the injection. This puts the cat in a state in which it is relaxed and free from pain. Sometimes mild tremors shake the body or the cat may release urine or feces. Sometimes it may gasp or cry out, although this is rare, but these sounds are not indications of pain nor that the cat is still alive. They are merely the muscles going limp as life leaves the body.

Decide ahead of time whether you want to be present when your cat is euthanized. Your veterinarian may encourage you to bring a family member or friend along for support and should not object to your presence during the procedure. Say your good-byes while the cat is still alive, and try your best to stay calm so the cat won't be frightened. If you don't want to be present while the cat is euthanized, that's okay, too.

If you are very emotional, it may be easier for you and your cat to allow the veterinary staff to give the injection in a less emotionally charged atmosphere. Instead, you may wish to view the body afterward. Whichever option you choose, your veterinarian should support you and should allow you the time you need to be with the body and make your peace with the situation.

Although the veterinary office is the most common and convenient place for euthanasia, some cat owners find it too cold and sterile for a final farewell. Others may believe a cat is in too much pain or will be too stressed by the trip to the office. To a grieving owner, euthanasia at home, in a place that is familiar and comfortable to the cat, may seem preferable, especially if the cat has always hated going to the veterinarian. If you have a close relationship with your veterinarian, a housecall may be arranged, but not all veterinarians are able to offer this service. In some cities housecall specialists may be an alternative. In either case, the cost will be higher, although it may be a small price to pay for your cat's comfort. Keep in mind, however, that euthanasia can be more difficult to face at home. An emotional owner often makes the cat upset. At this sad time, the kindest, most important thing you can do is to put your cat's comfort first.

If your cat is euthanized at home, make preparations ahead of time. Think about where the procedure should take place. If it is on the dining room table or in the kitchen, will you later have difficulty eating there? Is there a nice, sunny spot that your cat loves? Will it be most comfortable right in its bed?

In a perfect world, none of us would ever have to make such difficult decisions. Our cats would die at home, in our arms, with no pain. Or they would slip peacefully away in their sleep.

Unfortunately, we are not usually this lucky. Sometimes we must decide whether our cats' quality of life is such that euthanasia is a kinder alternative than a life of suffering. In many ways, this ability to provide a quiet, easy death is one of the greatest gifts we can give our cats. If we have made every effort to give our cats good lives, and if we trust our veterinarians' skill and advice, we should never feel guilty about making the decision to euthanize. Second-guessing the decision only prolongs the grieving process, making an unhappy situation unnecessarily painful.

AFTER DEATH

Making plans for burial or memorial is an important part of accepting the loss of a cat. A number of options are available for disposal of the body. It can be taken home for burial, buried or cremated at a pet cemetery, or disposed of by the veterinarian. Try to decide beforehand which method you prefer so that it will be easier to make arrangements.

Home burial has a number of advantages and disadvantages. If you have a large yard with a spot that is special to you or the cat, it can be an ideal place for a burial with a marker or a plant as a memorial. Usually, caskets, vaults and memorial markers are available for home burial from pet cemeteries or from companies that advertise in cat magazines. If you move, however, you can't very well take the cat's grave with you, and you run the risk that the new owners of your home will inadvertently destroy the site.

A gravestone for a beloved family companion.

Not everyone has access to a yard, and some city ordinances prohibit burial of pets in residential areas. If this is the case, cremation or burial at a pet cemetery are options. A pet cemetery is the equivalent of a combination human funeral home and cemetery. Most pet cemeteries offer a variety of services, enabling the pet owner to choose a cremation, burial or memorial that meets both emotional and financial needs.

Cremation exposes the body to intense heat, reducing it to skeletal remains, which are then processed to reduce them to small fragments. These "cremains" are then presented in a memorial urn that can be taken home or scattered in a special place, or placed at the cemetery. The cost of cremation varies, depending on whether the cat is cremated individually or in a mass cremation. Generally, a private cremation costs about one hundred dollars. The choice of urn or the decision to place the urn at the cemetery can increase the price.

Burial at a pet cemetery can be as simple or as elaborate as desired. The cost varies, depending on whether the burial is in-ground or above-ground in a crypt or mausoleum; the type of memorial stone purchased; and the type of casket preferred. An in-ground burial with a casket, land, and a marker can cost $200 or more. Mausoleum burial is more expensive than in-ground burial. Some pet cemeteries provide a common burial plot where pets are buried along with other deceased pets. Individual memorials may not be available at the communal plot, but many cemeteries provide a memory wall displaying plaques honoring deceased pets.

Decisions made under stress are not always well thought out. If possible, choose a pet cemetery before you need it. That way, grief won't blind you to its flaws. When choosing a pet cemetery, examine the grounds carefully. Does it look as if someone cares or are the plots grown-over and ill-kept? Talk to the owners. Are they open and friendly? Do they have a long-term commitment to the cemetery? Some pet cemeteries are deed-restricted. Ask what has been planned for the future. Will the cemetery be there in five years or is development planned for the area? Ask if the owners belong to the IAPC. The International Association of Pet Cemeteries upholds business ethics and practices, maintaining a strict code of ethics to which all members must adhere. Members must display the IAPC plaque and code of ethics. The IAPC also provides information to the public regarding pet burial or cremation. Its address is listed at the end of this chapter.

If burial at home or use of a pet cemetery is not feasible, your veterinarian can dispose of the body for you. You may or may not want to know what will happen to the cat's body. Practices vary from one veterinarian to the next, depending on local regulations. The body may be sent to a mass crematory or to a rendering plant where it is processed to ash used for fertilizer and other products. If this thought is distressing to you, remember that where the cat's body lies is not as important as the place it holds in your heart. And many people like the idea of a useful purpose for their pets' remains. Whichever method of disposal you choose, your veterinarian can discuss the options and help you come to the best decision for your situation.

PET MEMORIALS AND CEREMONIES

Creating a memorial or performing a ceremony is one of the most healing activities a grieving pet owner or family can undertake. From lighting candles to inviting friends over to reminisce about Smoky and drink a toast to his memory, pet owners are free to invent whatever will mean most to them and to the memory of a beloved pet.

One cat owner decorated a box and invited friends to come over and put something in the box that related to the pet—a note or a photo, for instance. Another created a dance for her pet. So graceful an activity is a particularly suitable feline memorial. Making a scrapbook or writing a journal can be therapeutic. Something as simple as framing a photograph, or wrapping Tiger's collar and tag and placing them in a special spot can help soothe an aching heart. Burying the body or ashes and planting a tree or plant in that location is a special living memorial. Some owners spread the ashes in a place that has special meaning. One type of memorial that can have lasting benefits for other cats is a donation to an organization that supports veterinary research into feline health problems, such as the Winn Feline Foundation or the Morris Animal Foundation, or establishing a memorial in the cat's name with a veterinary college or humane society.

A ceremony may also take place before the cat's death. In a case where the cat is being euthanized at home, the owner may perform a ritual such as playing special music, lighting a candle or reminiscing with the cat before the veterinarian arrives.

A cat is often a symbolic link to important people, places, or times in our lives. Perhaps it has associations with a friend or relative who has since died. Sometimes it has been a companion from childhood through adulthood, a part of happy summertimes, college, marriage and a first child. In other cases, there is a need to complete unfinished business before being able to let go. Whether it is arranging for a spouse to come say good-bye, or videotaping the cat, or taking it home one last time, if that act will make a difference, it is something that needs to be done.

Societal constraints may make people unwilling to share their feelings or unburden themselves in these ways, but it's important to remember that grief is a potent force. If a ceremony or memorial can make it easier to deal with, then by all means the desire should be honored. Only family and friends who understand the value of a pet's life should be invited to the ceremony. Don't make things more difficult by including people who don't understand the importance of your relationship with your cat.

DEALING WITH GRIEF

Euthanasia is among the most difficult decisions a pet owner will ever make. After a lifetime of companionship, he or she must voluntarily decide to end a beloved friend's life. The grief and guilt that accompany this decision can be overwhelming. Adding to the stress are concerns regarding the procedure itself. Thus, it can be the last straw to hear the words: "Don't be so upset. It was just a cat. You can get another one." The unthinking individuals who say this deserve our pity, as they are unable to experience the loving relationship between human and cat.

Fortunately, with the growing recognition of the human-animal bond, such insensitive statements are heard less frequently, which is good news for people who love animals. The bond with pets is as strong as that of any other important relationship, and it is no longer necessary to hide grief or to feel guilt over mourning "just a cat." Society has begun to recognize that the love of a pet is worthy of recognition and that a death requires emotional support, not judgment or dismissal.

To that end, a number of pet grief counseling groups and hotlines have sprung up around the country. Often sponsored by veterinary schools, they offer an opportunity to associate with others who have suffered a similar loss and who understand and are sympathetic. Trained counselors provide guidance in working through the grief.

Psychologists have defined grief in a number of ways, but generally they agree that it occurs in five stages: denial, anger, bargaining, depression, and acceptance. The length of these stages and the ability to get through them depends on the type of relationship with the pet, the depth and length of attachment, emotional state, and the availability of outside support and relationships. There is no "normal" period of grief, nor is there any one way to grieve.

The stages of grief may occur both before and after a cat's death. For instance, denial that a beloved cat is terminally ill, despite physical signs and test results, is often the first reaction. Then anger sets in, perhaps combined with the suggestion of a misdiagnosis by the veterinarian or a mistake by the laboratory. With acceptance that the cat is truly dying often comes a time of bargaining—making promises in exchange for the cat's life. Following the realization that bargaining isn't working, depression and, finally, acceptance, set in. These stages may be repeated after the cat's death.

Normal responses to grief include crying, loss of appetite, inability to sleep, lack of concentration, depression, loneliness, tightness in the chest or throat, and audible or visual hallucinations. Crying spells can go on for days. Just when you think you are recovering from the loss, a random thought will trigger a fresh round of tears. It is not at all unusual to glimpse the cat out of the corner of your eye, usually in its favorite spot, or to jump because you think you hear its meow. People often take these "sightings" as farewell visits from the cat and find that they give a sense of closure. As one owner put it, "I felt that they were saying, 'Don't feel bad; you treated me well, and now it's time for me to move on.'"

Dealing with grief and moving on with life is a four-step process. The first is to accept the reality of the loss. Denial is normal, but eventually you must come to the realization that the cat is gone. Next, it's important to accept the pain of the loss. This includes allowing yourself to cry or to otherwise express your grief. Do not be inhibited by people who believe it's silly or undignified to mourn for an animal. The third step is to adjust to the loss, which can be especially difficult if your cat was an integral part of your life. Life will be different, but it does go on. Finally, turn your attentions to other relationships or activities. This does not mean that you must forget about the cat. Rather, you must invest your emotional energy in living your life, while keeping a special place for the cat in your heart and mind.

If you feel that you can't cope with your cat's death, don't hesitate to seek help from a professional grief counselor. There is no stigma in needing help to recover from such a loss. The need for grief counseling has been compared to having a broken leg. Just as you would not ignore the pain and hope that the leg would heal itself, neither should you ignore your grief. A caring mental health professional can offer you the support you need. Your veterinarian may be able to refer you to an appropriate person, or you can look in the Yellow Pages under such headings as "Counseling," "Marriage, Family and Child Counseling" or "Psychologists."

WHAT TO TELL CHILDREN

Only one rule applies when a pet loved by a child dies: Never lie. Offering seemingly soothing statements such as "Fluffy's gone on a trip and won't be back" or "The vet had to put Snowball to sleep because he was in pain" not only don't answer a child's questions, they can also make a child unreasonably fearful of trips, sleep and pain.

Depending on the child's age and relationship with the cat, make your responses simple, yet answer questions sincerely and as fully as possible. Susan Phillips Cohen, director of counseling at New York City's Animal Medical Center, describes how children of various ages might react and offers suggestions on how and what to tell them.

Up to the age of five, Cohen says, kids have what is called "magical thinking." The differences between reality and make-believe are still a little fuzzy to them. That means giving concrete explanations in terms the child can understand: "Fluffy is dead. That means she's not breathing, she's not looking around, she's not moving, she's not growing, and she's not coming back."

Emphasize that Fluffy's death is in no way related to anything the child did, and avoid such phrases as "put to sleep" or "Fluffy's up there in heaven." Children at this age can be literal-minded, either becoming excited about going into high places to see if they can see Fluffy or becoming frightened of high places, fearing that they too will get snatched into heaven.

Children between the ages of 5 and 10 understand what death is, but they think they can work around it. Cohen says children of this age have a lot of questions about illness, death and methods of dying, and they sometimes personify death. They may routinely check doors and windows each night to make sure they are locked so no one can get in at night, or they may want a gun to protect themselves. It may seem gruesome or warlike to adults, Cohen says, but it is merely the child's way of trying to figure out how not to be dead.

Older children have a better sense of the life cycle. They understand that death comes to everyone and everything. For these children, roles and ceremonies can be important. Cohen suggests that the child be permitted to pick out the best place to bury Fluffy or choose a photo to have framed. Other comforting activities include drawing a picture of Fluffy or leading the family on a walk to all of Fluffy's favorite places.

Don't be too protective of a child's feelings. Children often understand more than we think they do. One child explained to her mother that it was okay to bury the family's parakeet because, she said, "He's not in there [his body] any more."

A pet's death may be a child's first opportunity to deal with life and death questions. He or she may want to know such things as why animals die, whether dying hurts and if the cat will ever come back again. Take the questions seriously and answer them to the best of your ability. When handled sensitively, a pet's death can be a sad but valuable learning experience.

THE SPIRITUAL SIDE

A concern for the afterlife of a pet is common, Cohen says. Many of her clients question whether they will be reunited with their pets after death.

In many cultures, cats are believed to have souls and to participate in an afterlife. Mohammed had a special fondness for cats, and his blessing is said to ensure them a permanent place in paradise. And ancient Egyptian civilization, of course, was well-known for its belief in a feline afterlife.

Although Christianity is not known for encouraging the belief that pets go to heaven, Christian Church pastor Kent Dannen says the Bible clearly indicates that animals have a place in heaven. In the gospels Matthew and Luke, God's love for sparrows and ravens is proclaimed, and in Romans 8:19-22, Paul writes that all of creation will be freed from death.

Pride has been struggling with common sense over this passage for centuries, Dannen says, with Catholic saints theologizing on both sides of the question of whether Paul was proclaiming salvation for nonhumans. Even Protestant reformer John Calvin wrestled with the passage, writing that logically it indicated that animals would be "renewed," but worrying, "If we give free rein to these speculations, where will they finally carry us?" Presumably, Dannen says, to John Wesley's commentary on the same passage—"Away with vulgar prejudices, and let the plain word of God take place." Wesley then goes on to speculate about what heaven is like for animals.

In other religions, the hope is that the cat will be reborn into another body. "I've run into plenty of people who believe in reincarnation, who hope to see their cat in this life, in some other body," Cohen says.

A belief of this type can lead to ethical concerns about euthanasia. Veterinarians or pet owners who hold these beliefs may believe it's wrong to assist in a death because it may interfere with spiritual development. The feeling is that even if it's a suffering life, the spirit will be angry because it was supposed to take a certain course.

Religious or spiritual beliefs of any kind may affect the decision regarding euthanasia, leading pet owners to ask themselves some difficult questions. A fear of "playing God" is strong in most people. It may help to realize that the disease is killing the cat, not the owner.

"What the owner must do," Cohen says, "is consider whether the animal is likely to have a gentle, peaceful death or a hard death. If it's likely to be a hard death, does the owner want to intervene and, if so, when? It's very complex, determining whether to wait until the cat is uncomfortable or deciding to euthanize before the cat becomes uncomfortable. It's all related to quality of life and people's interpretation of what the pet wants, as well as what they want for their pet."

MEMORIES

Although it may hurt to remember, tears are an important part of accepting and working through grief. And through the tears we sometimes laugh, remembering the special and sometimes funny things that we loved about our cats. Don't be afraid to stir up memories. It can help to repeat the cat's name out loud, to remember the funny things it did.

The wonderful thing about memories is that time smoothes their edges. They can be painful in the beginning, but the more you remember the better you will feel. You can rerun the memories in your head, time and again, and they will never wear out. A cat may have only nine physical lives, but it can live forever in your mind and heart.

RESOURCES

American Association For Marriage and Family Therapy, 1100 17th St. NW, Washington, DC 20036; (202) 452-0109. They provide referrals to state marriage and family

therapy associations, which can direct interested parties to
licensed therapists who do grief counseling.

American Psychological Association, 750 1st St. NE,
Washington, DC 20002-4242; (202) 336-5500. It provides
referrals to state psychological associations, which can offer
leads on area psychologists who do grief counseling.

The Delta Society, P.O. Box 1080, Renton, WA 98057;
(206) 226-7357. This society offers a nationwide listing of
bereavement groups. Ask for the Nationwide Pet
Bereavement Directory.

International Association of Pet Cemeteries, 13 Cemetery
Ln., Ellenberg Depot, NY 12935; (518) 594-3000.

Pet Loss Foundation, 764 Riley Wills Rd., Lebanon, OH
45036; (513) 932-2270. This foundation has a database of
pet cemeteries, suppliers of memorial and burial items, and
organizations that have support groups.

GRIEF HOTLINES

California: University of California at Davis, Pet Loss
Support Hotline; (916) 752-4200. Hours: 6:30 PM to 9:30
PM Pacific Standard Time, Monday through Friday.
Messages can be left 24 hours a day, seven days a week.
Calls are returned collect. The UC Davis hotline, established
in 1989, was the first grief-counseling service offered by
phone.

Colorado: Colorado State University Veterinary School,
bereavement program; (303) 221-4535. Call before 10 PM,
seven days a week.

Florida: University of Florida at Gainesville College of
Veterinary Medicine, Pet Loss Support Hotline; (904) 392-
4700, ext. 4080. Hours: Messages can be left 24 hours a
day, seven days a week. Calls are returned at no charge
between 7 and 9 PM Eastern Standard Time.

Illinois: Chicago Veterinary Medical Association, Pet Loss
Support Helpline; (708) 603-3994. Hours: Messages can be
left 24 hours a day, seven days a week. Calls are returned
7 PM to 9 PM, Monday through Friday.

Michigan: Michigan State University College of Veterinary Medicine, Pet Loss Support Hotline; (517) 432-2696. Hours: 6:30 PM to 9:30 PM Eastern Standard Time, Tuesday, Wednesday and Thursday. Messages can be left 24 hours a day, seven days a week. Calls will be returned collect.

Pennsylvania: University of Pennsylvania Veterinary School, bereavement program; (215) 898-4529.

PET MEMORIALS

A number of companies provide markers, headstones, urns, and caskets. Listed below is a sampling of what is available. Write or call for a brochure or information.

Binsfeld's Best (granite memorials), Rt. 1, Box 152, Big Stone City, SD 57216; write for free brochure

Blue Ribbons (caskets, urns, remembrance gifts, and St. Francis personalized mini-marker), 2475 Bellmore Ave., Bellmore, NY 11710; (516) 785-0604

Boyer International (cremation memorials), P.O. Box 847, Penn Valley, CA 95946; (916) 432-4100

Everlasting Stone Pet and Family Memorials, P.O. Box 995, Barre, VT 05641-0995; (802) 454-1050

Faithful Friend (caskets and vaults), P.O. Box 646, Bowling Green, OH 43402; (419) 352-3691

Larry Gomez Products (caskets), P.O. Box 517, Temple, TX 76503; (800) 722-7561

Guardian Products Inc. (caskets); (800) 778-PETS

Hoegh Pet Casket Co., P.O. Box 311, Gladstone, MI 49837-0311

Lifemark (eight-foot tree, metal plaque and certificate); (800) 977-1226

The Vase Place (ceramic urns), 65 Webb Cir., Reno, NV 89506; (800) 682-8273

Books on Bereavement

If you aren't able to join a support group or call a grief hotline, reading a book may help you cope with your loss. Sharing the experiences of others, even through words on a page, can be calming and comforting. Some of these books may be out of print, but look for them in libraries and secondhand bookstores.

Coping With the Loss of a Pet. Moira Anderson Allen. Peregrine Press; 1988.

How To Survive the Loss of a Love. Melba Cosgrove, et. al. Bantam Books, New York; 1976.

Maya's First Rose. Martin Scot Kosins and Howard Fridson. Random House, Villard Books, New York; 1993.

Death: The Final Stage of Growth. Elisabeth Kubler-Ross. Prentice-Hall, New Jersey; 1975.

On Death and Dying. Elisabeth Kubler-Ross. Macmillan, New York; 1969.

Coping With the Loss of a Pet. Christina M. Lemieux and Wallace R. Clark. 1992.

When Your Pet Dies: How To Cope With Your Feelings. Jamie Quackenbush and Denise Graveline. Simon & Schuster, New York; 1985.

The Loss of a Pet. Wallace Sife, Ph.D. Howell Book House, New York; 1985

Good Books To Help Kids Cope

Part of helping a child to mourn and understand the loss of a cat can include reading about the subject. *The Tenth Good Thing About Barney*, by Judith Viorst, is a good story that you may want to have on your son or daughter's bookshelf long before the family pet dies. It may be helpful for you and your child to read Viorst's book or one of the other books listed just before or immediately after your cat is euthanized.

Consider making it part of the ceremony celebrating the cat's life. The following books are helpful in explaining the concept of death to a child.

Lifetimes. B. Mellonie and R. Ingpen. Bantam Books; 1983.

Pet Loss: A Thoughtful Guide for Adults and Children. Herbert A. Neiburg and Arlene Fischer. Harper & Row; 1982.

Oh, Where Has My Pet Gone? Sally Sibbitt, B. Libby Press; 1991

The Tenth Good Thing About Barney. Judith Viorst. Aladdin; 1975

VETERINARY TIP

"Love them while you have them, and save the mourning until they are gone."

—Lenny Southam, DVM, West Chester, Pennsylvania.

Completing 11 the *Circle*

Grow old along with me!
The best is yet to be . . . —Robert Browning

When a cat dies, friends and relatives often recommend replacing it immediately. "Go out and get another one right away," they say. "Then you won't miss him so much."

Resist that advice. Only you can know when it is the right time to open your heart and home to a new cat. Don't let yourself be pressured into making a mistake by people who don't understand the importance of timing in a relationship. On the other hand, some people can't bear to be without a cat. For them, buying or adopting a new cat as soon as possible is the right decision. The point is that each situation is unique.

Not only is each situation unique, each cat is unique. Never acquire a new cat and expect it to be just like your previous cat. Cats may resemble each other superficially, but their temperaments and personalities can be miles apart. It's unfair to burden a new cat with expectations that it can never meet. Enjoy the cat for its own self, and don't make comparisons.

When you are ready to acquire a new cat, you have a number of options: You can adopt an adult cat from a shelter or breeder, buy a pedigreed kitten, or adopt a kitten from a shelter. Each alternative has advantages and disadvantages. Which you choose depends entirely on your situation, personality and expectations of a cat. Again, don't let anyone pressure you into making a decision that isn't right for your circumstances.

ADOPTING AN OLDER CAT

People have many reasons for the types of cats they acquire. Some are interesting in breeding or showing, others only in companionship. If your desire is to save a life, you can't do

Each cat is unique. If it's time to get another one, you have a lot of options.

any better than to adopt an adult cat—two years or older—from an animal shelter or humane society. Very few of the adult cats that land in shelters are reclaimed by their owners, and fewer still are adopted. Unless they are lucky enough to end up in a no-kill shelter, their futures are bleak.

Many people are reluctant to adopt an adult or geriatric cat, citing concerns about its health and longevity. But those who have taken a chance on a pre-owned cat with high mileage have been amply rewarded. Adult cats, especially those that are five years or older, have a lot going for them.

The advantages of adopting an older cat are many. These cats have settled down from kittenhood and often are content to sit in your lap or by your side for hours on end. If you haven't had a kitten in a while, you might not remember just how much energy they have. It can be exhausting to keep up with a kitten—hauling it down from the curtains, sweeping up broken figurines, being awakened at 2AM by a tiny fuzzball bouncing on your head. If a peaceful, gentle pet is what you're looking for, skip over the two or three years that kittenhood can last and go right for an adult cat.

Health, of course, is an important factor. Generally, cats in middle age—and even those entering their geriatric years—are very healthy and can even be less expensive than a kitten.

A prospective owner's fears of large veterinary bills are not necessarily rooted in reality. Indoor cats can live very healthy lives without much veterinary intervention, as long as they are kept clean and flea-free and given regular veterinary exams and inoculations.

Adult cats are also more predictable. Their personalities have formed, and you can better judge how they will fit into your household and how they will get along with your other pets. Adult cats are more likely to be litter box-trained and to have some house manners. A cat's destructive tendencies lessen as it matures.

You may want to adopt an older cat.

CHOOSING A SHELTER CAT

When you go to a shelter, it's a good idea to have a preconceived notion of what you're looking for in a cat so you won't be overwhelmed by numbers. Do you want a cat with a long or short coat, or one of a specific color? Sometimes popular pedigreed cats, such as Siamese and Persians, are available in shelters. If your home is filled with fine furniture, you are probably interested in a cat that is trained to use a scratching post or one that has been declawed. Cats that are declawed

The Next Step

- *Don't be pressured into getting a new cat before you're ready.*

- *Consider adopting an older cat from a shelter or from a breeder.*

- *Choose a healthy, outgoing kitten. Don't be swayed by pity for the shy kitten coughing in the corner unless you are prepared for potentially hefty veterinary bills.*

- *Question breeders carefully about their breeding practices, and expect to be scrutinized in return.*

- *Enjoy your new kitten or cat!*

are often found in shelters. Make a list of the qualities you want so you won't be distracted when you are looking.

A good way to make the selection is for the whole family to go through the shelter together. Make three sweeps of the facility. On the first go-round, just enjoy looking at all the cats. Don't try to make a decision yet. Walk through again. This time, each person should choose two cats he or she would like to adopt. The third time through, look at each cat chosen, comparing it to the list to see if it meets the criteria. Eliminate those that don't. Take your list of remaining cats and ask a shelter employee to tell you about them. He or she may have information about the cats that will affect your decision.

It's rare that you will be making a completely blind decision when you choose a cat from a shelter. Shelter personnel see the cats on a daily basis and can give you insight into each cat's personality and habits. If a cat was turned in by its owners, the shelter is likely to have more detailed information about its health, habits and personality than about a cat found as a stray. Often, shelter cats come with background information, such as whether they get along with children or other animals, or if they prefer men or women.

Ideally, the home situation you can offer will be similar to what the cat is used to living in. For instance, old cats may have a difficult time fitting into a home with very young children unless they came from a family with children. On the other hand, most outdoor cats adapt well to becoming indoor cats. A good indication of a cat's suitability as a pet is whether it uses the litter box regularly. If the shelter is one in which several cats are kept loose in a room, ask if the cat is good about using the box. A good appetite is another factor to consider. If the cat is eating well, it is probably healthy and emotionally stable.

Once you have discussed your choices with shelter personnel, you can meet with the cat or cats left on the list to make

Cats in a shelter are in a stressful, unnatural situation. Ask to take a cat you're interested in to the visiting room to better assess its personality.

your choice. Remember that a cat in a shelter is in an unnatural situation. It is likely to be stressed and frightened and may not show to its best advantage. Cats separated from their previous owners go through a period of mourning, and being in the shelter environment is an additional source of stress. Often, the enclosures are small with little room for the cat to walk around. A cat in these circumstances may be depressed and withdrawn, but a cat that shies away in the kennel area may loosen up once it's in a less stressful situation. Arrange to take the cat into a visiting room so you can get to know each other on a one-on-one basis. In this setting, the cat may relax, giving you a truer picture of its personality. Whether you want a kitten or an adult, look for a cat that is healthy and responsive to you. If it is friendly in a shelter environment, it is likely to be friendly in your home, too. In case of a tie, you may have to flip a coin or do "eenie, meenie, minie, mo."

Don't pass up a cat because of its advanced age. Adopting a very old cat can be a marvelous experience. There is something wonderful about them at that age: their kindness, their lovingness, their compassion. Cats as old as 17 have been adopted; in one instance, the cat is now celebrating its

19th birthday and has been very healthy. Although a cat this age may not be around as long as a younger cat, the rewards of ownership can outweigh the eventual loss. It's natural to be reluctant to become attached to an aged cat, but death is a part of life, and the unconditional love of the older cat far outweighs the pain of eventually losing it. People who adopt an old cat from a municipal shelter can take immense pride and pleasure in knowing that they saved a cat in its ninth life.

If you would like to offer a home to an older cat but are interested in a pedigree, consider adopting a retired show or breeding cat. Often, breeders who have a number of cats look for homes where their retired cats can receive the attention the breeder may not have time to give. This type of adoption is preferable for people who want to know a cat's medical and behavioral history or who have an interest in a specific breed. To find a retired cat for adoption, check the classified ads in newspapers under the breed in which you are interested, or contact breeders who advertise in cat magazines.

GETTING A KITTEN

There is no more joyous symbol of new life than a kitten. Its never-ending energy and curiosity make it more entertaining than just about anything under the sun. A kitten lives life to the fullest, going everywhere at a turbocharged rate of speed. The person who goes home with a kitten is in for a wild but delightful ride. These captivating creatures can squirm their way into a heart without lifting a paw. There is no lack of choice when it comes to finding a kitten. You can buy a pedigreed cat of any one of more than 40 breeds, or you can select a domestic long- or shorthair from a shelter or a neighborhood litter.

PERSONALITY AND PHYSICAL TRAITS

A kitten's development follows specific stages. In the days just after birth it is helpless: blind and deaf, able only to nurse and sleep, mewling if it is cold or hungry. At day five, its tiny ears become operational; soon afterward the eyes open. The serious work of play begins at weeks three and four, with the kitten rolling and tumbling with its littermates. At this stage, a kitten may begin tasting small amounts of wet food.

Social skills are learned between the ages of 5 and 12 weeks. This is a critical time in the kitten's life. What it learns during these seven weeks can have a lifelong effect on a kitten's relationships with people and other animals. Studies show that kittens handled every day for the first month of their lives develop faster physically, learn more quickly, and are less likely to react fearfully to new situations than other kittens. At three to four months of age, the kitten is ready to start a new life with a loving family.

Although these stages follow a set pattern, each kitten is an individual. Both environment and heredity can affect how it develops. Choosing the right kitten is a matter of carefully researching breed, health and personality as well as observing the kittens themselves. Whether you are buying a pedigreed cat, choosing from a neighbor's litter or adopting from a shelter, much of the same advice applies.

Choosing the right kitten is a matter of carefully researching breed, health and personality, as well as observing the kittens themselves.

Good health at an early age is paramount. Look for a kitten that is active and alert, healthy and outgoing. Its eyes and nose should be clear and clean, not red or runny. A potbelly can be a sign of intestinal parasites. Respiratory health is very important. Avoid the kitten that is coughing or sneezing. Lift the tail to check for evidence of diarrhea or inflammation. A foul-smelling anal discharge should set off alarm bells. Healthy kittens have clean ears, white teeth and pink gums. Their coats should be shiny, with no skin irritation, bald patches or red blotches. Always go for a bright, healthy kitten. Many people feel sorry for the runt, but these kittens are much more likely to have medical problems than their larger siblings. There are many healthy kittens looking for homes. Unless you are prepared for potentially high veterinary bills, don't risk heartbreak by choosing a kitten that has the deck stacked against it.

Personality can be judged, too. Choose the friendly kitten over the shy one that cowers in the corner. Avoid the kitten that is overly aggressive. If you are buying from a breeder, the kittens should be well-socialized and accustomed to children, other household pets, and visitors to the home. Frequent early handling and exposure to a wide variety of people, sounds and experiences are the keys to the development of a friendly cat that meets new situations head-on.

Avoid breeders whose kittens are raised primarily in cages. Lack of handling, little exposure to new situations, and lack of interaction with people can produce a shy or fearful cat that doesn't adapt well to changes and never enjoys life to the fullest. Kittens that trust people should be unafraid and willing to be cradled like babies or put on their backs to have their tummies rubbed. When you are choosing from a litter, make every effort to see the kittens more than once so you can get to know them before taking one home.

Look for the kitten interested in you. If you are in a situation where you can talk to the breeder, ask which kitten likes her kids or likes to climb in someone's lap rather than play with the other kittens. This is the kitten that will be easy to handle and will enjoy being a lap cat. If you choose the kitten that plays hard, won't hold still and likes to run up people's legs, you're not going to have a cat that will enjoy purring in your lap by the fireplace—at least not for several years.

BUYING A PEDIGREED CAT

A pedigreed cat is one whose ancestry can be traced back for generations to ancestors that had the same characteristics. People buy pedigreed cats for a variety of reasons. Some are interested in a cat with an unusual coat type, such as a

Cornish Rex or a Sphynx. They enjoy the attention the cat attracts or the advantages of a particular coat type: its nonallergenic properties, for instance. The Exotic Shorthair offers the look of a Persian, but it comes with a shorter coat that is easier to care for.

Other people look for specific beautiful markings, such as the points on the Siamese or the mitts of the Birman. Each breed has its own personality, too. Abyssinians are active and inquisitive. The Persian or Himalayan has a quiet, regal demeanor. The Siamese likes to "talk" all day.

Think about breed personalities before you select a pedigreed cat. Abyssinians are active and inquisitive.

Pedigreed cats can become a way of life. People who enjoy competition can show their pedigreed cats to earn championships. Unlike dog showing, even a spayed or neutered pedigreed cat can compete in shows, in what is called the "premier" class. Buying a pedigreed cat offers the purchaser an opportunity to acquire a cat that has been bred not only for a specific look, but also for health and temperament. The parents and sometimes the grandparents can be examined for good health and pleasant personalities.

If you know you want a pedigreed kitten and you have chosen a breed, the next step is to find a reputable breeder. Reputable breeders are committed to improving the breed. They

Kitten Layette

Go shopping before you bring your kitten home. Essentials you will need include the following:

- *A bag or cans of the same brand of food the breeder has been feeding. If you plan to change the kitten's diet, do so gradually, by mixing its new food with the old food over 10 days.*

- *A litter box, two bags of litter, and a litter scoop. You can use a slotted kitchen spoon as a scoop, but the best tool is a wide plastic or metal scoop from the pet supply store. Wait to buy clumping litter until your kitten matures. It can cause intestinal obstructions if eaten, and it can get in a kitten's eyes, matting them closed.*

- *A small airline crate or a soft-sided carrier for trips in the car to the veterinarian, groomer, or just for a ride around town. Riding in the carrier will protect your kitten in case of accident and will protect you from having a wild kitten jump on your head just as you are making that left turn.*

(continued)

belong to cat clubs and exhibit cats of their breeding. One of the goals of their breeding programs is the elimination of health problems by screening their cats for genetic disease. They are up-to-date on current information regarding vaccinations, diseases, and genetics.

To find a breeder, ask your veterinarian or other cat owners for referrals. Magazines such as *Cat Fancy, Cats USA,* and *Cats* are good sources of breeder advertisements. Breeders can also be found at cat shows. Attend a cat show and talk to breeders there. Look for knowledgeable breeders who are interested in talking about their breeds and are willing to take the time to educate a novice. Let breeders know what you're looking for in a cat —quiet, active, talkative, easy to groom—so they can tell you if their breed is appropriate. Ask about a breed's personality and temperament. What are its grooming requirements? Does it have special dietary needs? Is it accustomed to children or other pets? What genetic problems affect the breed?

Some breeders may have kittens available for sale at shows. A kitten bought at a show should not be an impulse buy, however; you should already have interviewed the breeder, seen his or her adult cats in their home environment, and be familiar with the breed and its needs. If you meet a breeder you like at a show, make an appointment to see his or her cats in their home setting. Without examining the cattery, it's difficult to know how the kitten has been socialized or in what conditions it has been raised.

As you examine the kittens, interview the breeder. A good one will welcome your concern and won't be offended if you ask any of the following questions.

- How frequently are litters produced?

- Does the breeder participate in a cattery inspection program?

- Do kittens come with a health guarantee or a veterinary health certificate?

- Can the breeder show proof and results of screening tests for health problems common to the breed?

- Does the breeder belong to a cat association and subscribe to its code of ethics?

- If licensing is required in your area, does the breeder have a license?

- Is the breeder willing and able to give references from other buyers?

A good breeder questions buyers just as carefully. The questions may seem personal, but the breeder's intentions are good: to ensure that his kittens go to loving, lifelong homes. Expect a breeder to ask some or all of the following questions:

- Are your current cats altered?

- Do you keep your cats indoors?

- How many other cats/pets/kids do you have?

- How long did your previous cats live and why did they die?

- Is anyone home during the day?

- Do you own your home?

- *Food and water bowls. Small metal bowls are long-lasting and easy to clean.*

- *A scratching post. The ideal post is about 36 inches high, wrapped in sisal or rope. The height allows a grown cat to stretch out to its full length when scratching. The sisal or rope covering is attractive to cats and it's different from other household surfaces, such as carpets or upholstered furniture, that the cat might be tempted to scratch.*

- *Nail clippers. You can use clippers made especially for cats, available at pet supply stores, or you can use regular nail clippers made for humans. Accustom your kitten from day one to having its nails trimmed. Regular nail trimming reduces the damage cats can do to furnishings.*

(continued)

Kitten Layette

- *A metal flea comb and a wire slicker brush, hand mitt, rubber curry brush or other brush, depending on the type and length of fur. Ask the breeder or a groomer for recommendations. Begin grooming sessions at an early age so your kitten will learn not only to enjoy them, but also to sit still for them.*

- *Toys. Cats are easily entertained. You can wad up a piece of paper for them to chase, roll a ping pong ball across a bare floor or bounce the beam from a flashlight on the wall. For more sophisticated play, look for catnip mice, fishpole-type toys and squeaky toys. Examine toys for safety, ensuring that eyes and tails are sewn on tightly so they can't be swallowed. Never leave your kitten alone with any toy that has a string or cord attached, such as a fishpole-type toy. Swallowing the string could kill a curious kitten.*

- Can you provide references from your veterinarian and from your landlord if you are a renter?

A breeder may also require you to sign a contract agreeing to certain standards of care, such as keeping the cat indoors or spaying or neutering a pet-quality cat. Some breeders withhold a kitten's registration papers until they receive proof that the kitten has been altered. However, if you are buying a show-quality kitten, expect to receive a pedigree indicating the names and registration numbers of the kitten's parents and several earlier generations. In addition, the kitten should be accompanied by registration papers, which record its date of birth, description, ancestry and ownership. To register your kitten, complete the registration form and send it with the requested fee to the appropriate registry. The cat registries are listed at the end of this chapter.

The breeder may also require you to return the cat if there ever comes a time that you can't keep it. In return for meeting such stringent requirements, you should expect to receive a healthy, well-socialized kitten at a fair price, as well as ongoing advice from the breeder regarding its care, grooming and feeding.

Finding such a paragon of a breeder is not always easy. There is no feline *Consumer Reports* or Better Business Bureau. Anyone can hang out a shingle proclaiming himself a cat breeder. As the buyer, it is your responsibility to screen the breeder carefully to ensure that he or she follows reputable, responsible breeding practices. To help you in your search, three registries—Cat Fanciers Association (CFA), The International Cat Association (TICA), and the American Association of Cat

Enthusiasts (AACE)—offer cattery inspection programs. Each program operates in a similar manner, with some minor differences. The breeder pays for the inspection, which is performed by a licensed veterinarian of the breeder's choice.

Catteries are evaluated for such factors as cage size, cleanliness, state of repair, ventilation, lighting, and overall appearance. The veterinarian notes whether litter boxes are clean; rates adequacy of food, water, bedding and exercise space; and observes whether there is an isolation area for sick cats, show cats and newborns. The breeder must exhibit good recordkeeping, including proof of vaccinations; proper storage of medications and vaccines; and appropriate parasite prevention. In addition, the veterinarian rates the condition of the cats and the socialization of the kittens.

The veterinary report is scored by the registry, which assigns the breeder an appropriate designation. CFA catteries may be labeled Approved Cattery or Approved Cattery of Excellence. TICA catteries may be designated Cattery of Merit or Outstanding Cattery. AACE offers four ratings: 1 Star Cattery of Excellence, 2 Star Cattery of Excellence, 3 Star Cattery of Excellence and 4 Star Cattery of Excellence. Catteries must be reinspected annually. A high rating is not a guarantee that you will receive a perfect kitten, but it is evidence of a breeder's commitment to high standards. Do not rely solely on the results of a cattery inspection when choosing a breeder.

As the CFA states in its literature: "The approval relates to the physical condition of the cattery at the time of inspection by an independent, licensed veterinarian. It is not intended to nor does it guarantee the physical condition or health of any cat or kitten housed in said cattery or owned by the breeder, nor is it an endorsement of the breeder." In the final analysis, your own good judgment is what counts most.

Whether you decide to buy a pedigreed kitten or one of unknown heritage, make your selection carefully. Ideally, you will be able to examine the kitten's surroundings to ensure proper socialization and a healthy environment, and evaluate its mother's personality. Kittens are particularly susceptible to infectious disease, so acquiring a kitten from unknown circumstances can be risky. For instance, while a kitten in a pet store may be cute, it's difficult to know what kind of background it comes from. A kitten that has been shipped a long distance may be stressed and more likely to become ill. If the pet store can't provide information about the kitten's health and origin, consider another source. For the same reasons, avoid taking home a kitten that's being sold from a box in front of a store. You have no way of knowing whether the kitten has been exposed to disease or in what kind of environment it has been raised.

PATIENCE AND PERSEVERANCE

The kitten you choose will be with you for 15 years or more, so don't buy impulsively. Once you find a good breeder with nice cats, understand that you may have to wait for the kitten of your dreams. Litters are not available year-round, and many breeders keep a waiting list of potential buyers. If you are buying a kitten long-distance, some breeders may not be willing to ship it until it is 12 weeks old. Your willingness to wait for the right kitten rather than rushing out and buying the first one you find will undoubtedly pay off, however, in a healthy cat and a good relationship with the breeder, who can be your best friend during the kitten's adolescence and into adulthood.

Once you have a date set to pick up your kitten, make an appointment with your veterinarian to examine it on the same day. Your agreement with the breeder should include provisions for returning the kitten if it does not receive a clean bill of health. This first exam is also a good time for the veterinarian to give the kitten any booster shots it may need.

To help the kitten adjust to its new life, confine it to a small, quiet area for the first few days. Gradually permit it access to other rooms. It's also a good idea to establish a routine. Feed and groom the kitten on a set schedule.

HAPPILY EVER AFTER

A new kitten is an opportunity to start with a clean slate, but even an adult cat can get a boost from a change in circumstances. Life offers no guarantees, but by providing an indoor lifestyle, quality nutrition, and preventive care such as home exams and regular veterinary checkups, you can give your cat a head start to a long life.

CAT REGISTRIES

American Association of Cat Enthusiasts, P.O. Box 213, Pine Brook, NJ 07058

American Cat Association, 8101 Katherine Ave., Panorama City, CA 91402

American Cat Fanciers Association, P.O. Box 203, Pt. Lookout, MO 65726

Cat Fanciers Association, 1805 Atlantic Ave., P.O. Box 1005, Manasquan, NJ 08736-1005

Cat Fanciers Federation, 9509 Montgomery Rd., Cincinnati, OH 45242

The International Cat Association, P.O. Box 2684, Harlingen, TX 78551

Canadian Cat Association, 83-85 Kennedy Rd. S., Unit 1805, Brampton, Ontario, Canada L6W 3P3

VETERINARY TIP

"Each cat is different, so don't look for the new cat to replace the one you lost. Just appreciate the differences. And remember that although you're in need of the cat you just lost, there's a cat out there that needs you."

—*Christine Wilford, DVM, Cats Exclusive, Edmonds, Washington.*

Appendix:
Resources for *Cat Owners*

BOARD-CERTIFIED FELINE PRACTITIONERS

The following veterinarians have met the requirements to become specialists in cat care. This specialty is still new, and as yet only 22 veterinarians have applied and qualified for it, but with cats being the fastest growing group of pets, expect to see more veterinarians with this specialized knowledge. For more information, contact the American Association of Feline Practitioners, Kristi Thomson, Executive Director, 7007 Wyoming NE, Ste. E-3, Albuquerque, NM 87109.

Arizona

Robert Bruce Koch, Phoenix

California

Tom Elston, Irvine
Margaret F. Horstmeyer, San Bernardino
Elyse Marie Kent, Santa Monica
Susan Diane Steinberg, Costa Mesa
Vicki Lynn Thayer, Walnut Creek
Elaine Wexler-Mitchell, Orange

Connecticut

Margaret McIsaac, Bloomfield

Georgia

Douglas Weigner, Atlanta

Illinois

Jeffrey Lee House, Hoffman Estates

Indiana

Alice Juel Johns, Indianapolis

Missouri

Elisa Sundahl, Kansas City

Pennsylvania

Jean Marie Pittari, Philadelphia
Robert Bebko, Pittsburgh

Texas

Mary Louise McCaine, Missouri City
Cynthia L. McManis, Spring
Gary D. Norsworthy, San Antonio
Alice M. Wolf, College Station

Virginia

Lynn M. Gulledge, Alexandria

Wisconsin

Ilona Rodan, Madison
David Rosen, Glendale

Canada

Margaret A. Nixon, Vancouver, British Columbia

ANIMAL BEHAVIOR CONSULTANTS

The behaviorists listed here are certified members of the Animal Behavior Society, belong to the American Veterinary Society of Animal Behavior, or are diplomates of the American College of Veterinary Behaviorists. They are listed alphabetically by state of residence.

Alabama

Lawrence J. Myers, DVM, Ph.D., College of Veterinary Medicine, Auburn University, Auburn, AL; 36849; (334) 844-4568

California

Benjamin L. Hart, DVM, Ph.D., Behavioral Service, Veterinary Medical Teaching Hospital, University of California, Davis; (916) 752-1418

Colorado

Dan Estep, Ph.D., Animal Behavior Associates, Littleton; (303) 932-9095

Suzanne Hetts, Ph.D., Animal Behavior Associates, Littleton; (303) 932-9095

Florida

Walter F. Burghardt Jr., DVM, Ph.D., Behavior Clinic for Animals, Coral Springs; (305) 755-0055

Jack C. Hunsberger, Ph.D., Animal Behavior Consultants, Tampa; (800) 359-3295

Georgia

John C. Wright, Ph.D., Psychology Dept., Mercer University, Macon; (912) 752-2973 or (404) 524-5500

Illinois

Dennis H. Passe, Ph.D., Hebron; (815) 648-4542

Massachusetts

Amy R. Marder, VMD, Cambridge; (617) 868-4830 or (617) 522-7282

Stephanie Schwartz, DMV, Newton; (617) 527-1128

Missouri

Debra Horwitz, DVM, St. Louis; (314) 739-1510

New York

Peter Borchelt, Ph.D., Animal Behavior Consultants, Brooklyn; (718) 891-4200

Linda Goodloe, Ph.D., Animal Behavior Consultants, Brooklyn; (718) 891-4200

Katherine A. Houpt, VMD, Ph.D., Dept. of Physiology, College of Veterinary Medicine, Cornell University, Ithaca; (607) 253-3450

North Carolina

Donna Brown, Ph.D., Bahama; (919) 471-4522

Virginia

Suzanne B. Johnson, Ph.D., Animal Behavior Associates, Beaverdam; (804) 449-6654

West Virginia

Kennon A. Lattal, Ph.D., Dept. of Psychology, West Virginia University, Morgantown; (304) 293-2001, ext. 608

SELECTED BOOKS, MAGAZINES AND NEWSLETTERS

BOOKS:

Carlson, Delbert, DVM, and James Giffin. *Cat Owner's Home Veterinary Handbook (rev. ed.)*. New York: Howell Book House, 1995.

Daly, Carol Himsel. *Caring for Your Sick Cat*. Hauppauge, New York: Barron's Educational Publishing, 1994.

Hawcroft, Tim, BVSc, MRCVS. *First Aid for Cats: The Essential Quick-Reference Guide*. New York: Howell Book House, 1994.

Humphries, Jim, DVM. *Dr. Jim's Animal Clinic for Cats*: What People Want to Know. New York: Howell Book House, 1994.

Pitcairn, Richard. *Dr. Pitcairn's Guide to Natural Health for Dogs and Cats*. Emmaus, PA: Rodale Press, 1982.

Siegal, Mordecai, ed. *The Cornell Book of Cats: A Comprehensive Medical Reference for Every Cat and Kitten*. New York: Villard Books, 1992.

MAGAZINES:

Cat Fancy Magazine, P.O. Box 6050, Mission Viejo, CA 92690. A monthly magazine devoted to responsible cat care. Articles include breed profiles, behavior, health, and care.

CATS Magazine, P.O. Box 290037, Port Orange, FL 32129. A monthly magazine celebrating cats, with articles on health care, behavior, breeds, and the quirks of cat ownership.

Cats USA Magazine, P.O. Box 6050, Mission Viejo, CA 92690. An annual guide to buying a pedigreed kitten. Extensive breeder listings, as well as articles on finding a breeder, preparing for a kitten's arrival, grooming and training, and nutrition.

NEWSLETTERS:

Catnip Newsletter, Tufts University School of Veterinary Medicine. $24 per year. To subscribe, write to Catnip, P.O. Box 420014, Palm Coast, FL 32142.

Perspective on Cats Newsletter. Published by Cornell University and the Cornell Feline Health Center. For more information, contact the Cornell Feline Health Center, 618 VRT, Ithaca, NY 14853.

CAT RETIREMENT HOMES

If you have ever worried about what would happen to your cat if you died or became incapacitated, you are not alone. Concern about a surviving cat's welfare is common to many owners. However, with thoughtful planning, you can ensure quality care for your pets.

The *Committee on Legal Issues Pertaining to Animals* of the Association of the Bar of the City of New York has prepared a brochure that explains how to designate caretakers, provide funds for pet care, arrange for short-term pet care and prepare a will. To order a copy of this brochure, send a $2 check or money order (made out to the Association of the Bar) to the Association's Office of Communications, 42 W. 44th St., New York, NY 10036-6690. The brochure is frequently out of stock because of its popularity, so before ordering call the Bar at (212) 382-6695 to make sure it's available.

Lifelong shelters are another alternative. Although they are few in number, some humane organizations provide retirement living for animals whose owners have died or can no longer care for them. Among them are the Bide-A-Wee Home in New York City and the Bluebell Foundation in California.

Bide-a-Wee runs the Golden Years Retirement Home, which offers a homelike facility where cats can live with "round the clock" supervision and regular veterinary care. Pet owners who wish to join the program must make a prearranged contribution to cover the cost of the cat's stay for its lifetime. For more information, write to Pet Retirements, Bide-a-Wee, 410 E. 38th St., New York, NY 10016; or call (212) 532-6395.

The Bluebell Foundation was founded in 1987 by Bertha Gray-Yergat to care for her remaining cats after her death. This cat sanctuary can house up to 150 cats and accepts cats for retirement on a space-available basis. For more information on Bluebell's facilities and costs, contact the director at 20982 Laguna Canyon Rd., Laguna Beach, CA 92651; (714) 494-1586.

Another option is the retirement plan offered by the veterinary college at Texas A&M University. The Stevenson Companion Animal Life Center provides lifelong care for pets in a homey environment. The cost of enrollment is $25,000. The interest paid on the enrollment fee goes toward the expenses for the cat's care. When the pet dies, the principal goes to the veterinary college. The money can be designated to support a program of the owner's choice; for example, one that advances veterinary education or animal health. For more information, write to the Stevenson Companion Animal Life Center at Texas A&M University, College Station, TX 77843.

CATS-ONLY CLINICS

More and more veterinarians are specializing in specific species, and not just exotics such as birds or reptiles. The popularity of cats means that in the past decade a number of veterinarians have set up clinics devoted only to cats. By caring exclusively for cats, these clinics can offer veterinary visits free of the stress of encountering dogs and other animals, as well as a staff that is educated in and committed to feline health. There are many cats-only clinics around the country. To find a cats-only clinic in your area, look in the Yellow Pages under the headings "Cats" or "Veterinarians" or contact your state veterinary medical association for a recommendation.

RADIOIODINE TREATMENT CENTERS

In addition to the veterinary colleges at Auburn University, University of California-Davis, University of Georgia, University of Illinois, Purdue University, Kansas State University, Louisiana State University, University of Minnesota,

University of Missouri, Cornell University, Ohio State University, University of Tennessee and Texas A&M University, the following clinics offer radioactive iodine therapy.

Arizona

Southwest Veterinary Oncology, 141 E. Ft. Lowell, Tucson, AZ 85705; (602) 327-8131.

California

Veterinary Nuclear Imaging, 34 Creek Rd., Ste. D, Irvine, CA 92714; (714) 559-7289.

Veterinary Tumor Institute, 2585 Soquel Dr., Santa Cruz, CA 95065; (408) 476-5777.

Veterinary Oncology Specialties, 225 Carmel Ave., Pacifica, CA 94044; (415) 359-9870.

Florida

Veterinary Radiology Services of South Florida, University Animal Hospital, 9410 Stirling Rd., Cooper City, FL 33024; (407) 479-0460 or (305) 432-5611.

Massachusetts

Angell Memorial Hospital, 350 S. Huntington Ave., Boston, MA 02130; (617) 522-7282.

New Mexico

Aardvark Veterinary Clinic, 217 E. Marcy St., Santa Fe, NM 87501; (505) 989-4343.

New York

The Animal Medical Center, 510 E. 62nd St., New York, NY 10021; (212) 838-8100.

Ohio

The Veterinary Referral Clinic, 5035 Richmond Rd., Cleveland, OH 44146; (216) 831-6789.

Oregon

Feline Thyroid Clinic, 1045-F Gateway Loop, Springfield, OR 97477; (503) 744-2966.

Texas

Animal Radiology Clinic, 2353 Royal Ln., Dallas, TX 75229; (214) 484-5637.

Washington

Feline Hyperthyroid Treatment Center, 22226 Hwy. 99, Edmonds, WA 98026; (206) 771-2287.

VETERINARY SCHOOLS

Alabama

Auburn University, College of Veterinary Medicine, Small Animal Clinic, Auburn University, AL 36849; (334) 844-4690.

Tuskegee University, School of Veterinary Medicine, Patterson Hall, Tuskegee, AL 36088; (334) 727-8460.

California

University of California, Davis, School of Veterinary Medicine, Davis, CA 95616; (916) 752-1393.

Colorado

Colorado State University, College of Veterinary Medicine and Biomedical Sciences, W102 Anatomy Building, Fort Collins, CO 80523; (970) 491-7051.

Florida

University of Florida, College of Veterinary Medicine, P.O. Box 100125, Gainesville, FL 32610-0125; (904) 392-4700.

Georgia

University of Georgia, College of Veterinary Medicine, Athens, GA 30602; (706) 542-3221.

Illinois

University of Illinois, College of Veterinary Medicine, 2001 S. Lincoln, Urbana, IL 61801; (217) 333-5300.

Indiana

Purdue University, School of Veterinary Medicine, Lynn Hall, Room 113, West Lafayette, IN 47907; (317) 494-7608.

Iowa

Iowa State University, College of Veterinary Medicine, Ames, IA 50011; (515) 294-1242.

Kansas

Kansas State University, College of Veterinary Medicine, Anderson Hall, Room 9, Manhattan, KS 66506-0117; (913) 532-5690.

Louisiana

Louisiana State University, School of Veterinary Medicine, South Stadium Dr., Baton Rouge, LA 70803-8402; (504) 346-3100.

Massachusetts

Tufts University, School of Veterinary Medicine, 200 Westboro Rd., North Grafton, MA 01536; (508) 839-4000.

Michigan

Michigan State University, College of Veterinary Medicine, A-120E East Fee Hall, East Lansing, MI 48824-1316; (517) 355-5165.

Minnesota

University of Minnesota, College of Veterinary Medicine, 1365 Gortner Ave., St. Paul, MN 55108; (612) 624-9227.

Mississippi

Mississippi State University, College of Veterinary Medicine, Box 9825, Mississippi State, MS 39762; (601) 325-3432.

Missouri

University of Missouri, College of Veterinary Medicine, Columbia, MO 65211; (314) 882-3768.

New York

Cornell University, College of Veterinary Medicine, Ithaca, NY 14853-6401; (607) 253-3000, general information; (607) 253-3414, Cornell Feline Health Center.

North Carolina

North Carolina State University, College of Veterinary Medicine, 4700 Hillsborough St., Raleigh, NC 27606.

Ohio

Ohio State University, College of Veterinary Medicine, 101 Sisson Hall, 1900 Coffey Rd., Columbus, OH 43210; (614) 292-3551.

Oklahoma

Oklahoma State University, College of Veterinary Medicine, Stillwater, OK 74078-0353; (405) 744-6595.

Oregon

Oregon State University, College of Veterinary Medicine, Magruder Hall 200, Corvallis, OR 97331-4801; (541) 737-2141.

Pennsylvania

University of Pennsylvania, School of Veterinary Medicine, 3800 Spruce St., Philadelphia, PA 19104-6044; (215) 898-4680.

Tennessee

University of Tennessee, P.O. Box 1071, Knoxville, TN 37901-1071; (423) 974-8387.

Texas

Texas A&M University, College of Veterinary Medicine, College Station, TX 77843-4461; (409) 845-2351.

Virginia

Virginia-Maryland Regional College of Veterinary Medicine, Duck Pond Rd., Virginia Tech, Blacksburg, VA 24061; (540) 231-7666.

Washington

Washington State University, College of Veterinary Medicine, Pullman, WA 99164-7010; (509) 335-7073.

Wisconsin

University of Wisconsin, School of Veterinary Medicine, 2015 Linden Dr. W., Madison, WI 53706; (608) 263-7600.

Glossary

Acute: Having a sudden or severe onset and pronounced symptoms.

Amino acids: The chief components of proteins, synthesized by living cells or provided through the diet. Of the 22 amino acids, 10 are essential for cats. These essential amino acids are not produced by the cat's body and must be provided in the diet.

Anemia: A condition in which the blood has a lower than normal number of red blood cells or is deficient in hemoglobin or in total volume. The result is insufficient delivery of oxygen to the tissues. Anemia is often secondary to bone marrow suppression, which could be due to FeLV, kidney disease, toxins, chronic infection or poor nutrition.

Benign: Used to describe a tumor that is not malignant (cancerous). The names of these tumors usually end in the suffix *-oma*; for instance, lipoma. Even if a tumor is benign, its location or size can cause problems. For instance, a small benign tumor in the brain could be trouble, or a benign tumor could grow so large that it disrupts the function of other organs.

Calculus: Calcified deposits that form on or around the teeth.

Carcinogen: A substance that causes cancer.

Cataract: An opacity of the lens of the eye or of its capsule, obstructing the passage of light.

Chemotherapy: The use of chemicals or drugs to treat disease, usually cancer.

Chronic: Recurring frequently or lasting for a long period.

Ciliary body: The tissue that produces the eye's fluid.

Congenital: A condition that exists at birth, but is not necessarily hereditary.

Conjunctiva: The pink mucous membrane that lines the inner surface of the eyelids and the front part of the eyeball.

Cornea: The transparent anterior portion of the outer fibrous coat of the eye.

Cryotherapy: The use of controlled freezing to remove or destroy diseased tissue.

Diabetes mellitus: A condition in which the body is unable to metabolize carbohydrates; indicated by excessive thirst and urination, excessive amounts of sugar in the blood, and excessive hunger and loss of weight.

Digitalis: A drug derived from the foxglove plant; used to improve function of the heart muscle.

Diuretic: A substance that causes increased production of urine.

Endocrine gland: Any gland, such as the thyroid or pituitary, that secretes hormones.

Enucleation: Surgical removal of an entire tumor or organ, such as the eye from its socket.

Enzyme: A large, three-dimensional molecule/complex protein that initiates chemical changes in the body.

Feline Calicivirus (FCV): an upper respiratory virus against which cats are vaccinated.

Feline Immunodeficiency Virus (FIV): An infectious disease that cannot be prevented and is transmitted between cats via bite wounds.

Feline Leukemia Virus (FeLV): A virus against which cats are vaccinated that can be highly contagious to other cats.

Feline Panleukopenia: A virus whose symptoms resemble parvovirus in dogs, and against which cats are vaccinated.

Feline Rhinotracheitis (FVR): an upper respiratory disease against which cats are vaccinated.

Gingivitis: Inflammation of the gums.

Glaucoma: Increased pressure within the eye.

Glucocorticoid: An anti-inflammatory, immunosuppressive corticoid, such as hydrocortisone, that affects the metabolism of glucose.

Hereditary: A condition that is transmitted from parent to offspring.

Hypoglycemia: An abnormally low concentration of glucose in the blood; low blood sugar.

Idiopathic: A disease in which the cause is unknown.

Immunosuppressive: A drug or chemical that can suppress an immune response.

Immunotherapy: The stimulation or suppression of immune response; i.e., vaccines to stimulate immunity or corticosteroids to suppress immune response.

Incontinence: Inability to control urination; passive urination at rest or during sleep.

Lethargy: Inactivity; lack of energy, alertness or vigor.

Lymphoma: Cancer of the lymph nodes; the most common type of cancer in cats.

Malignant: A condition that is resistant to treatment and frequently fatal, i.e. malignant tumors. A malignant condition is one that exhibits uncontrollable growth with invasiveness or dissemination to other organs. Malignant skin tumors usually end with the suffix *-carcinoma* or *-sarcoma*.

Mast cell: A type of connective tissue cell that plays a role in the formation and storage of certain active substances. Mast cells are found in higher concentrations in areas that are inflamed.

Metabolism: All biochemical processes in the body; the process by which cells assimilate food and create energy. Occurs through chemical changes in body tissues.

Metastasis: The spreading of a disease or tumor from one part of the body to another.

Musculoskeletal: Relating to the muscles and bones.

Nuclear sclerosis: The thickening and hardening of the fibers in the center of the eye's lens.

Ovariohysterectomy: Surgical removal of the ovaries and uterus; called a spay.

Palpate: To examine by feeling and pressing with the palms of the hands and the fingers.

Patella: The kneecap.

Periodontal: The area surrounding the teeth.

Periodontitis: Inflammation and destruction of the structures around the tooth; i.e. gums and alveolar bone.

Plaque: A film of bacteria on a tooth.

Polydipsia: Increased frequency and amount of water consumption stimulated by excessive thirst.

Polyuria: Increased frequency and amount of urination.

Prognosis: The foretelling of the probable course of a disease.

Pulmonary edema: An excessive accumulation of fluid in the lungs.

Radiograph: The machine used to produce an image (a radiogram) on X ray film. The image is created by exposure to X rays. Commonly but incorrectly referred to as an X ray.

Sclera: A dense, fibrous, opaque, white covering that encloses the eyeball, except for the cornea.

Senility: The physical and mental infirmity caused by old age.

Spay: See ovariohysterectomy

Subcutaneous: Beneath the skin.

Tartar: A hard yellow coating on the teeth consisting of food residue, saliva and salts such as calcium carbonate.

Toxic: Poisonous.

Uremia: Means "urine in the blood." This accumulation of waste products, such as urea nitrogen, in the blood is due to kidney failure and causes toxicity and death.

Urethra: The canal through which urine is expressed from the bladder.

Urethritis: Inflammation of the urethral lining.

Zoonosis: A disease that can be transmitted between humans and animals.

Index